MW01640228

MAGYAR WOMEN

Also by Chris Corrin

SUPERWOMEN AND THE DOUBLE BURDEN: Women's Experience of Change in Central and Eastern Europe and the Former Soviet Union

Magyar Women

Hungarian Women's Lives, 1960s–1990s

Chris Corrin
Lecturer in Politics, Glasgow University

Consultant Editor: Jo Campling

St. Martin's Press

First published in Great Britain 1994 by
THE MACMILLAN PRESS LTD
Houndmills, Basingstoke, Hampshire RG21 2XS
and London
Companies and representatives
throughout the world

A catalogue record for this book is available
from the British Library.

ISBN 0–333–56039–6

Printed in Great Britain by
Ipswich Book Co Ltd
Ipswich, Suffolk

First published in the United States of America 1994 by
Scholarly and Reference Division,
ST. MARTIN'S PRESS, INC.,
175 Fifth Avenue,
New York, N.Y. 10010

ISBN 0–312–10689–0

Library of Congress Cataloging-in-Publication Data
Corrin, Chris, 1956–
Magyar women : Hungarian women's lives, 1960s–1990s / Chris Corrin
: consultant editor, Jo Campling. — 1st U.S. ed.
p. cm.
Includes bibliographical references and index.
ISBN 0–312–10689–0
1. Women—Hungary—Social conditions. 2. Feminism—Hungary–
–History. 3. Hungary—Social conditions—1945– I. Campling, Jo.
II. Title.
HQ1610.5.C67 1994
305.42'09439—dc20 93–4301
CIP

To Eva Corrin with love and thanks

Contents

List of Tables and Figures

Tables

Figures

Preface and Acknowledgements

The origins of this work lie far back in 1982 when I read a book by two excellent Hungarian sociologists György Konrád and Iván Szelényi called *The Intellectuals on the Road to Class Power.* This work was a Marxist critique of 'actually existing socialism' with the authors building from their research into urban inequality a thesis about the new class oppression in 'Eastern Europe'. In my desire to pursue these lines of thought I began a dissertation which eventually metamorphosed into a critical study of the situation of women in Hungarian society. Doubts concerning 'studying women' were then being voiced in women's groups in terms of objectification and careerism. I eventually made my peace with these arguments as the aim of my research was to privilege women's experience of change, in close contact with many women in Hungary over the past seven years. I am glad to have written this work in order to 'feed it back' into the women's groups which are now developing in Hungary and elsewhere in central and eastern Europe.

My way of working was ethnographic in that I spent as much time as I could with women discussing everyday concerns, particularly aspects of their lives in terms of work, child care, money, personal identity and sexuality, and political change and sometimes taping more formal 'interviews'. The taped interviews formed the basis for much of my reasoning in the original work, yet I was warned by 'Oxford academia' not to include too many 'unsupported quotes' from women. It is precisely these discussions which are the most valuable insight into how women in Hungary have experienced the changes since 1948. It was from 1948 that conscious decisions were being made to alter Hungarian economic and social decision-making radically within a new form of political organisation.

For this book I transcribed documentary and other materials written by Hungarian sociologists on various aspects of women's situation and theories of 'socialist families'. I also interviewed various people in Hungary who had worked on areas associated with the 'woman question'. It was relatively easy to spend time with women from various backgrounds and age groups in Budapest, but it became more complicated when I wanted to visit women in other towns. This was in part because my Hungarian was never good enough to have long interviews without interpretation and partly because the time and energy needed to organise such visits meant that I usually had to set up taped interviews rather than being able to get to know the women over time and 'just talk'. The title of this work 'Magyar Women' signifies my work with Hungarian women. I had neither enough opportunities nor the detailed linguistic and cultural knowledge required to work with many Roma women in Hungary. To do justice to the different lives of Roma women in Hungary would require at least as much research and another book. I hope it will not be too long before such research is in progress.

The nature of the taped interviews usually followed a pattern. I explained what the research was about and why it was being carried out, and asked certain open-ended questions about women's experiences of change, their expectations and things they might like to see developed for women. What was most surprising to me was that almost without exception I was not only welcomed warmly into people's homes and lives, but also that women were so willing and sometimes very enthusiastic to be able to talk about themselves and their own lives. The comment from Eszter that 'It is good to talk, to be able to think it out loud and to put my thoughts into a kind of whole somehow' was not uncommon. All the names of women have been changed but I am sure some will recognise themselves and each other. When I was only to meet a woman once we always ended our session with a general question-and-answer part for me to answer questions about women in the 'West' – about child-care, contraception, feminism, sexuality, work or lesbians. I can certainly say that to be given the opportunity to spend 7–8 months travelling in Hungary talking with women about their lives was an honour. I thank the Isle of Man Board of Education and the British Council for their financial support in 1986 which enabled me to do this.

Since 1986 I have visited Hungary many times but always for much shorter periods of 2 months or less. During these visits I have been able to notice and discuss the tremendous social and political upheavals which have taken place in Hungary and the impact such changes have had on women's situations and possibilities. In writing up this work for publication I hope it will make a small contribution towards enabling Hungarian women to draw together the threads of their shared experience and to build on some of the analyses to be able to support each other in their various activities.

I would very much like to thank everyone who helped me to carry out this work in Hungary – those who gave of their time and energy to share their days and nights with me, sociologists with whom I could discuss my ideas and thoughts, women who introduced me to their sisters, daughters, grandmothers, aunts and mothers and especially to those women who snatched a few hours from incredibly busy schedules, often whilst their children slept, to discuss their lives with me.

CHRIS CORRIN

List of Abbreviations

CMEA	Council for Mutual Economic Assistance
COMECON	Council for Mutual Economic Aid, or Assistance (Communist nations)
EFSF	European Forum of Socialist Feminists
ELTE	Eötvös Lóránd University
FKgP	Smallholders Party
FIDESZ	Federation of Young Democrats
GDP	gross domestic product
GYES	child-care allowance
HCA	Helsinki Citizen's Assembly
HSWP	Hungarian Socialist Worker's Party
KDNP	Christian Democratic People's Party
LIGA	League of Industrial Trade Unions
MDF	Magyar Democratic Forum
MDP	Hungarian Worker's Party
MSzP	Hungarian Socialist Party
NEM	New Economic Mechanism
OTP	Hungarian National Bank
SzDSz	Alliance of Free Democrats
SZETA	Foundation for the Assistance of the Poor
SZOT	National Council of Trade Unions
TARKI	Social Science Information Centre, Budapest
TDDSz	Democratic Union of Scientific and Research Workers
WHO	World Health Organisation

1 Introduction

Since 1989 the countries described as 'Eastern Europe'[1] have experienced revolutionary changes, so much so that the political and economic map of Europe has been transformed. These so-called 'ex-socialist'[2] countries are now experiencing the rolling back of the Stalinist state forces from many of the areas previously kept under the tight grip of 'the power'.[3] There have been important changes in many spheres of these societies which have had far-reaching impact on both external and domestic frameworks. This book addresses questions concerning the changing situations and positions of women within Hungarian society both in the proclaimed moves towards socialism/communism in which women were to become liberated through 'socialist' development, and in the political liberalisation which has been occurring since the mid-1980s. The drive towards 'socialism' was associated with an interventionist state within a heavily planned economic framework and a communist bureaucracy which was influential in many areas of social life. In turn, families acted to protect themselves from undue and unwanted state interference. The current period is associated with the withdrawal of the state from the public sphere. The 'rolling back' of the state and the marketisation of the economy are being carried out in an atmosphere of political pluralism which rejects the authoritarian rigidity of the previous regime. Questions about how these developments are affecting the position of women in Hungarian society and, importantly, how women are responding to these changes – working in groups and through various networks or within families, at workplaces and through political parties – form the concluding sections of the book.

WOMEN

As always it must be noted that nowhere in the world do women occupy one category. Societies differ in so many ways in terms of cultural, traditional, religious, ethnic and class complexities that conceptualising 'women' and women's oppression takes care. In

Hungary there were of course, Party women, richer women, poor women, Roma women and elderly women, and their concerns are nuanced and various. For the purposes of much of this study, 'women' is taken to mean the majority of those women who are affected by the particular policy measure or political change, under discussion. That is, the 'socialist' authorities, and now the new politicians and policy-makers in Hungary produced specific policies based on the collective of 'women' as an entity in terms of policy decisions regarding work, child-care, family policies and in other arenas. This official identification of women cut across traditional social and economic divisions. Within different areas of this work the fundamental differences are assessed between women in Hungary – in economic activities, household patterns, living arrangements, rural and urban differences – yet official decisions and policies are often made with a blanket entity 'women' in view. At other times, of course, official recognition of women is in relation to men – either as wives, mothers or carers. As is shown in Chapter 5, because decisions regarding benefits were based on 'women' as 'women workers' or 'mothers' or 'wives' this meant that no provision was made for those women (such as elderly women) who were no longer part of any of these categories.

Another aspect of studying 'women' is that women suffer inequalities on the basis of their ability to give birth and are assigned gender qualities which are socially, and often officially, constructed. The whole debate concerning rights/duties is instructive here in that women are seen to have duties in both the public and private spheres, whereas men's duties tend to be only within the public sphere. In terms of 'rights' men tend to have rights in both spheres whereas women appear only to have limited rights within both spheres, especially in terms of controlling their fertility. This gendered notion of 'rights' and 'duties' also includes the psychological and emotional factors in terms of so-called 'failures'. If men see themselves as failing within their economic responsibilities towards their families they can rationalise this in various ways, whereas if women believe themselves to be 'failing' in any one of their multifaceted obligations, then this is often viewed as something of a personal failure, a problem for themselves. Many (over)expectations placed upon women result in their direct and indirect oppression, as *women*. With this in mind, much attention is given within this work to those areas of health (Chapter 6) and social policy (Chapter 5) which vitally affect *women*'s lives, physically, psychologically and in terms of women's images of themselves (Chapter 7).

MAIN AIMS

There are two main strands to this work. The first is concerned with the situation of 'how things were/are for Hungarian women'. In outlining the changes that have occurred in Hungarian society over the past thirty years particular attention is given to the attempts by policy-makers to implement policies in relation to 'women' and child-care, and some of the debates surrounding the effects of such policies on aspects of gender equality. In certain areas policies are based on principles of equality yet there is inequality in practice: wages and child-care are two examples, and this difference between policy and practice requires explanation. Power relations are important features of any social change and this book asks how women's lives have been affected by different official conceptions of women's social roles in terms of pro-natalist policies, labour-power goals and incentives. Women have often been viewed as a flexible workforce, at times depending on whether the state needs more women-workers, more mothers or both, as is often the case.

The contention of this work – and this underlies the second strand – is that women did not become 'liberated' in any genuine sense in Hungary, in large measure because women were expected to take on extra 'duties' without a consequent problematising of men's duties/obligations. Women were needed as workers, during the intensive phase of development of the Hungarian economy up to the late 1960s and were also always needed as mothers. In addition much of the apparent paternalism *vis-à-vis* social relations engendered through the bureaucratic administrations in Hungary has to some extent become internalised by Hungarian men and women. Issues with gender dimensions such as the domestic division of labour, sexuality, domestic and sexual violence, sexual harassment, and even to some extent rape, were all 'non-issues' within Hungarian everyday thinking and sociological research. In terms of attitudes towards women in Hungary, it can be argued that there is strong patriarchal resistance to women organising for themselves. Whether this resistance, from men and from various social groups generally, stems also in part from the 'split' nature of Hungarian society before the communist takeover, must also be considered. By this is meant that before the Second World War Hungarian society consisted of (at least) two distinct groupings – a semi-feudal set of social relations, peasant culture within the country-side and an industrialised, urban petty-bourgeoisie existence in towns and Budapest.

As will be seen in the concluding sections of this book, although it may be harder for women in Hungary to begin to organise autonomously as *women*, overcoming this resistance may in part give them a very definite sense of purpose and strengthen their resolve to change those outdated social relations. It is a complex interrelationship, changing over time, which is best explored in relation to differing aspects of women's everyday lives.

That Hungarian women's 'liberation' became subsumed within a reduced marxist analysis of 'liberation through paid, public work' actually meant that working mothers within Hungarian society suffered under the much-discussed 'double burden'. This double burden or double shift meant that women were not only exploited by this so-called 'emancipation' but were now very keen to move away from any such notions. This has particular importance in terms of any consideration of feminist analysis and the projection of women organising towards 'liberation'. Many Hungarian women who have experienced the so-called 'socialist liberation' may well begin by asking 'Whose ideas of 'liberation' are involved and what are the costs to women?'.

This woman-centred analysis focuses on the construction, implementation and effects (intended and unexpected) of policy decisions as they affect women in Hungary within the broader framework of socio-political change. Feminist analyses are used throughout this work to illuminate certain considerations of the failure of 'socialist' policies to realise equality for women. The centrality of attitudes is stressed, and how such attitudes are formed and shaped. The main concentration is on those decades between 1948 and 1991, in which two revolutions took place. There are parallels between Hungary's two revolutions – the first against the 'Stalinist' system in 1956 when people might still have followed a communist road, with Imre Nagy, and the second in 1989 when moves were made away from the statist authoritarian regime of so-called 'Soviet socialism'. In the most recent changes there appears little talk of 'socialist' or collective action and yet, given the strong internalisation of state paternalism within much discussion in Hungary – certainly in terms of the right to work and to a minimum standard of life, such issues are likely to raise all types of debate, including the not-totally discredited social democratic arguments. For women, issues of social welfare are pivotal, given their position as primary 'carers'. Marketisation will radically affect women's lives not least in differentiating between different groups of Hungarian women – women entrepreneurs, women politicians, feminists. Hungarian women are making their voices heard within their changing environments.

It is evident that two major factors mediating the situation of women in Hungary, other than actions by women themselves, are state forces and family formations.[4] Each are given consideration in terms of power differentials, and how both state forces and families mediate women's oppression. The state authorities have legislative power over women and the power to reinforce (or not) implementation of certain policy decisions. Families in the Hungarian 'socialist' context can be seen not only as the site of women's oppression and as mediators of such oppression but also as a unit of resistance against the intrusion of the state. There were parallels here with some black family situations in Britain in terms of the way that people live within a hostile environment.

Feminist analysis is subject-centred so that women's views, aspirations and experiences are central. I had a humbling first encounter with a very friendly and extremely busy woman on a large housing estate outside Budapest. She eagerly agreed to speak to me about her life experiences in having her children, her work, and living with her husband and children in various situations, by saying 'No one has ever been interested in what I think before. I am happy to share with you my feelings and views about what *I* think' (Ágnes, 1985).

INTERVENTION TOWARDS CHANGING SOCIAL RELATIONS

Just as material change cannot bring about psychological changes, so legislation cannot bring about social change. If the people on whose behalf the legislation is designed do not have a belief in the 'rightness' of the development, or do not have the will to try to work out different ways of dealing with changes, then either the intended effects of the legislation will often not be felt or unintended consequences may arise. An example can be seen in the parental child allowance which is taken up by less than 1 per cent of Hungarian men. Equally, if legislators have a rigid hierarchy of values then the prioritisation of particular goals will often preclude certain avenues of social intervention. Of course unexpected effects of legislation can be felt regardless of the way it is implemented. Policy-makers cannot successfully predict long-term consequences of various measures, so a certain amount of redefinition takes place.

Important questions considered include: 'What are the contradictions and parallels between changes affecting women's situations – both towards a "socialist" future and away from the "socialist" development?' Consideration of the important question 'How can Hungarian women gain a more forceful voice within their society?' ends this book. It is clear that answers to this particular question remain ambiguous because the reasons women would wish to gain a greater voice differ. Certain women's groups which are very much in favour of making motherhood the top priority for all women and which argue for a woman's right to remain in the home being cared for by her husband find themselves at odds with feminist groups who believe primarily in *choice* for women to have opportunities to organise their lives in ways which they choose. Without pre-empting our consideration it can be clearly stated that, from a feminist perspective, no society exists in which women (or children and men) are truly liberated. For women to be liberated, power imbalances must be changed and men need to be liberated from some of the narrow and defensive attitudes which have shaped their consciousness.

WOMEN'S POLITICAL PARTICIPATION

Consideration is given to the conditions in Hungary which could aid or hinder the development of wider political participation by women at all levels of society, with some reference to the new parties which have been emerging since 1988–9. Within this the dissolution of the old hierarchical regime has created some openings for women to be actively involved in political activity. Yet women tend to be involved 'behind the scenes'. At the first round of the elections when visiting several of the offices of the new parties when election programmes were being prepared, it was obvious that many women were busy and organising much of the work. In discussing their involvement one woman summed it up: 'We mainly support our husbands, my husband is standing and I have always supported his political work ever since our early days in the 1960s' (Ilona, 1990). Generally women spoke of their lack of time for direct political intervention, yet they seemed to spend a good deal of time organising for candidates and on other aspects of the political work. Of the 386 Members of Parliament elected only twenty-eight were women, which is the lowest ratio for four decades.

Yet it must be remembered that the formal participation by women in quotas within the 'socialist' hierarchies was actually destructive of any women's initiatives that were not officially led. This political context, in which the official Women's Council in Hungary was actually a major factor blocking the establishment of representative groups for women is fully explored in Chapters 7 and 8. As will be seen a quantitative approach is totally inadequate to encompass the discrepancy between formal and actual equality and representation of women.

Women are beginning their own struggle in the political arena. One women's group in Hungary, associated with the Young Democrats successfully organised protests against the hydroelectric dam project. Feminist organisation and networking is evidenced by the activities of the new *Feminista Hálózat* (Feminist Network) founded in May 1990. What 'feminist' has come to mean within Hungarian intellectual circles and in the everyday sense is considered in Chapter 8. It is highly unlikely that Hungarian women will wish to replicate western European feminist ideas in that their different herstories, cultural experiences and expectations for the coming years are bound to feed into different priorities and directions. This is not to say that feminist analyses of situations, their own historically and in current times, will not be made use of by Hungarian feminists and activists, but that the various directions and changes that they choose will not necessary be similar to those of the majority of white Western feminists.

The group of women involved in the Feminist Network held an important open meeting in Budapest in June 1990 to discuss the threat to abortion rights. The interplay between the members of the Network, several of whom have participated in various Europe-wide feminist conferences since 1990, and the women involved in political parties will be something to consider in Chapter 8. As youth culture is playing an increasingly important role within Hungarian society, the increasing popularity of the Federation of Young Democrats (FIDESZ) since the 1990 elections is important for younger women. Young people were very disillusioned with the old system and impatient for change. One facet of young women's culture seems to entail a definite rejection of aspects of their mothers' lives. Some young women in Hungary today can remember as children the strains under which many of their mothers lived – the dual burden – and many young women want something 'different' from the lives their mothers experienced.

With increasing unemployment facing large sections of the Hungarian population, particularly certain groups including many women such as unskilled textile workers, health and educational employees, and some school-leavers, the effects of consequent hardship and poverty on women, directly and indirectly, will be significant and diverse. Women working in trade unions and in community groups have important roles in attempting to intervene and to try to ameliorate and change certain situations.

TERMINOLOGY AND SOURCES

Much has been written on 'women and socialism' yet detailed concentration on European 'socialist' countries other than the USSR has been limited. A few words on the use of the term 'socialist' are needed here. This term is used partly for brevity ('so-called actually existing socialism' or some other such descriptions are a bit long-winded) and partly because this is how Hungary was often labelled in writing and discussion during this period of history. Quotation marks are used around the words 'socialist' and 'socialism' as an indication that this term is used as a short form rather than descriptively. The societies which took up the Soviet development process cannot be considered as a monolithic bloc. 'Eastern Europe' is not a particularly useful label and both Hungary and Czechoslovakia are generally considered 'central European' along with Austria and Germany. The vast changes which have taken place in this region since 1989 have caused some discussion on such labels yet most Hungarians have never considered their country to be merely part of 'Eastern Europe', rather it is Hungary, with all the distinct historical phases and developments that have led up to the present-day society. To view Hungary as having been merely a Soviet satellite would be both harmful and short-sighted, just as ignoring the large Soviet influence apparent within Hungarian society since 1948 would be mistaken. Accordingly, Chapter 2 outlines the complexities of Hungarian history in the post-war period, up to the early 1990s.

The transformations which state and social relations have undergone over several decades in Hungary have shaped certain behaviour and ways of thinking. Changes in social relations take place slowly in Hungary. Certain of the historical–cultural developments apparent before the Second World War were actually interrupted by 40 years of 'socialist' intervention. To some extent one can see these historical processes re-emerging to continue developing in an integrative process. Something of this process was apparent in the break-up of the former Yugoslavia in the re-emergence of ethnic tensions which had been subsumed under an authoritarian regime which dictated 'rights' to citizens, rather than allowed for the protection of ethnic minority rights as full human rights within a federal situation. In Hungary, the re-emergence of older developments is taking the pattern of attempts to consolidate the rural and urban Hungarian ways of life. That is, for both life-patterns to coexist and receive equal recognition as 'Hungarian'. Within the changing situation of openings to the Western market forces, this development is not necessarily smooth and harmonious. In part, the Western orientation favours extensions of urban-bourgeois social relations, yet the loss of agricultural markets in the former Soviet Union may mean that peasant cultures and social relations remain a bedrock for rural Hungarians. The two are not mutually exclusive, but the shifting balance between the dominance of one or other projected life-pattern does underlie much of the political debate concerning the way forward for Hungarian society into the 1990s and beyond. This in turn, affects how women's situation is viewed within different spheres and how women themselves look forward to change.

SOCIAL POLICY

There is much to be learnt from the Hungarian experience, particularly in the area of social policy. Whilst there are specific areas in which Hungary can be seen as something of a forerunner in policy implementation for women, there are also common threads between Hungarian policies and those of the former Soviet Union and neighbouring 'ex-socialist' states. One major factor which helps to build up a detailed study of certain aspects of life for women in Hungary is the enthusiasm and relative freedom with which Hungarian writers, academics, professionals and others expressed 'opinions' on aspects of daily life and expectations within society, in addition to carrying out work on many varied themes. Yet it is noted that such major and obvious social issues as poverty were not able to be officially recognised in Hungary from the 1940s to the early 1980s because all such ills had been 'overcome in the socialist transition'. As poverty did not exist, so the argument ran, it would be useless to make any researches into such a subject and it could also have proved politically disastrous for one's career. Indeed activists such as Ottilia Solt who were involved with helping poor people in Hungary through SZETA, the Foundation for the Poor, were harassed by the authorities as if they were criminals. Several times I discussed with these activists the levels of harassment for political oppositionists which in 1986–7 reached severe limits, such as placement in psychiatric care. Acknowledging the existence of poverty, either by writing of its proportions, or by actively helping poor people, including the large numbers of Roma *(csigani)* families, was seen as anti-state activity.

It is relevant here to mention the reliability of data from the centralised offices of the Central Statistical Office – given that absolute poverty was not recognised. By far the more useful data on income levels came from some of the *samizdat* (underground) publications such as *Beszélö* (*The Talker*) which described as accurately as possible, real situations, verified with material data. Some of the data from the Central Statistical Office is used in this work, as well as material from journals, papers and discussions in the media. Attempts are made to try to locate such material, to explain the methodological approach used or the political stance of the author(s), thereby gaining something of the background value that different studies provide. With regard to material from the Central Statistical Office there is a wealth of statistics available which concern women but little use has been made of this as the statistics presented are very much in the 'official' mould, are generally aggregated and tend not to provide a sound basis on which to build up a broader picture. There is a group of radical statisticians at work in the CSO in Hungary who aim to carry on working to formulate some more reliable and socially useful data.

WOMEN AND 'SOCIALISM'

Two major types of studies are available concerning 'women and socialism'. First, there are case studies of women's position within Soviet-type 'socialist' states.[5] Second, there are comparative analyses which point up the similarities between policies concerning women in various 'socialist' states, some of which argue the pros and cons for women's liberation under socialist and/or capitalist systems.[6] From a feminist perspective many of these studies are partial because they do not attempt to examine critically the reasons and intent of the studies undertaken, nor to build up a woman-centred analysis. Much of the work that has been carried out on 'women and socialism' is insightful, even though some of it rests on assumptions about 'the woman problem' or considers women as the 'other' in men's worlds.

In their studies both Scott and Heitlinger give comparative analyses of the situation of women in the Soviet Union and Czechoslovakia, each assuming certain 'models of development'. Within Scott's analysis it is proposed that part of the failure of these countries to promote actively and practically full equality policies for women lies in the fact that a commitment to women's equality is but one of the progressive priorities of these societies. Within this framework various possible areas of change towards a broader equality are proposed. Research into the 'politics of equality' project has been problematic in several key aspects as Hilary Pilkington points out in her work on women's situation in Russia and the former Soviet republics (see Pilkington in Corrin, 1992, p. 186). Given the relational nature of equality and the cultural construction of the category 'women' any attempts as blanket 'measurement' of equality are at best contradictory and at worst doomed to failure. In her work Heitlinger includes certain factors accounting for the failure to implement policy, despite some commitment to 'liberation' and within her analysis she is less optimistic about the possibilities for change (Heitlinger, 1979).

In her case study concerning women in Soviet society, Gail Lapidus makes the point concerning 'revolution from above', which she believes can give an 'intentional character to outcomes that were the secondary or even unintended consequences of other choices', with women's position being shaped, 'by the broader forces set in motion by the Soviet regime and by economic and political choices in which a concern for sexual equality played a negligible role' (Lapidus, 1978, p. 5).

In similar vein Barbara Jancar's work on women's participation in Yugoslavia's national liberation movement emphasises that 'socialist' mobilisation can occur for a number of reasons, and that to achieve women's liberation as a byproduct of 'socialism' is probably the least effective mobiliser (certainly in comparison with economic necessity). Such studies tend to emphasise these factors, of exactly how women's 'liberation' is to come about, in terms of the political structure of 'socialist' societies of the Soviet type, yet little is said about what this 'liberation' involves for differing groups of women in their everyday lives or what feminists would like it to involve. Differing groups of women will define and assess their interests in various spheres in different ways and one would not expect it to be otherwise. Within her work Sharon Wolchick stresses the instrumental use of women by the male Party and governmental élite in Czechoslovakia, in terms of the cyclical mobilisation of women (Wolchik, 1979, p. 594). Certain elements of the 'mobilisation' of large numbers of women in the Hungarian context, especially with reference to such aspects of women's lives as their paid work and their 'duty as mothers', are important for this study.

Writings which attempt to compare and contrast women's lives in different countries can sometimes offer us a more nuanced framework of analysis. Such comparative works are, of course, dependent upon evidence from the specific case studies. In comparing the status of women in Eastern Europe and the Soviet Union with that of women in the USA, Sharon Wolchick considered as part of her work, her hypothesis that sexual equality would have been more likely in 'socialist' states. This would have been the case for two reasons: (i) that the official ideology supported women's equality which was reflected in legislation prohibiting discrimination against women in education, work and wages; and (ii) that the communist élites appeared to have 'a greater capacity to produce desired social changes' (Wolchik, 1979, p. 446). Such arguments were quite common from Western feminist analysts in the 1970s and 1980s. Yet as this work shows, there were often serious reductionist aspects to some of these analyses, and overestimations about what could be achieved for 'women' by the limited legislation of the 'socialist' hierarchies, and indeed about the actual intentions of such policy-makers.

In her discussion paper on women's emancipation under socialism as a potential model for the 'Third World', Maxine Molyneux discusses the significant advances made by 'socialist' states in promoting women's equality, whilst considering the inherent inequalities in the policies of the states analysed. Molyneux notes that such inequalities 'are often hidden behind the formal equality that women have acquired and behind the accession of women to previously unconventional occupations' (Molyneux, 1981, p. 36).

Several authors point to the persistence of the sexual division of labour in employment and the failure to lessen women's load in terms of housework,[7] or to equalise wo/men's domestic labour and responsibilities, as significant difficulties facing 'socialist' states. Reference is also made to the crucial role which 'the family' (however defined) still plays in many 'socialist' societies.

From my own observations, a central point noted in the failure to achieve a more egalitarian environment in Hungary, is the dual nature of women's oppression linked to the ways that women are 'viewed' by men generally and how such sexism is institutionalised and reinforced. The notion of patriarchy as an analytic tool is very useful here to avoid objectifying women as 'victims' of state forces and policies. Sexism is what is being dealt with in much of this work. Not only the sexism which comes from state structures in terms of 'equal' policies that are not put into practice, but the sexism which is often much more pervasive and more difficult to get to grips with, that intrudes into people's everyday lives whether at home, school, office, factory. This sexism consists in thinking of women as having certain, specific (if not 'natural') roles that they *should* perform because they are women and it is the weight of these sexist attitudes that inform much of Hungarian women's discussions about the 'superwomen' expectations and the guilt of not being simultaneously a 'good' mother, daughter, worker, wife, whatever. Linked with notions of personal failure if all 'duties' are not carried out successfully, the picture emerges of some women living under great stress within their everyday environments.

It is the case that most women in Hungary are discriminated against in employment and by what is expected of them in connection with housework and child-care.[8] There is something to be learnt in terms of the active, official promotion of gender equality by analysing legislation, such as that in Sweden which is committed to 'achieving equality between the sexes by changing the role of men as well as that of women' (Scott, 1982, p. 3). Here, too, the debate concerning issues such as 'equal pay for work of equal value' in terms of say, EC Directives, could be useful (see Eberhardt, 1991, p. 37). Distinctions are made throughout this work between the impact on certain groups of women of specific government policies concerning women's equality, from the consequences of broader patterns of economic change. In other respects the distinctive orientations and priorities of Hungarian policy-makers are noted as is their impact, as well as the duality of interests apparent between researchers and planners and more importantly, between women themselves.

IDEOLOGY OF 'SOCIALISM'

Hungary has its own 'specifics' in terms of historical development and experience. One of these has been the experience of rule by Communist party forces, introduced to Hungary when Stalin was in power within the USSR. Any discussion of women's changing situations needs to consider the way in which Soviet-styled Marxism–Leninism influenced attempts to introduce 'socialist' policies, but there is no wish in this work to carry on the jargon-laden debates that seem to have characterised much marxist writing concerning women. Obviously, any ideology is modified when put into practice. Marxism–Leninism was affected by Stalinism. The variety of Marxism–Leninism, and within that the policies concerning women, which were adopted in Hungary after 1948 have to be seen in this light. The input of Hungarian theorists, interpreting marxism (Lukács) and constructing humanist theories (Hegedüs *et al.*) was important.

WOMEN'S LIBERATION THROUGH 'SOCIALIST' DEVELOPMENT

At the outset it is important to consider what is meant by 'women's liberation'. In the sense in which it is used here, women's liberation is concerned with the abolition of oppression from which half of the adult population suffer because of their gender, because they are women. The term 'gender' is used here instead of 'sex' because the former takes into account all of the social phenomena which overlay the basic biological differences between men and women. Only women can give birth to and suckle children, yet all other child-care duties can be undertaken by either men or women. Such a division of labour by gender has not occurred 'naturally' but has been socially constructed and can thereby be changed by people's actions. This has nothing to do with biology but a great deal to do with what societies have come to expect of women. It is evident that throughout the world caring for children is mainly carried out by women and is seen as a 'woman's role'. The majority of domestic work – such as cooking, cleaning, shopping and general caring duties – is carried out by women. Yet in most 'socialist' states women were expected to engage in paid, public work. Indeed it was the very encouragement of women to become part of the public workforce that Engels viewed as one step on the way to liberating women from domestic slavery.

It is useful here to remember the distinction between liberal rights and socialist duties – in relation to productive labour. Whilst women in western Europe were struggling for the 'right to work', women in many of the central and eastern European countries were oppressed by their 'socialist' duty to work outside (and inside) their homes. Much of the debate currently being undertaken in central and eastern European countries is in terms of *choice*. That women will now have some choice over employment (*less* regarding unemployment) is a situation which will be new to many and future choices will be viewed within this context.

DOUBLE BURDEN

The socialisation of domestic work was envisaged by early marxists as another stage on the way to equalising relations between men and women in society. Yet the contradictions of the so-called double burden from which women can suffer in all societies, and did suffer in 'socialist' societies where the majority of women were involved in paid work, are all too apparent. Much has been written about Engels's work on women and the family, both because this is one of the classic marxist documents on the family and because there has been a vulgarisation of Engels's work by many theorists (east and west), reducing his analysis to 'if women have *public paid* work then they become liberated'. The idea of liberation through paid work was but one aspect of the original marxist conception of human liberation. Engels has much more to say in terms of household work becoming privatised under capitalism, and in terms of women's position as 'slaves of the workers', each alienated from the other, etc. Yet it is clear in Marx's and Engels's work that the working class is the agency for human liberation. Liberation will be gained by workers' efforts to control the external world of work. There is no systematic study of the specific oppression of women. In his *Origin,* [9] Engels gives an account of some aspects of the development of sexual and family relations under capitalism and he is clear in interpreting the hypocritical sexual relations under capitalism as containing adultery and prostitution within monogamous marriage. The vital point is made about 'the family' – as a changing entity. He is also clear on the essential preconditions for women's emancipation: women's participation in the workforce and the *socialisation of domestic work*. Women would leave the private sphere of domestic production and broaden their horizons through participation in public production. Engels gives each premise equal stress:

> the first premise for the emancipation of women is the reintroduction of the whole female sex into public industry, and that this again demands that the quality possessed by the individual family of being the economic unit of society be abolished (Engels, 1976, p. 501).

This task could be begun under capitalism but would obviously proceed much more rapidly under 'socialism' as the costs involved in unifying the processes of domestic labour and commodity production could be spread throughout the whole society. Yet Marx's and Engels's thought is, of course, a product of its time and the discussion of women's emancipation in the abstract almost inevitably meant that the pressures working against the socialisation of domestic work were underestimated. It is evident that Marx and Engels (and later Lenin) were concerned with the 'woman question' in so far as they wrote of the developments in society affecting women, changing their analysis when new information came to light, yet their analyses remain one-sided.

As their consideration of women's oppression is constructed within the general, theoretical emancipation of humankind through the transition to communism, the specifity of women's oppression is not fully realised. After all, as Sheila Rowbotham points out, despite their theoretical capacities, Marx and Engels were a couple of bourgeois men in the nineteenth century, so they 'were bound to see the women's situation through the eyes of men, and working-class women through the eyes of middle-class men. Inevitably this affected how they saw and where they looked' (Rowbotham, 1972, p. 62).

The importance of this is that in their analysis of the socialisation of housework and child-care tasks, the economic benefits of women's participation within the public sphere were overestimated, or rather the high costs (to men) of making available public utilities for meals, laundry and child-care were radically underestimated. As Heitlinger points out, Lenin only thought of the savings in labour time when housework would be socialised, but another outcome is that previously unpaid domestic work becomes waged work, thus requiring equivalent payment to other paid work, so that it becomes more expensive.[10] So far as the division of labour within the home is concerned no mention is made of the need to equalise relations and responsibilities.

'SOCIALIST' FEMINISM

It is in this area that the arguments of some 'socialist feminists' are applicable. In a suitably broad definition of the aims of 'socialism', Christine Pelzer White states that:

> socialism aims at transforming the world as it is presently structured by neocolonialism, capitalism, patriarchy, racism and sexism into a better world characterized by political self-determination by producers and equality between the sexes (Pelzer White, 1989, p. 172).

Within such a context the theoretical underpinnings of 'socialist feminist' thought on the female/male problematic can be assessed in terms of equalisation of work, renegotiation of acceptable/respected values, which have generally been regarded as a threat or an exaggerated emphasis on difference by most male 'socialist' thinkers. In this way, although some 'socialists' have argued that the 'woman question' has been answered at least in part, by 'socialism(s)' in various countries, socialist-feminists would argue that because women as a grouping had not consistently contributed to the theories of 'socialism', then current practices are lacking. Having 'women's issues' on the public agenda is not enough – so-called 'women's problems' are generally societal problems and need to be recognised as such. Something of this realisation is present within some of the new women's groups forming throughout central and eastern Europe. However, it is essential to point out that few women within these movements describe themselves as feminists, let alone socialist-feminists, as discussions have highlighted.[11] Debates on what the various political changes mean for women are important and varied, as will be seen later in considering of the choices and activities women are making towards new goals or towards a return to or retention of historical, gendered choices for women.

THEORISING WOMEN'S OPPRESSION

What are the consequences of the one-sided development of women's 'liberation' under 'socialism' for constructing a theory of women's oppression? Many aspects of Hungarian policy towards the 'emancipation' of women (never clearly defined in the official literature) appear to succumb to the vulgarisation of marxist theory in terms of women achieving full 'emancipation' through employment. In this context it is readily apparent that Hungarian men were not fully emancipated through public waged labour. There are contradictions here between the state policy in terms of women's public participation and the various kinds of encouragement aimed at increasing birth-rates. Policy-makers in 'socialist' states such as Hungary did not simply 'forget' the need for equal relations between men and women within the domestic sphere but actively proposed images of women as primarily mothers, child-carers and homemakers. Engels's important premise concerning the socialisation of domestic chores was used as a screen for ignoring those domestic relations which cannot be socialised – without revolutionising familial relationships – which was never a serious consideration in Hungary.

Here lies much of the confusing pressures which women face in terms of their 'social roles and responsibilities'. There are contradictions too concerning the reasoning behind, and outcomes of, certain social policy measures concerning the socialisation of child-care. As will be seen there is often a recourse in official rhetoric to women's 'natural' roles which is on a totally different level from that of the principles of historical materialism which analyse the causes of women's subordination in social and economic terms. As Molyneux points out this elevation of production above other areas of policy forms a barrier in terms of improving women's material situations and expanding consciousness of sexual inequality 'this "productivism" and the appeal to the general "needs" of society legitimises the reproduction of sexual divisions both in the workplace and in the home' (Molyneux, 1981, p. 13).

Yet the productivism and needs of 'socialist' societies do not require a *sexual* class division, only, it would appear, a class division along the lines of waged/unwaged labour. It will be seen that whilst in many areas over 80 per cent of Hungarian women participated in paid employment, this could not be considered as 'liberating' in any sense.

This shows the need for a more complex perspective from which to analyse women's oppression. Whereas Marx and Engels do not develop an agency for women (distinct from that of the working class) feminist theorists believe that women constitute the agents for changing their situation. This multifaceted debate includes various arguments concerning the nature of science/sociology/politics.[12] Feminist analyses separate knowledge from experience and offer critiques of social organisation. Such analyses are anti-élitist and reject a high culture which universalises white male heterosexism. In this study then, not only is the statistical evidence of women's employment given, along with the (male) orientation of the collection, but information on the ways in which such employment affects women's consciousness is given a central role. The historical development of Hungarian families demands consideration, as does the way in which most women experience the consequences of life within nuclear and other familiar settings for different periods of their lives. Official values concerning 'good mothers/workers' deserve consideration alongside the 'guilt feelings' which many Hungarian women suffer about not being 'superwomen'. It is signficant that the rates of mental illness in Hungary, as in many 'socialist' countries, are higher for women than for men.

Within this analysis, the nature of the so-called 'socialist family' is considered. In this context it can be seen that potentially the two most major exceptions so far as feminism is concerned are, first, that traditional marxists failed to analyse the ideology of domesticity which is involved in reproducing a particular form of family and the relations of male domination and female subordination, whilst, second, they critically presumed that the monogamous (heterosexual) family would disappear as women were drawn into social production.

FAMILIES AND EMPLOYMENT – IDEOLOGY

State ideologies in many countries work on the basis of an 'ideal' family in which live a man, a woman, two or – in some contexts – more children.[13] That this 'ideal' family situation rarely exists in practice does not detract from its powerful influence – for policy-makers and in terms of people's everyday lives. In contemporary life the dilemma still exists for those who are widowed, separated, ill, unskilled, mothers of 'illegitimate' children and many others, of how they fit into this 'ideal type' of family, when they patently do not. Somehow, such people are expected to reconcile the very different ways of life and work and household management that they experience, with the increasingly dominant ideology. When this dominant ideology is questioned and some of the underlying assumptions that make it up are analysed, it becomes clearer just how much certain attitudes about such things as motherhood (e.g. maternal instinct, natural mothering, biological determination) are deeply imbued with it. In the analysis of families in the Hungarian context the differences between ideals and reality are explored and the ways in which familial groupings have changed, and are changing, over time.

Given the ups and downs of market-oriented (un)employment and a distinct lack of continuous, official encouragement to working women in some Western countries such as Britain, the different context in Hungary regarding the processes whereby 'official' views feed back into women's consciousness – of their part in society and the ways in which they can achieve an harmonious, balanced and fulfilled life – is given detailed consideration. That there is much debate in Hungary in terms of what is 'natural', indicates an underlying tension in discussions on women's equality which has a political content, concerning the terms of those for and against full human equality. The very nature of what is meant by equality is important, in that most feminist theorists stress that within the present socio-political conditions this equality would necessarily be only partial as the terms on which it would be achieved would largely have been developed in a patriarchal framework of male institutions and male-oriented policies. When this dominating framework is broadened enough to be able to grasp the needs of women in their emancipation then the conditions will exist for women and men to work towards full human liberation on equal terms.

FEMINIST METHODOLOGY

Criticism of feminist analyses is often made in terms of their being visionary – not creating an analysis of the differences between women as a social entity, a driving force in history, and say, the working class as an agency for change. Certainly there is a visionary aspect to feminist analysis, one which many consider essential to any theory of liberation. In her consideration of the development of movements concerned with the liberation of women, Sheila Rowbotham has a vision of the future:

> It is only when women start to organize in large numbers that we become a political force, and begin to move towards the possibility of a truly democratic society in which every human being can be brave, responsible, thinking and diligent in the struggle to live at once freely and unselfishly. Such a democracy would be communism, and is beyond our present imagining (Rowbotham, 1972, p. 12).

There are several points to be made in terms of this feminist vision, not least that, in common with other creative visions, there are several bodies of theory arguing for different ways of achieving liberation. It is important to remember that feminist analysis is rooted in experience – the experience of being woman and this fundamental *common* experience underlies the creation of feminist work. This is not to suppose that merely by 'being' all women share common concerns, this is blatantly absurd given the differences for women in various cultures, across different herstories and in different situations of so-called 'development'. It does mean though, that such events as childbirth and child-caring have common aspects for women and as such can be discussed cross-culturally in terms of gains/losses (possibly due to certain policy measures) and lessons can be learned from changes in legislation, treatment, community care and action that have benefited women's situation (see Priya, 1992). Still, in this context it needs to be borne in mind that because 'woman' is a cultural (not a biological construct) then there are various cultural constructs of women. What feminists are working towards is the recognition of these different cultures within a woman-oriented perspective.

It is well to point out here that whilst feminist methodology is used within this work to give a critique of certain aspects of social policy and state intervention within Hungarian society, no 'prescriptions' from the Western experience are applied in the Hungarian context. At the outset of her study on feminist practice, Chris Weedon notes that:

> Feminism is a politics. It is a politics directed at changing existing power relations between women and men in society. These power relations structure all areas of life, the family, education and welfare, the world of work and politics, culture and leisure. They determine who does what and for whom, what we are and what we might become (Weedon, 1987, p. 1).

Weedon points out that the politics of feminism, which she is addressing, arise out of the Western Women's Movement, and as such are not directly applicable within different cultures. As will be seen, women's attitudes towards 'feminist politics' in Hungary show differing developments.

The difference for our purposes between the feminist emphasis and other emphases hinges on the stress given to women's experience *in their own account*. The considerations and comments made by women in Hungary to the author, are included here as equally important as other conceptions of 'how life is' drawn from academic researches. The intention is to avoid objectifying women as a focus of study and to view and review women's own perceptions of their situation. Another point to note here is the 'interdisciplinary' nature of feminist analysis which rejects the male-oriented tendency towards compartmentalism. Arguments are developed through sociological and psychological conceptions, anthropological evidence, political analysis as well as with poems, songs and womenlore. In this context there are many examples of male-oriented perspectives within the various 'disciplines' – the use of the term sounds authoritarian in itself. Oakley gives several examples of this within sociology, such as the sociological literature on women's employment, which:

> until quite late in the history of sociology, [women's employment] did not exist and when it did, focused almost entirely on the so-called 'social problem' of the employment of married women and the hazards this might pose to the satisfactory functioning of marriage as an institution and to the physical and psychological welfare of husbands and children (Oakley, 1976, p. 204).

Within her critique of sociology Oakley emphasises a central feature of feminist argument which restates the importance of the subjective experiences of women themselves. In writing about women from the male-oriented perspective women remain the objects of study and have no opportunity to take part in the study as subjects.

In this context extracts from discussions and interviews with the author are used in this work precisely to redress the imbalance often apparent in works which miss out the subject. Most of the discussions and interviews took place over a period of eight months in 1986 with many shorter visits from 1987 to 1992, in an environment in which there were exchanges between the author and the women who were sharing experiences, information and insights about their lives in Hungary. No enforced effort was made by the author to be detached and dispassionate and frequently questions were asked by each of us. Building up an atmosphere of trust in which open discussion of our everyday lives as women and all that this entails in terms of feelings and emotions connected with senses of self, hopes, fears, ambitions, expectations, romance, caring, the search for and/or assertion of identity, was essential to get beneath the surface impressions gained from questionnaires or formal interviews. This is not to say there is no place for general surveys, questionnaires and structured interviews, all of which have been included within this work. There is a need to emphasise, as a vitally important ingredient, the *experience* of women themselves. In answer to questions concerning the objectivity and impartiality of knowledge, Jaggar notes that:

> Women's subordinate status means that, unlike men, women do not have an interest in mystifying reality and so are likely to develop a clearer and more trustworthy understanding of the world. A representation of reality from the standpoint of women is more objective and unbiased than the prevailing representations that reflect the standpoint of men (Jaggar, 1983, p. 384).

In so saying Jaggar is not claiming that only the oppressed can realise and analyse the nature of their oppression, nor that women have a monopoly of understanding their situation. What Jaggar and other feminists do claim is that the experience of being woman means that women are free from some of the narrow and often defensive constraints which patriarchal socialisation places upon men.

Just as Engels's work on women's liberation has often been reduced in practice to 'liberation equals paid work for women' so there is a danger within the male-oriented perspective of attempting to reduce complex feminist analyses either to a form of women's rights within the male world or to vulgarise them by dismissing arguments as being female supremacist. In this context Rowbotham makes the point that:

> Just as the abolition of class power would release people outside the working class, and thus requires their support and involvement, so the movement against hierarchy which is carried in feminism goes beyond the liberation of sex. It contains the possibility of equal relations not only between women and men, but also between men and men, women and women, and even between adults and children (Rowbotham, in Evans, 1982, p. 79).

Another strand of male-oriented criticism is in terms of feminist theories being merely 'Utopian'. This however, is practically and easily disproved by the variety of analyses which concentrate on how to change the 'here and now' problems which women face daily in contemporary societies. It is exactly this combination of long- and short-term analysis and discussion of alternatives that gives the feminist contribution its strength. In terms of social policy, feminists include within their criticisms questions concerning the underlying assumptions about the family and the sexual division of labour which are generally implicitly included in welfare measures.

AIMS AND STRUCTURE

The primary aim is to look at the material conditions in which Hungarian women have gone, and go, about their everyday lives in the context of the interventionist measures designed to change certain aspects of their existence. In this context the state forces in Hungary are analysed over time, in terms of the way that policies are formulated, the direction to which planning was leading, as well as noting how welfare policies were administered and controlled, and whether or not barriers are evident in terms of the recipients of certain benefits/allowances. New sets of social relations were created in the moves towards 'socialism' and the extension and consolidation of these relations shaped new forms of power relations. Hungarian society was not developing into a 'socialist' society but became a distinctly Hungarian form of Kádárism, in which power and status were differentially accorded to officials within the regime. In order to 'get on' people had to make some compromise with the regime, in terms of either joining the Party or not opposing its ritualistic form of rule. Within these new social relations, well-being and status were primarily tied to political social relations, although within underground circles of course some status attached to active opposition to the regime. In time this statist 'socialism' became not only discredited but displaced and a political pluralist, market-oriented system is now being developed in Hungary. The ensuing changes within social relations are very much affecting women's lives and women in turn are effecting change within certain areas.

Obviously relations between state forces and societal elements play a major part in people's lives, and a major factor in the ways in which state forces affected women's lives under 'socialism' was the psychological element. In any transitional period, be that

Hungarian society from 1948, or from 1988, the development of new social relations is bound to be uneven, and to some extent limited – by existing attitudes or lack of money. One of the barriers to bettering women's situations in such transitional periods is that 'hangover' of former attitudes and beliefs, which to a large extent become internalised and so reproduced within the consciousness of succeeding generations. In this context the work of Irene Dölling is important in terms of considering the patriarchal paternalism which she argues was internalised by many women who experienced 'socialist emancipation' in various contexts within central and eastern Europe.

Both the quantitative and qualitative aspects of life need to be changed in order for new social relations to emerge. In a highly industrialised late twentieth-century society such development entails social upheavals which are fraught with complications and are bound to necessitate a certain amount of rethinking along the way. As regards women's liberation, complex sets of relationships would need to undergo change – those between women and men in terms of rights/duties and expectations, between particular groups of women and certain state forces, mediation between specific ideologies and the realities of women's situations, between changes in family structures and state structures, and between women's domestic and public work – to note but a few. For 'socialist' societies, such as Hungary was viewed for 40 years, a framework within which women's position was seen as largely shaped by state policies and ideology, with state forces constructing ideology to some extent, was very destructive, not only for women's images of themselves and their opportunities, but for hindering the development of more progressive social expectations of women's strengths and future possibilities. State policies were constrained by changes in family structures caused by industrialisation and urbanisation, to a certain extent. The role of domestic (largely women's) labour in the economy, which in turn affects the position of women and each other is considered within the general framework of work – valued/undervalued, paid/unpaid – in both the 'socialist' and the so-called democratic context.

In Chapter 2, major social and political developments in Hungary since the 1940s are assessed together with some of the recent social changes following from the economic reforms of the late-1960s and the political developments since 1989. In Chapter

3 women's situation in connection with paid work is considered in order to gauge what women gained materially from 'socialist production' and how their domestic environments, considered in Chapter 4, are interlinked to their paid working situations. Generally the pivotal link between these two working contexts for women, are the activities involving families. Certain aspects of family theory are outlined to give background to some of the 'socialist' claims as well as to highlight some possible changes within the new political climate of liberal economics coupled with conservative socio-political attitudes.

In Chapter 5 the strengths and apparent weakness of certain social policy issues are considered. Much importance is attached to the debates surrounding the implementation of the child-care leave within Hungary. As this was one of the earliest instances of a much wider policy introducing payment for women to care for their children at home, its repercussions for women's lives was, and remains, important. Some of the stresses and strains faced by women in their various working lives are considered in Chapter 6, on health. Particular health needs of women in terms of child-bearing and child-caring are assessed against the background of health service crises. In the concluding section of this book attitudes towards femininity, sexuality, feminism, women's rights as well as those surrounding pornography, rape, prostitution and Hungary's most modern industry – the sex industry – are considered. What all this has meant for women who choose to organise in order to change certain patriarchal attitudes and to support actively campaigns for extending women's rights in various arenas is the subject of Chapter 8. In conclusion the questions raised throughout are reconsidered against the background of transitional changes, in terms of future possibilities for women within Hungarian society.

2 Transformations

This chapter outlines the unique transformations that went towards making Hungarian society what it is today. Various transformations that occurred within the Hungarian state structures are assessed, as are the ways in which certain policies resulted in various social consequences. In turn the focus is upon the impact that societal developments had upon the statist structures. A major aim is to look at changing balances of power and within that political participation, especially in terms of later developments in the 1980s and early 1990s. Events in 1989 in Hungary cannot be seen as a knock-on effect as some commentators have viewed developments in the former GDR and Czechoslovakia. The rise of Solidarity, ably chartered by Garton Ash (1985), certainly forms a backdrop to changing interrelations in Hungary, but more significant are the attempts at economic reform from the late 1960s and the widespread influence of the second economy throughout Hungarian society (see Swain, 1992). A particular focus for this study will be women's participation in, and views of, some of these changing power relations.

Politics concerns the mediation of power throughout society, and in the 'socialist' phase of Hungarian development relatively clear power cleavages between state structures and social forces were apparent. In the rigidly controlled early phase, 1948–56, political power was exercised by a small ruling élite attempting extensive control over all elements of Hungarian society. With the revolution in 1956 some rethinking occurred and over time the 'Kádárist compromise' became a living reality in the form of intensive economic development to build integrative links between rural and urban populations. This development attempted to eliminate rural poverty within the framework of full-employment policies.

People made choices in such a situation – to join the Party for career advancement, to actively oppose the Party/state authorities within the small oppositional groupings, or to divide themselves between the so-called First and Second societies – the external world of survival in a controlled socio-political situation and the internal world of private, everyday life. These distinctions were never clear as inevitably these worlds merged and to some extent coalesced (see Szelényi, 1989).

With the economic reforms beginning in 1968, being slowed down in 1972 only to restart around 1979, Hungarian society was undergoing massive change – not least, the 'cracks' in Party/state administration were becoming more obvious. The development of the second economy added enormously to the changing developments in both 'worlds' but principally in people's everyday existence. Economic reforms within such an intertwined political-economy as Kádárist Hungary could not be carried out without challenges being made in the socio-political sphere. These changes were something unique to Hungarian society and cannot be underestimated, either in terms of the path which political democratisation took in 1989/90 or in the likely directions to which Hungarian goals will be targeted in the 1990s and beyond. As will be seen, it could be argued that it was not that the Party structures in Hungary were 'overthrown' but that their 'leading roles' had become superfluous.

In basically chronological order consideration is given to the changes after 1948 in terms of the 'top-down' authoritarian approach of the communist bureaucracies wishing to shape society towards a 'socialist future', Kádár's so-called normalisation policies and within this the development of economic reforms and the second economy and its consequences. Events in Hungary from the mid-1980s can be seen as a culmination of the need for socio-political reform to enable accommodation to various economic developments which had changed social relations. The changeover of power from the Party in the multi-party elections is considered with some of the consequences for Hungarian society and women's participation within politics. Externally, the 'Gorbachev' factor cannot be discounted, impacting as it did in Poland and Hungary very early on, and some saw the development of economic reforms in Hungary as a 'test-bed' for potential changes throughout the region. Bearing this in mind, it is possible to consider developments in Hungary from 1948 to 1989 as something of a continuum with obvious breaks and realignments.

In terms of how such transitions affected Hungarian women it is important to remember that 'women' cannot be analysed as an entity. There were always Party women, richer women, poorer women, Roma women, and differences between Hungarian women by class – or around access to the mechanisms of the redistributive process. Yet, as the Party/state policy-makers did view 'women' as a policy entity, be it 'women workers' or 'mothers', then it is possible to consider some of the particular policies aimed at 'women' in terms particularly of paid work and childcare and family policies and how these added or detracted from Hungarian women's active participation within politics and social relations.

It was within the period from 1948, following the 'liberation', that Soviet 'socialist' ideology became incorporated into official government policies in Hungary.[1] Much of the impact of change was experienced particularly by women, who were being introduced into the workforce in large numbers and were becoming 'liberated'.[2] It was during the later period, from the 1960s to the present, that the impact of the economic reforms was being felt within Hungarian society. A major focus will be on changes within the economy from 1967 to 1990 which in turn initiated developments within society sometimes referred to as 'second society thesis'.[3] Certain social consequences arising from the various phases of the economic reforms are analysed including the changes in living standards, with rising prices and differing opportunities for earning.

HISTORICAL BACKGROUND

There are many good accounts of Hungarian history including recent sources such as Heinrich (1986); Hare, Radice and Swain (1981); and Hankiss (1990). Hungarian society between the wars was marked by a rigid class system and a virtually feudal situation in the countryside with massive inequalities. As Macfarlane points out: 'There were half a million landless peasants while 1 per cent of the land-owning population held 43 per cent of the land' (Macfarlane, 1990, p. 163). The country was governed by successive conservative administrations under Admiral Horthy. Hungary was allied with Nazi Germany from 1941 until October 1944 when an armistice was agreed.

The Soviet presence in central and eastern Europe ensured the establishment and maintenance of 'socialist' political systems in Hungary and certain neighbouring countries. In these states the Soviet Union largely determined the form, though not necessarily the substance, of each regime's policies, especially with respect to the promotion of economic and social transformation. A provisional National Assembly was convened in December 1944 when much of the country was occupied by the Soviet army. The provisional national government which was elected gave the Communist Party, Social Democratic Party and Smallholders Party each two portfolios, with one for the Peasant Party. It was clear from the beginning that the Communists and the Soviet authorities were in control and were determined to remove all domestic opposition and secure the 'election' of a Communist government. Between 1947 and 1950 power was concentrated in one of Stalin's followers, Rákosi, who presided over the liquidation of all other political parties.

In the 'reconstruction period' in post-war Hungary, the quantitative social transformations were apparent in the economy, the labour force, educational and governmental institutional structures. As always, the qualitative impact is less easy to illustrate, yet in terms of the changing labour force, especially the entry of many more women and the rising educational level of workers, there was quite apparent transformation.[4]

It is generally accepted that the decade after 1947 was one of immense change. In Hungary its status as an ex-enemy country of the USSR was decisive. The Hungarian nation had suffered massive destruction in the summer and autumn of 1944, and large-scale plunder of the national wealth occurred under the Fascist Arrow Cross and the Nazis. After the cessation of hostilities concerns financed by Germany were taken over by the USSR as German assets and operated for reparations. It became clear that Hungary entered the post-war 'liberation' period under the burden of many Soviet economic liabilities. Unlike the situation in Poland and Czechoslovakia, there was relatively limited nationalisation in Hungary at the end of the war. Yet the break with the West in 1948 brought about massive transformation in the political and economic climate of Hungary. Between the 1948 nationalisation law (16 March) and December 1949, the state sector absorbed all enterprises of more than ten employees, plus all foreign concerns except those whose ownership was based on laws passed in January 1945 (i.e Soviet acquisitions). By late 1949 the state sector had absorbed approximately 90.5 per cent of total employment in manufacturing, with only 4.7 per cent remaining in the private sector, 3.6 per cent in the Soviet-owned groups and 1.2 per cent in cooperative and municipal ownership.(Spulber, 1975, table 2).

These developments were paralleled by an upswing in industrial production after 1947. This reconstruction of industry did not mean a basic restoration of its pre-war structure as a restructuring of output occurred. The food industries and light industry generally still lagged behind the pre-war productive level, while output in heavy industry considerably surpassed it. Here the shift in favour of heavy industry was justified as a necessary consequence of the demands of reconstruction and reparations deliveries and set the trend for the basic Stalinisation of the economy, favouring heavy industrial expansion above consumer needs. Several writers (Mellor, Heinrich) note that Hungary began developing its heavy industry along new lines to fit the concepts of autarky during the Stalinist period. This rapid development, a form of 'rushed industrialisation', was to have important consequences for the introduction of women into the workforce and for the ability of state policies to meet welfare demands. Yet in the agricultural realm, in which women had long played a very active role, no such productive upswing was apparent. Investment targets for agriculture, set out in the three-year plan were not fulfilled. Instead of the 7700 new tractors prescribed by the plan, for example, only 4500 were actually put into use (Berend and Ránki, 1974, p. 187). Such restrictions on peasant production for the market as the limitations of credit to agriculture, were definite obstacles to growth and proved harmful to agricultural production.[5] The proportion of agricultural output reaching the market was even smaller, for the poor peasants were markedly increasing their consumption at this time so that the amount of produce available for market sale was considerably smaller than can be calculated from the crude figures of agricultural production.

POLITICAL, SOCIAL AND ECONOMIC CHANGES

Distinct developments were emerging within the nature of political life in Hungary. By 1949 Hungary can be seen as a member-state in the group of Soviet-styled 'socialist' nations which had emerged in central and eastern Europe. With the dissolution of the governing coalition and the unification of the Communist and

Social Democratic parties in June 1948, the new Hungarian Workers' Party (Magyar Dolgozók Pártja) came to power. In economic terms, centralisation necessitated planning, whilst in social terms measures were taken towards encouraging 'socialist' policies in an Hungarian environment. One obvious difference in the policies of the new ruling bodies in post-war Hungary was that because 'socialist' societies were supposed to be actively moving towards the future goal of 'socialism' (then communism) so processes of industrialisation, urbanisation and social mobility in general were to be accelerated by deliberate efforts of the new central authorities. Zsuzsa Ferge assesses the revolutionary changes in social and economic relations in post-war Hungary:

> Hungary is one of the East European socialist states where an unusually rapid social and economic transformation took place in the years following the Second World War. The old structure, part-feudal, part-capitalist, was dismantled in a revolutionary way in the years after 1945. Many members of the former ruling classes lost their position. The events of war, the various radical measures such as the land reform, the nationalisation of capital assets and the dismissal of many people highly placed in the administration, drove a great number of them out of the country; those who stayed became 'downwardly mobile' in many respects (Ferge, in Andorka and Kolosi, 1984, p. 193).

As 'socialist' state ownership needed planning, the government necessarily aimed at a control mechanism within the economy which best supported its goals, and enabled their direct realisation. Under the new system, the whole workings of the economy, production as well as distribution, were controlled by binding directives precisely spelled out in facts and figures. Production was according to detailed plans worked out for every year and every company – plans based on an amazingly large number of indicators.

The central decision to minimise as far as possible the 'element of chance' in economic life, was reflected in the 1951 price reform which removed the direct connexions of the price level and movements of 'consumer prices' and of the producers' prices. In essence, the resulting price system was one in which the cost price bore no fixed relation to the sale price – a great many primary industrial materials were sold below cost with large state subsidies. On the agricultural side, the situation was further aggravated by the big difference between the market price of agricultural goods and the price which producers received when they delivered to the state. In an effort to reduce the unfavourable effects of the price fluctuation which the Korean war boom caused on the world market, there was a changeover to fixed prices in Council for Mutual Eonomic Assistance (CMEA) foreign trade so that the right-price system of the CMEA market emerged as totally independent of the world-market price level and price ratios. Although this obviously made planning easier by removing spontaneous effects of price fluctuations, this price system went no way towards stimulating economic activity and efficiency. The conseqences of these decisions were indeed far-reaching as the events of 1989 were to show.

Whilst the remnants of the old conservative, capitalist order in Hungary were being destroyed, new elements concerned with creating Soviet-styled 'socialism' were introduced. Many of these new elements were becoming distorted, both in economic and socio-political terms, due to the prevailing Stalinist orthodoxy. Reducing this complex, all-encompassing process to its basic essentials it is apparent that the system introduced in Hungary from 1948 was one which was fraught with tensions and contradictions. As the government had 'top priority' aims in the economic sphere (geared primarily towards this prevailing Stalinist theory of rapid, autarkic industrialisation), the economic goals and the means of achieving them were chosen largely on the basis of political considerations, so that the needs of the population were ignored.

Policy decisions based on political expedience soon proved to be defective. At the beginning of the 1950s there was a decline in real wages and real incomes. Social benefits had remained at the level of their introduction in the 1940s so in like manner their relative level decreased. Women workers, often heads of households, were having to work at full-time jobs to care for their families financially in a situation in which there were very few child care facilities available. Dependence upon – generally women – relatives, neighbours or friends was fundamental. There were few workplace canteens or public laundries in existence in Hungary at this time so the 'double burden' aspect of women's lives within the 'socialist' context was an early feature of the period.

The majority of Hungarians were becoming much worse off. Workers in factories were aware of the reality of the so-called 'global' fulfilment of the plan, which had become common practice – a company may overfulfil the plans for heavy casts but neglect the manufacture of light ones. In this way enterprises accumulated increasing stocks of unsaleable goods which embodied large amounts of material and labour. Despite some good growth statistics, it soon became evident that this system of overcentralised planning was proving incompatible with one basic principle of economic development – higher productivity. As Berend sees the situation, growing bureaucracies and worker/administrative cleavages were also beginning to emerge:

> The enormous information hunger of the system of central planning and the flood of regulations brought with it a phenomenal expansion of the administrative machinery. In 1941, the blue-collar:white-collar worker ratio in Hungarian industry was 9.1, by 1953 it was 4.1 (Berend and Ránki, 1974, p. 263).

Many experts agree that it was this paralysing identification of the established economic model with the 'socialist' system which was at the root of the vast majority of social and eocnomic problems in Hungary at this time. An attempt was made to try to stem the vast growth of the bureaucracy and measures were taken in the summer of 1954 to reduce the administrative staff by a certain percentage. Although these checks temporarily cut-back the steady and unusually rapid growth of the administration, the fact that the economic mechanism remained unchanged necessarily reproduced the problem.

After Stalin's death in March 1953, this period began to be seen in a truer light, in terms of the propaganda matching, or not matching, the reality of Hungarian conditions. Yet it needs to be remembered that the discrepancy between official statements and public beliefs was much less in the late 1940s and early 1950s than it is now. For example, many people genuinely believed that women were becoming 'liberated' – these beliefs had not yet been tested. One professional woman who was just beginning her career in 1948 told me of the real belief she and many of her colleagues had in what they were being asked to do:

> and yet we had such high hopes, real enthusiasm. We did believe that it was possible to work towards a fairer future in which there was less of a difference between rich and poor. It is easy to forget that now with all that has happened (Nora, 1986).

After Stalin's death there was a 'new course', in which this grim reality became better-known and the general public and party opinion were less likely to be deceived by propaganda, films, or broadcasts. The famous Polish *Poem for Adults* is a forceful example of the dreadful realities behind some of the myths of the glorious 'building of communism'. In this work the situation on the 'star' construction sites is retold in stark reality. On such sites as Nova Huta and Duna Város, people worked in sub-human conditions in which it was not uncommon for women to have to drown foetuses on the building sites. Such was the reality behind the propaganda.

Much has been written on events in 1956 and I do not propose to detail this. It is widely accepted that the October revolution in Hungary marked a turning-point in Hungarian history and its political significance had worldwide repercussions. Of Hungarian people's expectations in political terms, Heinrich points out that:

> As a result of Soviet intervention and American non-intervention most Hungarians began to adopt a pragmatic attitude towards both superpowers: they had to live with Soviet occupation and give up their illusions about the United States as an unselfish champion of human rights (Heinrich, 1986, p. 32).

The massive impact of Stalinism within Hungarian society cannot be overestimated. As Konrád and Szelényi put it: 'There was no sphere of private life; in every aspect of his life he was compelled to profess his faith in the political system' (Konrád and Szelény, 1979, p. 195). This meant that not only were impromptu political meetings called at workplaces which all were expected to attend, but also that agitators were constantly asking questions to which there were 'correct' answers, and that even at weekends people were expected to do 'social labour' which could vary from building work, to editing a wall newspaper for an apartment house. Yet the Western ideal of the separation of public and private life did have deep roots in Hungarian society so that apart from notable exceptions, such as children informing on their politically incorrect parents, the political realm did not overwhelm everyday family life. This was to have important repercussions when the second economy began to develop and again later in terms of a 'reactivated civil society' becoming politically involved in campaigns. For women's lives and their own identities the importance of 'family life' also had direct consequences.

'NORMALISATION'

By November 1956 Kádár returned as head of an almost non-existent and thoroughly discredited Party, in a country torn by civil war, united only by a hatred of Soviet occupation. It was a curious phenomenon by which Kádár emerged as one of the most popular leaders in the region. In his first few years in office Kádár had to struggle against those in the workers' councils who would not 'give up'. According to estimates about 20 000 people were arrested, 2000 executed and many thousands were exiled to the Soviet Union (Kovrig, 1979; Heinrich, 1986). To show new beginnings, the name Hungarian Socialist Workers' Party was taken but the reconstruction of this party was difficult because of opposition from both the Nagy group and supporters of Rákosi-type politics. At the same time as purging the party of all Nagy supporters – Nagy himself was executed in 1958 after another Soviet attack on the Yugoslavs – Kádár was instituting economic reform. Yet progress in economic recovery was slow. Until Stalin's death economic development in Hungary had been based on self-sufficiency and limited trade with the Soviet Union. After 1953 this emphasis changed, and states neighbouring the Soviet Union began to trade more with each other. Any impetus for the formation of multinational and regional coalitions and associations, which might have challenged Soviet authority was blocked. Such coalitions would also have made it more difficult for the Soviets to have played one country off against the other. Yet steps were being taken in agriculture which although not producing immediate results, laid the basis for the modernisation of agriculture. It was around this time (January 1962) that János Kádár made his famous statement about 'those who are not against us are with us'. Rákosi had said 'those who are not with us are against us'. This came to typify Kádárist politics, and the Alliance Policy which promised gradual liberalisation in the future. In March 1963 a final amnesty was granted for all those fighting the regime in 1956. Within the Party the secret vote was viewed as a step towards more inner-party democracy. It was also beginning to be realised at this time that economic decisions do not necessarily solve social problems.

CHANGES IN POLICY-MAKING

Hungarian policy-makers up to the early 1960s believed that changing economic relations inevitably led to progressive social development. Eventually though, politicians realised that they could not expect to change and shape social reality without at the very least some information in the form of social statistics and some data on policy options. To attempt to shape policy in a vacuum had proved disastrous by this time and planners realised that some information concerning the mechanisms of power relations in society and the interests of people operating in real life were vital to social progress, indeed to social cohesion. Such information could only be gained by the development of social research. Following from this realisation there has been a sharp rise in the production of social statistics and a rapid development of historical, economic and social research.

Yet it must be borne in mind that this perceived need to make the decision-making structure less rigid and to gain help from other sectors of society (sociologists and historians as well as economists) was severely constrained in many ways. Any discussion of 'real' levels of poverty within Hungarian society remained outside the purview of social researchers until well into the 1980s.[6] At the time though it was argued that policy-making would need to take into account the wants as well as the needs of the population. By 1960 Kádárist politics associated with creating policies based on some measure of social reality, built from survey data and reports, was beginning to be discussed. In this context, the population census of 1 January 1960 provided an opportunity, given the apparently encouraging political conditions, for some large-scale surveys within different sections of Hungarian society. The difference between surveys carried out from 1960 and earlier research, was in terms of concentration upon specific aspects of social reality rather than general, global comparisons of economic circumstances. These surveys attempted to find out what things were really like for people in Hungary and to report this to policy-makers. This development of a partial type of interactive social policy is one feature of the Kádár years, with the later development of certain societal 'problems' being discussed within the pages of national newspapers and magazines, academic journals and monographs, on television and on radio. Such discussion developed in a limited way throughout the 1960s along with the debates concerning the economic reforms, which eventually resulted in the introduction of the New Economic Mechanism.

ECONOMIC DEVELOPMENTS SINCE THE 1960s

A primary push towards social change concerned developments in economic relations between various groups in Hungarian society in the 1960s. It was apparent from the 1950s that the Hungarian Socialist Workers' Party (HSWP) favoured political solutions to problems yet the traditional command model of the economy was not well-suited to Hungary's needs. Hungarian economists were aware that without sufficient raw material resources, their small country could not withstand potential crises without some structural reform. This was less obviously apparent in the earlier phases of intensive development yet by 1965 the HSWP had taken a decision to initiate economic reform and to accumulate reserves. This was not envisaged as a grand design to change the entire socio-economic system, unlike the situation in Yugoslavia or Czechoslovakia, but was only along the lines of improving or reinterpreting the system of planning. There were four basic elements involved:

1. Abolition of target planning and physical allocation of resources; no formal subordination of central plans and enterprise plans; free exchange of information.
2. Investments – enterprises received freedom in investment but this was basically controlled from the centre on big projects.
3. Incentives – determine general function of maximisation of profit from enterprises. Increases in average wages were linked with increases in profit (with a ceiling on maximum wages). The fund created in relation to profit was divided

into two parts: (a) development fund; and (b) sharing fund (for bonuses, etc.). Both were linked to profit.

4. Change in pricing principles – (a) change in price formula used as the starting-point for price determination (recognising that costs of capital must be reflected in the price); and (b) linking starting price with world market – foreign trade price must be taken into account in determining domestic trade price.[7]

These elements made up the basics of the Hungarian Economic Mechanism, which ebbed and flowed over the twenty years up to 1988. János Kornai called the system that developed in the Hungarian state-owned sector 'indirect bureaucratic control' compared with the old command system of 'direct bureaucratic control'. This showed that the dominant form of coordination remained bureaucratic control. Here it must be noted that the terms 'bureaucracy' and 'bureaucratic control' refer to the role played by the Party apparatus (Fehér and Arato, 1991, p. 44). In this context the development of the second economy was of great importance.

The transition from a system of central planning to that of a more market-determined system was vaguely scheduled for fifteen years. Such change was supposed to be discreet, not involving any politicial change, despite the fact that there was a decentralisation in the political bodies, among which the lower members of the hierarchy of councils were furnished with increased powers. Indeed, given events in Czechoslovakia in 1968 it was important for the authorities to stress that economic reform had nothing whatsoever to do with politics. In reality of course, governments cannot choose to change 'parts' of society as economics and politics are interrelated in all societies but more especially in those actively attempting to change the social relations. Economic changes affect the way people live and interact with each other and with the state forces. This trend towards decentralisation which was supposed to become apparent in socio-political terms, by greater emphasis on participation within the enterprise, remained more ideal than factual. This was one of the essential contradications of the Hungarian economic reforms, and contributed to the economic crises of the late 1980s.

In the 1970s these processes came to a standstill in some economic spheres and in others there was a reversal. The

Hungarian authorities had decided to 're-centralise'. This recentralisation took different forms – from the 'visible' decisions to put a few dozen major enterprises under direct ministerial supervision and the revision of the pronounced liberal attitude towards the independent craft enterprises, to the less-obvious areas such as the change of direction in the field of price policy, where the proportion of centrally administered prices increased in many branches yet contracted in others. Amongst the arguments put forward as to why this reversal occurred, the fundamental economic one is that to have free prices a system needs functioning markets, which in turn work from some measure of competition. In Hungary, for various reasons, the number of suppliers was very limited, so whilst the principle of an open market was introduced in 1968 it could not be successfully implemented straight away.

As would be expected, of the four elements mentioned above, whilst the first two involved some decentralisation of decision-making it was within the second two that the possibilities for dislocation and disparities were present. Giving workers incentives is a basic market principle, yet doing this within a framework which includes some non-profit-making industries is a dangerous project. For a profit-oriented system to operate successfully, the profit motive must be predominant both for enterprise managements and workforces so that their behaviour is guided by the link between personal income and enterprise profits. In this context Vajna states that, from a survey carried out amongst managers, the fear of losses caused some managers to be shy of taking risks, as they could lose up to three months' salaries (Vajna, in Nove, 1982, p. 208). Certainly, by 1973–4 some heavy industry factories were on the verge of disintegration due to workers leaving in search of better jobs. It is understandable that working people would move to the best job situation which often created situations in which industrial workers would take up employment in enterprises that could not always use them. As Vajna notes: 'The waves of movement between jobs made the clash between central, enterprise and personal interests plain' (Vajna, in Nove, 1984, p. 192).

By the mid-1970s the Hungarian economic mechanism can be said to have reached a watershed. It had to go one way or the other – to have more tolerance or more administration. The Hungarian authorities chose more administration so that by 1976 enterprise wage-policy was confined within narrow limits and there was a 'minimum wage increase' fixed for every enterprise, independent of results. The new trade agreement entered into by the Hungarian authorities in January 1975 quickly worsened the economic situation. Previously the Hungarian economy had been sheltered from the sharp increase in oil prices, whereas in this agreement the terms of trade worsened and COMECON (Council for Mutual Economic Aid) prices were changed to include the principle of a sliding average based on world market prices over the previous five years. By 1983 Hungary had incurred a loss equalling its entire annual GNP over a period of ten years (Heinrich, 1986, p. 41).

IMPACT OF ECONOMIC CHANGES

What did all this mean for the average Hungarian? Given the difficulties within the original project the two areas which most affected working people were those of wages and prices. Perhaps the most major impact on lifestyles during the 1980s was that of price increases. Much of the involvement within the second economy was from economic necessity. By the 1980 price reforms it was possible to see the 1968 theoretical conceptions being put into practice. Basically, this meant that consumer prices were linked to producer price levels. The differences were so great that this had to be a relatively gradual process. As prices had been subsidised for so long, though, these price changes were bound to affect working people and those on fixed incomes badly, and the price increases in 1980 were shocking for the majority of Hungarians. The price of bread, which had been stable for twenty-eight years as a political price, was raised on average by 50 per cent. The price of meat and meat products increased by 26 per cent, sugar by more than 20 per cent and there was also a steep rise in dairy products. Yet, these increases still did not cut the absolute burden of food subsidies on the state budget – only bread was being sold at a price which directly related to producers prices. It was not only foodstuffs which became much more expensive, as the rises in energy prices show. The price of electricity, which had been the same for fifteen years, again for political reasons, was raised by 50 per cent but would need to have been raised by 90 per cent to cover the subsidy. The price of district heating was increased by 40 per cent, which only covered about one-third of its actual cost (Vajna, in Nove, 1984, p. 209).

These price increases added at least 5 per cent to the cost of living. As domestic budgeters and managers, women generally bore the brunt of such radical changes in the purchasing power of their incomes. Obviously for those people on low and fixed incomes this was a disastrous state of affairs. Whilst some income supplements were introduced to contain popular dissatisfaction these were insufficient to cover the total increases in living costs, so some people's standards of living markedly deteriorated. Certain groups of people in Hungary then became poorer. It was around this time that pensioners and those with large families became 'confirmed' as two major sections of society which were very much lagging behind in incomes, and thereby in living standards. Both of these groups remain amongst the poorest people in Hungary as well as Roma families who are discriminated against in many ways and usually suffer acute poverty. Amongst the 'new poor' were now included those without work and so, without regular income. Unemployment became a reality of Hungarian life.

Movement between jobs became common to 'get the best deal' but some workers were unable to do this successfully so income differences became noticeable. Some workers could bargain for higher wages during the 1970s and 1980s but the changes towards marketisation strategies have tended to prohibit bargaining of the old sort whereby changing jobs, going to factories with better conditions then returning to their old workplaces, certain workers could receive higher wages than before. For managers up to the mid-1980s, their selection and appointment remained within the purview of the top bureaucracy. Kornai notes that until the legislative changes in 1985 it was understandable 'that one of the main objectives of managers was to please their superiors' (Fehér and Arato, 1991, p. 35). In this context the development of the second economy and the analogous *second society* thesis (Hankiss) was viewed by some as crucial to the development of differentiated social spaces and independent thought.

SECOND ECONOMY AND SECOND SOCIETY

The *second economy* should not be confused with the so-called *shadow economies* in Western countries. In Hungary the *second economy* was an important activity *within* the national economy so it has more parallels with the term *informal sector* used within Western research terminology. Work within the second economy can take many forms ranging from informal work which is actively encouraged by the state to work that is illegal. All those who for decades, whether in rural or urban areas, had been growing fruit and vegetables on their plots or allotments for themselves and to sell on the market were taking part in the second economy. In his work Hann notes that the majority of households in Hungary which engage in small-scale farming market some of their produce and have regular sources of wage income. In urban areas anything from using factory machines in the evening to fulfil outside orders or using your car as an unofficial taxi came within second economy work. Often, though, the legality of work did not compare with its social standing perhaps because the *Power* was not only the prime employer but also the primary oppressor so that to work slowly or to steal from the state were often seen as laudable.[8] The extent and range of activities within the second economy is very wide. Iván Szelényi notes that 'By the mid-1980s 70 per cent of the households in Hungary earned incomes from the second economy, and about a fifth of the income earners received a third or half of their incomes from private business activities.'[9] So far as women are concerned many women who are classified as 'inactive' or 'housewives' are also active earners within the second economy. Although aspects of alternative economic activity such as that of the second economy in Hungary are visible elsewhere, it is generally noted that the sheer extent of such activities makes the Hungarian situation unique.

Yet opinion is divided over the *second society* thesis proposed by Hankiss. Essentially Hankiss argues that in Hungary a so-called *double* or *split consciousness* was common during the 1950s and early 1960s – one mind/soul for official life and another for family environment or second society. There could be parallels here with the personal/public distinctions that feminist analysts make about opening up politics to encompass the personal, everyday political aspects of our lives.

As noted, the Communist take-over in 1948 aimed to 'control' society which, over time, became systematically atomised. Whilst Hankiss outlines how traditional social networks – local, professional, cultural, religious – were destroyed, he argues that fragments survived and by the mid-1960s the regeneration of social networks began, despite renewed efforts by the party and local oligarchies to thwart this process (Hankiss, 1991, fig. 3.1). By outlining this view briefly the aim has been to give a framework in which to consider the basis of societal developments which led to the renewed activism within Hungarian society in the 1980s and within this women's activism in various spheres.

Various scenarios of how Hungarian society was changing were being discussed in the mid- to late 1980s. At least three schools of thought were apparent concerning what would bring about a transformation of the country:

1. those who believed the second society was *the* emerging alternative which would expand within the existing political system, and would grow into the challenger of the system;
2. those who believed that the institutional system of the first society needed to be transformed initially; and
3. those who felt that a combination of a regenerated civil society with legal-constitutional transformation of the first society was necessary for change.

Table 2.1 gives an idea of how some such scenarios were phrased. During the 1970s and 1980s there were active oppositional groupings within Hungarian society and whilst these remained small and largely intellectual, their ideas were influential. The publication in 1987 of *The Social Contract: Pre-conditions of a Way Out* by János Kis, Ottilia Solt and Ferenc Köszeg through *Beszélö*, caused a great deal of discussion and rethinking of future political developments. Within these particular proposals were ideas concerning a second chamber in Parliament. It could be argued that the present system in place in Hungary suffers from the lack of this bicameral arrangement and that the Councils which have been set up over the period August 1990–1 are in fact attempting to play the role of a second chamber in Parliament. Yet such groupings remain privileged as membership is selective. This is not to say that this was a conscious programme but the very nature of having to register officially as a group, to become a member of the 'Social Council' which was formed in August 1991

Table 2.1 Organising principles at work in the two spheres of the first society, the second society and the alternative society

The first society	*The second society*		*The hypothetical alternative society*
The formal, manifest and legitimate sphere	The informal, latent and 'non-legit.' sphere		
Central planning redistribution	'the administrative market'		Market mechanisms?
(Market mechanisms)	Clientelism	(Market mechanisms)	(Central planning?)
Statism One Participatory party system (State corporatism, or 'bureaucratic pluralism'	Oligarchy	(Elements of self government social corporatism syndicalism)	democracy?
(Enlightened absolutism)			Social corporatism?
'Socialist culture'			Syndicalism?
(Elements of European traditional culture)	(Elements of European consumerist culture)	(Elements of European traditional and consumerist cultures)	

Source: Hankiss, 1991.

meant that it was those groups who had registered in 1990 that were invited to join. In terms of the involvement of trade unions, employers and employees within the Council for Reconciliation, again the selective membership makes the democratic process difficult, as do questions of representativeness.

By 1987 and 1988 strong groups began to militate and fight openly for various interests. The important point here is that such groups were not seen to be active for interests within the latent second society but within the first society, or within a Hungarian society where these divisions were becoming blurred again.

DEVELOPMENT OF POLITICAL CHANGES IN 1989

Much has been written on the events of 1989; my concentration here is on the broad framework of the 'opening up' of society rather than the catalogue of events. Both the two major parties now involved in Hungarian politics – the Hungarian Democratic Forum (MDF) and the Free Democrats (SzDSz) began very much as movements rather than parties. The speed of growth of these opposition movements during the spring of 1989, whilst the old Party was finding its 'new course', was amazing. Aware of the erosion of the Party's power (or the decline of 'the Power') these movements began peeling power away from the Communist Party. By summer 1989 the opposition groups had jelled to some extent and round-table negotiations took place. These were tripartite negotiations between the Party, the Opposition Roundtable and a third grouping representing several social organisations such as trade unions and the People's Patriotic Front. Opposition groups proceeded to extract concessions from the Party regarding the shape of the new party law, the new Constitution, and the political processes which Hungary was to include as the basis of the new political structure. During this time there was an understandable dislike of 'parties' and associations with that hierarchical, power-seeking method of organisation.

Something of the history of those involved in these groupings is pertinent to aspects of their later development and style of working. Of the three parties in power in coalition – Hungarian Democratic Forum (MDF), Smallholders and the Christian Democratic Peoples Party – the MDF is the most powerful, with a total of 164 seats out of the 386 in Parliament (see Appendix I for election results). The MDF can be viewed as essentially a nationalist party, which supports Hungarian values (nowhere clearly defined), traditional views concerning the family, and religion (Catholic not Jewish), and this style of politics has a long tradition within Hungary. There is wide popular support for this party throughout the country and the ideas of land redistribution centre on ideas of all farmers becoming smallholders. These *magyar farmerek* ideas echo those of the American ideal of small farmers with traditional values. Members of the MDF also hold strong positions on the rights of Hungarians in Transylvania and other minorities outside Hungary. The two smaller parties in this coalition can be seen as 'historical' parties basing themselves on the kind of parliamentary democracy that existed in Hungary between 1848 and 1948. Despite their different outlooks the ruling coalition parties share a Hungary-centred popular–national set of values, Christian ideals and liberal economic outlooks.

In the opposition coalition, consisting of the Alliance of Free Democrats (SzDSz), the Hungarian Socialist Party (MSzP – ex-Communists) and the Alliance of Young Democrats (FIDESZ), the Free Democrats hold the majority of seats with ninety-two. The Free Democrats are certainly viewed in many Western political circles as having a pedigree of oppositional histories. Certainly many authors of *samizdat* publications such as *Beszélö* (*The Talker*), *Tájékoztató*, *ABC Bulletin* and *Hírmondó* (*The Messenger*) – that is Miklós Haraszti, Ottilia Solt, László Rajk, Tamás Gáspar Miklós, Gábor Demsky and others – are members of the Free Democrats. FIDESZ has become a popular grouping within Hungarian society. The original members had to be under thirty-five years old and these young MPs are often prepared to challenge some recognised viewpoints. The old Communist Party, reformed into the MSzP is also becoming more respected within the political system as time goes on.

There were two striking features about the political structure which was emerging in 1989–90. First, the parties which developed did not form for the expression of particular group/social interests but were actually seeking members to represent.[10] There was much talk of these groupings as social movements and organisations, rather than political parties. Several women with whom I discussed this stated that they would leave the 'movement' (generally either MDF or SzDSz) if it became a 'party'. Such reservations are understandable given the fear and dislike of 'the Party' image. In practice, prior to the elections there were no great distinctions between the parties in their political practice and with regard to the social groups and ideas they wished to represent. A situation arose in which some groups of different parties had more in common with each other, than with other wings of their own party. This was partly due to the speed with which the reform wing of the old Party gained ground, and the opposition forces mustered strength simultaneously. In effect, the changes in the political system were legally instituted in less than eighteen months.

For Western observers Hungarian politics remain difficult to comprehend fully, primarily because the 'historical' parties have few direct Western parallels, although Christian democracy has its equivalents. In addition, many Western observers seem hesitant and confused as to why the economic/welfare discussions do not seem an important issue within the Hungarian Parliament, as no matter what their disagreements over rural/urban issues, strengthening local government, educational policies, and so on, all parties are agreed on the need to speed up the process of marketisation, at almost any cost. None of the parties are proposing a comprehensive social welfare policy, which some outside observers believe is a necessary concomitant to a radical economic restructuring. The cardboard cities, soup-kitchens and poverty apparent in cities such as London, Birmingham, Glasgow and elsewhere in the UK are now becoming part of Hungarian reality. These issues, regarding the currently increased visibility of poverty and its causes, are discussed again in later sections.

INTELLECTUALISATION OF POLITICS

In terms of considering why change occurred, it is important to remember that in the Hungarian context the impetus for these developments did not emerge overnight. A central feature has been the language of 'reform' which has not changed so much since the early 1950s. In this sense very particularly, the people in central and eastern Europe are living in 'post-Communist' rather than 'non-Communist' societies in that the ideas of the first party reformers are mingled within the present slogans. It is important to consider not the 'defeat' of the leading role of the Communist Party in Hungary, but the reasons why it became superfluous. Basically, the party became familiarised within Hungarian society by three combined developments – the party apparatus trying to build the 'new society', the end of the search for enemies and the spread of reformism within and outside the apparatus. This combination provided a reinforcement of the continuous stream of civil or popular resistance, and was able to accommodate demands coming from below. This made possible a silent compromise, made life in the system tolerable and slowly eroded the enormous gap separating the Party and the population. Yet at the top level of ideology, politics and public image of the party, nothing had changed. It was the intellectualisation of politics that played an important role in enabling the party and society to permeate each other. Party workers no longer fitted the images of brainwashed *apparatchiks* harassing the peasants to join agricultural cooperatives. They were instead often quietly-spoken intellectuals with a degree in economics or law, or both. In the Hungarian case it is notable that even the leaders and candidates of the populist party, the Democratic Forum, are intellectuals. Quite what this means for people's everyday identification with the politicians who represent them is another question. In Britain, the fact that John Major left school at sixteen, seems to be generally viewed as a positive point by voters. That Hungarian politics are so (over-) intellectualised could widen the gap between voters and politicians.

In some of her work Erzsebet Szallai has argued that the new political parties occupied themselves too much with the top of the power structure and too little with the processes occurring deep within society. In her view this results from the fact that their programmes typically describe an ideal society – usually resembling parts of western Europe or America – but do not concern themselves with the question 'which attitudes, aims and efforts of which social strata they will build on in order to reach this ideal' (*Beszélö*, no 26, 1989). In an attempt to look at the interrelations between state structures and societal forces within Hungary into the 1990s, Szonja and Iván Szelényi have constructed the figure which appears here as Figure 2.1.

In their work Szonja and Iván Szelényi aim to make the point that the social-democratic constituency is still considerable in Hungary, but has not yet become mobilised. As to why none of the political parties in Hungary has tried to mobilise this constituency, the argument is that during the electoral campaigns of 1989–90 social-democratic interests remained unarticulated for mainly institutional reasons. In their view unless the necessary centre-left force emerges in Hungary, then 'the dominance of the Christian-nationalist forces could last a millennium' (*New Left Review*, no. 187, 1991, p. 137). In the worst-case scenario the possibility of a right-wing force entering Hungarian politics is envisaged, which could fill the gap which a centre-left grouping had failed to occupy.

Figure 2.1 The class structure and political fields in post-Communist Hungary, 1990

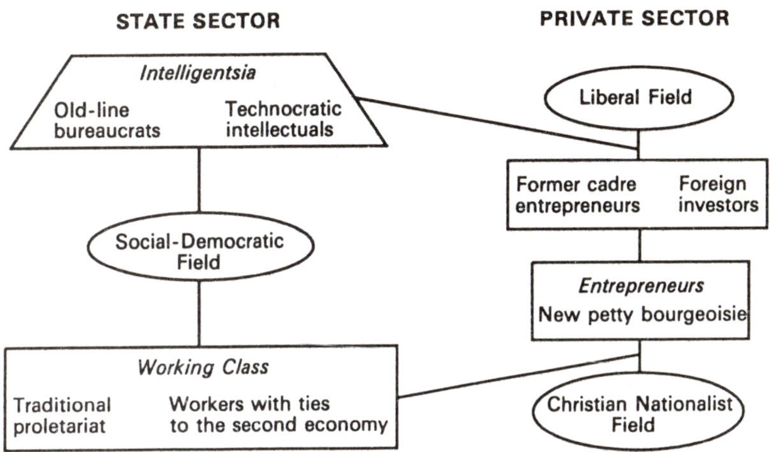

Source: Szonja and Iván Szelenyi, *New Left Review*, 1991, no. 187.

WOMEN'S PARTICIPATION

At this point it is useful to view women's participation in this whole process in order to see what questions are raised as to how these changes have affected, and are being effected by, women in Hungary. The major distinction in terms of participation is between the 'socialist' period and the situation following the changes in 1989. In the various phases of the 'socialist' regime, as has been shown, differential opportunities for participation in politics emerged. Basically pre-1989 the main opportunities to engage in other than Communist Party politics were within the democratic opposition groups. It remains the case that women's participation within these circles was limited. It is unclear as to exactly why this was the case, yet certain observers have remarked that women were not welcomed on an equal footing with men.

Writing in 1982, Piri Márkus sounded gloomy in terms of the recognition of women's situation:

> There is no general understanding about women being oppressed, and the subject is laughed at. There are hardly

> any *samizdat* books in the *samizdat butik* written by women, and extremely few women are involved in the decision-making leadership of the intellectual 'opposition' (Markus, 1982).

For women to set up groups officially in the pre-1989 period was vetoed by the existence of the official women's council, supported by the Party. No other groups could officially exist in such a climate, which is why some encouragement and discussion of women's priorities would have been useful within oppositional circles.

That gender divisions remained within the home may well have meant that the important (and in the pre-1989 period *dangerous*) world of opposition politics remained largely the preserve of men. Yet certainly within the environmental and peace groups women were active participants. It was through the organisation of some young women within FIDESZ circles that initial moves were made to protest against the Danube dam. Yet such participation is largely unrecorded, and to some extent unrecognised.

Women who were active within the official context in the pre-1989 situation had mainly formal roles to play, in large measure this was connected with the quota system of participation which coopted women in the rigid structures of the old regime. It was a relatively uniform phenomenon that within the old statist structures women were often coopted in higher numbers at the lower levels of political activities than in Western countries, but the formalistic nature of their involvement and the lack of opportunities for extending their political education meant they often appeared as 'token' women within male-oriented bureacracies.

In terms of women's active participation within the electoral setting of 1989–90 this remained largely organisational, in terms of attending at polling booths and 'behind the scenes' in party offices, rather than on election hoardings. Of those women elected, few wish to highlight directly the situation of women within their parties. In interviews with several women MPs during 1990/91 it was made clear to me that these women believe, as do many other prominent politicians throughout Europe, that their primary task is representing their party outlooks and if women's issues are not given priority within their party positions, then they will not be seeking any separate initiatives regarding women. This is a common feature regarding the duality of women's lives and situations in which there are contradictions for women 'as women' which will be considered in Chapters 7 and 8.

In August 1991 several active women's groups in Hungary were invited to participate in setting up a new Council, the Social Council. Such Councils have been forming since 1990, one of the first being the Council for Reconciliation of Interests which is concerned with industrial relations and labour-market training. Yet questions of representation and openness remain vital if these Councils are actually to form a type of 'second chamber' in Hungarian politics. It is in no current members' interests to change the Standing Orders of the various councils to introduce more serious discussion concerning how to make those within it actually representative of the varying interests and how to reconcile different group interests. If one group has fifteen members and another group 15 000, how are their equal rights guaranteed? For those trades unions involved in the current Council they can represent their members within it, but for those not currently within the Council whilst they can attempt to influence with proposals, they have little weight within high-level decision-making. In addition the important question of Party representation within the various councils is a fundamental one. In this context, the independent league of trades unions (LIGA) can be said to represent some of the interests of the Free Democrats, whereas the old communist-directed unions within MSzOz tend to represent the 'socialists' within the MSzP, with the Workers' Council movement to some extent putting forward views from the Democratic Forum, yet these distinctions are often blurred and it is not a good principle for representation, as only political interests are represented and these councils supposedly exist to encourage citizens' independent representation. These subjects will be reconsidered in the concluding sections. In Chapter 3 the consideration of women in paid work begins with an assessment of what this meant for women within the 'socialist' framework.

3 Women's Paid Work

INTRODUCTION

In this chapter women's experience of paid work is considered in terms of women's introduction into the workforce in a planned and directed movement. With the changed situation from the late 1980s many aspects of women's employment are being questioned. Notions of 'family/male wages' are being proposed. The element of *choice* is central here. Women in Hungary were 'liberated' as workers and had a duty as mothers, there were few options for women to decide their own priorities. The initial focus in this chapter is on basic information in order to inform the consideration of what being a working woman and working mother meant for women in Hungary. These dual aspects of women's work – paid/unpaid, valued/undervalued, public/private – have been divided into two separate studies because although interrelated these aspects of women's lives cannot easily be reduced or be compressed together. This focus on paid work, education and training, equal opportunities and pay, forms the basis for the study of women's domestic environment and family situation in Chapter 4.

Many changes have occurred which have affected the lives of Hungarian women and men. It is important to consider the attitudes engendered by some of these changes. So far as the 'liberation' of Hungarian women is concerned, some of the attitudes concerning the 'roles' which women are expected to take up and also the actual and relative discrimination from which women still suffer in terms of personal, financial and social inequalities are examined. Women's working situation in the 'socialist' period from 1948, during the economic reforms from the 1960s to the 1980s and following the changes in 1989 are assessed against the transformations discussed in Chapter 2. What sorts of work women do, and the opportunities open to them were heavily constrained in the 'socialist' period, yet market constraints may well dictate their present opportunities.

INTRODUCTION OF MORE WOMEN INTO THE WORKFORCE

During the Second World War large numbers of Hungarian women did essential war work and took over many of the jobs left vacant by men fighting at the front. Yet whilst many women worked during wartime, their movement into permanent working situations was a result of conscious policy decisions taken by the communist leadership from the late 1940s. It was within the fifteen-year period (1948–63) of intense social upheaval, that women were being introduced into permanent jobs in the workforce in large numbers.

In Hungary, unlike some other European states, industry did not start with an emphasis on textile industries which are generally considered prime female employers, and significant involvement of women in industrial occupations did not begin until light consumer industries developed around the early 1900s. There was a 'spurt' of growth in women's employment figures around 1930 when industrial growth was accelerated, but it was during the Second World War that women began to be employed in large numbers. As in most other European countries during wartime, women workers in Hungary were in great demand. With men away working as soldiers, their places in the factories were taken by women in ever-increasing numbers. By the time the war ended, with Hungary 'defeated' almost 200 000 men had died, disappeared or been captured. In this situation, women began to play more important roles than ever in supporting millions of families. The increased demand for labour, and the consequent increase in paid employment opportunities for women meant that in the period 1949–60 almost 75 per cent of the increase in the number of economically active people were women who had newly joined the labour force.

There are several aspects to the debate concerning the ways in which women were introduced into the workforce and the 'equal' role that these economically active women were allowed to play. One view of the early period is that women suddenly became equal partners with men in building the 'socialist' future in Hungary:

> With 1945 a new era began for Hungarian women; they received their full share of legal equality with the electoral

> law of 1945. More important, following the four-year reconstruction period, they became full participants in the national transformation of industry begun in 1949 under Communist rule (Volgyes, 1977, p. 20).

Whilst the above statement is technically correct, the costs of women's participation in the 'transformation of industry' were great. That women would become 'liberated' through paid work was at best a simplified marxist interpretation of social developments following changes in economic relations. At worst it was seen as a calculated and hypocritical attempt on the part of the Hungarian authorities to disguise women's exploitation under the banner of ideological slogans. Yet there is some agreement that, at the time (before 1953) the mass entry of women into the workforce was genuinely seen as a situation of significant opportunities, and people had some belief in the activities of the government authorities in making the social situation easier in terms of potential domestic problems.

It is difficult to imagine just what it would have been like for a woman with three children who had worked during the war; when her husband did not return, she would have had to carry on working. The options open to such women would have been severely limited. Given that there were no child-care facilities in place in the late 1940s and that there was much poverty, the lives of such women would certainly have been hard. It is apparent that from the earliest times within the Hungarian post-war economy women suffered *vertical segregation*, as they were generally amongst the most poorly paid workers in low-grade jobs, and *horizontal segregation* as these jobs were in different areas. Typically, women remained at the lower wage levels and in areas of work which were often in the caring and servicing sectors.

During the period from 1948 to 1956 the introduction of women into the workforce had much to do with rushed industrialisation and the annihilation of agriculture, so that women were desperately needed in the workforce. Given the Stalinist political climate in the 1950s in Hungary, many men were arrested for various reasons so that the burden of work in many cases fell to women. The idea of 'liberation through work' fitted with Soviet conditions at the time. This is not to say that there was total cynicism about women's liberation through work, but given the social conditions such as the appalling lack and inadequacy of housing in this period, many women had to work and care for families, often as heads of households, in appalling conditions with little or no social provision to ease their situation. In this situation, those women who were working harder than ever in a home environment which was very poor would have found it difficult to regard this kind of 'liberation' in a positive way. In reality, this period of rapid industrialisation was most notable in terms of the new central authorities' belief in solving almost all problems with political–economic solutions. In this context, there was a marked *absence* of a perceived need for a general, theoretically based, societal policy. Given that women were still bearing and caring for children during these years, the lack of welfare policy was obviously felt keenly by the many women struggling as heads of households. There were several women-specific areas which were ignored in this period, along with other major developments which were given no attention by policy-makers.

LACK OF POLICY PROVISION FOR WORKING WOMEN IN THE EARLY YEARS

For working women, the major difference between their situation and that of men is women's ability to give birth, and when this is neglected or relegated in importance, it becomes a direct cause of social inequality. In this initial period very little was done to alleviate the direct effects of this inequality for women. So far as the development of services is concerned, before 1950 child-care provision for children under school-age was scarce and those institutions which were available were ill-resourced with staff and equipment. Of the two types of child-care institutions made available in Hungary from the late 1940s, crèches were for children under 3 years and kindergartens were for children between 4 and 6 years. Since primary schools worked on a half-day basis many new day-care centres were set up within schools for children whose parents were in paid employment but the supervision was generally inadequate. As Table 3.1 shows, there was a steady increase in the provision for child-care up to 1960 but this was neither sufficient in quantity nor satisfactory in quality.

Table 3.1 Data on child-care institutions, 1938–60

	Crèches		*Kindergartens*		
	1950	*1960*	*1938*	*1950*	*1960*
Number of institutions	189	816	1140	1773	1865
Number of children registered (in thousands)	7.3	32.0	112.1	106.0	184.0
As percentage of relative age group	1.4	7.4	–	23.5	33.7

Source: Ferge, 1979, p. 105.

Whilst the availability of institutional child-care services did rise progressively up to the 1960s the actual numbers of children registered in kindergartens fell in the period between 1938 and 1950, partly because fewer children were born in the war period.

URBAN WORKING SITUATION FOR WOMEN FROM THE 1960s TO THE 1990s

Budapest is an unusually dominant centre in Hungary, where a significant percentage of Hungary's industry is centralised. Despite a drop in this proportion during the 1960s, when there was some relocation of industries to the provinces, the increase in private enterprises has meant that, in effect, there are even more workers in Budapest than the officially registered number of persons employed. Since housing was, and remains, severely limited, the influx of workers into the capital settled in neighbouring towns and villages. In this way an 'agglomeration circle' developed around Budapest to a radius of up to forty kilometres. Over 40 per cent of the population of this circle commute to Budapest to work, making up almost half of the 400 000 or more commuters who travelled to the capital. So far as the types of work carried out by the urban workers, there has been a noticeable change in that heavy industrial outlets have been moved away from Budapest and the non-industrial elements, including workers in central government and the tertiary sector, have increased. It remains the case though that whilst women are present in most industrial enterprises and as members of cooperatives, some occupations have become almost exclusively female. Examples of this are found primarily in light industry, the food industry, trade and services. Also at least 66 per cent of employees in weaving, spinning, sewing, textiles, leather and shoe-making, beauticians, hairdressers, shop assistants, nurses, dairy industries and processing, are women. In addition women predominate or make up 50–60 per cent of opticians, surfacers, galvanisers, metal-polishers, medicine manufacturers, typesetters, furriers, computer operators and data processers, restaurant employees and fast-food sellers (Ladó, 1990, p. 2). Women's representation in office work and administrative jobs during the 1980s was over 90 per cent, as it was in child-care, teaching and certain areas of the health service (nurses and assistants).

Many women would take up part-time work if it was available. During the 'socialist' administration part-time work was considered expensive to implement and was not encouraged. Such aspects of employment policies as job-sharing were never given consideration. Within the new climate though, part-time work may well become available to women, but given the demands of certain market forces, part-time workers tend to become exploited more easily than full-time workers who have more job security. With regards to this choice the comment by Rózsa is not untypical:

> I did try hard at first – to find a job that I may be able to work more some weeks than others, to fit in more with the children but it was not possible. My bosses are not very understanding but at least they don't ask too many questions . . . I would definitely work part-time if I could get a job like that, certainly while the children are so young (Rózsa: Corrin, 1986).

As has been noted, the feminisation of professions which employ mainly women is apparent in that these sectors generally pay lower wages, and with technical, economic and/or social changes, the status of the particular profession or job begins to decline. Mária Ladó notes that occupational segregation has been reinforced by 'socialisation' in that:

> Occupations employing a large proportion of women, e.g. feminised careers, are stereotyped or socially ascribed as occupations destined for women. Socialisation transmits and

reproduces the values established in the division of labour, which is then realised in practice in the career orientations of women (Ladó, 1991, p. 4).

It is apparent that those industries where more than 50 per cent of the staff were women, were telecommunications and vacuum engineering, printing, textiles and the leather, fur and shoe industry, the textile clothing industry, and 'handicrafts and homecrafts'. In the higher forums of public life, such as executive decision-making committees, local councils and the National Assembly, the representation of women has been poor, whereas in the higher echelons, such as the Council of Ministers and the Politburo it was practically nil. In the twenty years from 1960 to 1980, the numbers of women in leading positions increased, as Table 3.2 below shows.

Occupational status plays an important role in influencing the earnings and the living conditions of women. Women usually occupy lower occupational status positions and their placement is accompanied by less power. Often the lack of qualified women is given as a reason why men are more easily assigned to leading posts. Whilst this is one explanation it addresses only part of the problem. Women are often employed in jobs not suited to their skills and qualifications. In addition certain attitudes on the part

Table 3.2 Proportion of women in leading positions, 1960–80

Occupation	*Proportion of women among total employed in each managerial company (as percentage)*		
	1960	*1970*	*1980*
Managers of enterprises, directors of institutions	7.4	6.4	12.1
Directors of cooperatives	2.4	2.9	5.6
Leaders in public administration	8.1	11.8	19.6
Leaders in municipal administration	12.5	15.3	29.1
Technical managers, chief engineers, works managers	1.7	4.2	3.1
Financial managers, business executives	21.0	33.8	40.9

Source: Kulcsár, 1981.

of employers and managers towards working mothers limit the amount of responsibility they are given. There are still a number of misconceptions and prejudices surrounding the training, employment and promotion of women, which are not always acknowledged, let alone criticised.

There appears to have been a general belief within Hungarian management circles that, as leading positions demand the total attention of those employed in them and often practically unlimited working hours, women cannot do such work. Women in Hungarian society, as in many other countries, generally have to make a choice between leadership occupations or family duties and child-care. This applies to women between thirty and forty years of age, and generally women choose the latter – family duties and child-care. Whether this could be seen as an actual 'choice' is questionable.

It would be more helpful to improve the actual conditions rather than to emphasise the contradiction between motherhood and a top job. Existing conditions which limit women from attaining leading positions can be changed but as is often the case attitudes would have to change first, especially regarding the myth of age. At forty, when women are generally relieved of the problems of raising young children, women are considered to be too old for training, and for placement in leading positions. Yet this is clearly not the case with men, who are considered to be at the peak of their intellectual and creative force at forty or forty-five. Such an attitude is at least mistaken, and in some contexts totally prejudicial to women's employment opportunities. It is frequently commented that the standards which women have to achieve in their work, sport, art or whatever, are frequently much higher and more exacting than those for their male counterparts. The comment 'I have to prove myself better than the men to show them I can do it' is not an uncommon one.

WOMEN WORKING IN AGRICULTURE AND RURAL AREAS

In considering the position of women in agriculture, it is important to recognise the unusually high proportion of workers in Hungary who commute from an agricultural home environment to an industrial working environment. Generally, it is men from outlying areas of Budapest and other settlements who commute into Budapest and other urban centres, leaving women in rural areas to carry out the majority of work associated with the land. In the past thirty years Hungary has become self-sufficient in major agricultural products, and even exports some agricultural produce. This process has gone on at the same time as a massive decline in agricultural employment, as a result of the increased investments in large production units and the import of Western harvesting and processing technology. New working combinations have been employed, as Heinrich points out:

> In addition, a unique form of cooperation was found between the private and the socialized sectors of agricultural production an arrangement that supplied around 30 per cent of the total agricultural output, provides employment and private activity for a large part of the population and is nevertheless monitored by the government (Heinrich, 1986, p. 42).

What have these changes meant for the employment of women in agriculture? Many women work very hard in agriculture. In the early 1980s women performed about 40 per cent of all types of work on the agricultural cooperatives and about three-quarters of all manual work. Dr Rózsa Kulcsár illustrates the proportion of active earners amongst women and men in agriculture as shown in Table 3.3.

Women are to be found, above all, in horticulture and gardening, fruit-growing and poultry-breeding. These areas are particularly labour-intensive with little or no mechanisation. The vast majority of private-plot farming, which is carried out by traditional primitive means, falls on the shoulders of women.

Table 3.3 The proportion of working women and men in agricultural activity, 1980

	Plant production		*Animal husbandry*		*Horticulture and forestry*	
	Men	*Women*	*Men*	*Women*	*Men*	*Women*
Per cent	57.2	42.8	45.7	54.3	44.8	55.2

Source: Kulcsár, 1981, p. 7.

Although women-members of agricultural cooperatives can theoretically attain the same jobs (and wages) as men, in practice the average annual income of women reaches approximately 85 per cent of that of male members – it was as low as 56 per cent in 1973. One factor relevant in this connexion is the deep-seated male prejudice against women working in the same jobs, yet even if this were absent, women continue to be disadvantaged as they still do not receive training in the necessary skills. Less-educated women suffer most in such circumstances.

Managers realised in the mid-1980s that they would be relying heavily on their women employees in the future – due both to generational change and the intensive phase of development of the cooperatives, and they began to draw on the large reservoir of younger women. Yet many of the women cooperative members under thirty years old did not have an 8th-grade primary school education which meant that they were considered unsuitable for certain types of training.

New employment opportunities are becoming harder to find in rural areas and this results in many women remaining in their original agricultural occupations. It is in the more industrialised areas such as plant production, that male labour power is absorbed by demand for skills. As in other areas of work, opportunities are open to men to find professional non-agricultural work without being separated from the usual environment. As Dr. Zsuzsa Kovács-Orolin is quoted as saying:

> Agriculture becomes increasingly mechanized; modern technology, the use of chemicals, herbicides and pesticides are widely distributed. The women, however, are anyway ousted from this process of transformation, without any chance to participate in up-to-date production processes. Instead, they remain stuck to the hard manual work performed under severe conditions of enlarged production where production processes cannot be mechanized for a while (Kulcsár, 1981, p. 8).

The outcome of this trend means that there is an increasing differentiation between men and women in agriculture, when compared with earlier periods in which agricultural work was commonly carried out by traditional means and techniques. For the present though, it seems that women in rural areas are either working in traditional rural activities or they do not find work at all. Table 3.4 shows clearly the differences in the earner-dependent ratios between towns and villages.

Whilst we can see that in Budapest in 1980 more than 75 per cent of women were earners it is apparent that in rural areas this proportion is less than 66 per cent. It is not only women who have difficulty in finding work in rural areas: many men also have to leave their localities to seek work in urban areas.

COMMUTERS

Various studies have been carried out which examine the life of commuters and attempt to define the stratum of commuting workers. István Kemény wrote of the commuters as a subgroup pouring from the villages to the towns, describing commuting as 'an endless form of wandering' (Kemény, 1972).[1] In their study György Konrád and Iván Szelényi (Valoság, 1971) attempted to provide a complex sociological definition by tracing this particular part of the social structure within the larger relations of society. The debate is a complex one which cannot be given just consideration here. However, some of the aspects of this commuting phenomenon can be noted.

One obvious point is that there are different types of commuters. Some commute shorter distances (ten to twenty kilometres) daily, whilst others return home only at weekends, or once a month. Between 1960 and 1980 there was a massive increase in the numbers who commuted. By the end of the 1970s there were over 1 047 000 commuters and weekly or monthly lodgers (Balint, 1983, p. 91). In the 1980s Budapest attracted over 300 000

Table 3.4 Distribution of female population by activity and settlement:

Area	*1960* *Earners*	*1960* *Depdts*	*1970* *Earners*	*1970* *Depdts*	*1980* *Earners*	*1980* *Depdts*
Budapest	55.7	44.3	71.3	28.7	75.2	24.8
Towns	36.6	63.4	54.4	45.6	62.9	37.1
Villages	30.8	69.2	45.1	54.9	59.5	40.5

Source: Kulcsár, 1981, p. 8.

commuters from over 250 settlements. A majority of commuters consisted of young, skilled labourers who were attracted by better-paid jobs. Those workers who commuted weekly or monthly lived in lodgings at their places of work. So far as the ratio of men to women commuters is concerned, Table 3.5 shows that whilst men were still clearly in the majority, the percentage of women commuters more than doubled in the twenty-year period.

Many commuters are caught in a situation which points up the differences arising out of their two ways of life, that is rural home situation versus industrial working environment. Yet there is evidence that many commuters would not wish to live in the cities, and prefer to retain their rural home life. This rural–industrial fusion is reflected in the high proportion of mixed peasant–worker households. In 1980 only 55 per cent of the collective farm households were purely 'rural', the rest were mixed in that they had one spouse belonging to worker or other occupational categories. It was amongst the unskilled or semi-skilled that the proportion of 'homogeneous' households was highest.

In analysing the social background of commuters Böhm and Pál emphasise the need to include the decades of 'society-shaping socialist development' yet outline four factors for consideration: the transformation of the peasants, the village, the village families, and the social structural effect of the mobility between classes. The authors expand their analysis to include changes in families – many commuters are found in the widest-spread family model with the husband employed in industry and the wife working in the cooperative. Böhm and Pál conclude that these commuters form a distinct stratum within Hungarian society.

Table 3.5 Commuters among the active earners (per cent), analysed by gender

Year	*Men*	*Women*
1960	16.9	7.0
1970	24.6	13.4
1980	24.9	15.3

Source: Kulcsár, 1981, p. 9.

HOSTEL LIFE

Before turning to look at the underlying reasons why women do certain work, it is important to consider another group of women workers who, unlike the commuters, actually leave their rural environment and make their homes in the many industrial hostels in the towns and Budapest. Such women generally move away from their villages when they are quite young (sixteen years upwards) and have no experience of urban life. In the 'feminised' industries such as the textile industry, some hostels have as many as 1000 members. Often the rooms are filled to capacity with some sleeping on floors or with ten beds to a single room. The young women are in the same accommodation as older women and many have difficulties settling in. Jutca who worked in a textile workers' hostel between 1977 and 1985 said that:

> The biggest problem was 'fitting in' and there were some who realised after one or two days that this was not what they wanted, they missed their parents and wanted to go back. So some started crying and started to neglect their food (Jutca: Corrin, 1986).

Much has been written in Hungary on the kind of life that the young women in such hostels lead.[2] It is often a very bleak and disappointing experience for many of these women. The main point made by all studies is that of 'status'. Living in such hostels is considered to be of very low status and conditions within the hostels do not help the women to improve their situations. Although the girls are told when they leave the countryside that they will be educated, and indeed most factory hostels do provide lessons, the environment in which such education is expected to proceed is not at all conducive to learning. Often the girls complain that the money on lessons is wasted, whereas if hot water were provided it would at least be useful.

In this bad situation, there is seen to be only one way of 'escape' – marriage. Yet, as all the romantic and sexual life of these women has to take place either in bars or on the street, the outcome of many romances is abortion and shame for the women involved, coupled perhaps with bitterness and cynicism. Even when it was realised by staff that some girls would be better off returning home it was very difficult to arrange. Jutca again noted that:

> There were some girls who I told would be better going back. They were total strangers in the town and they had nobody to talk to, so it was quite hard. But when I told a girl that she had best go home I was told off by the bosses, so the bosses didn't like me when I tried to help those girls in this way (Jutca: Corrin, 1986).

Often the women cannot return to their villages as this would be breaking the contract they have signed, and without the money to buy themselves out of such obligations they are forced to make the best of a very difficult situation.

CHANGES IN POLICY PROVISION FOR WOMEN WORKERS

During the late 1960s several important changes took place within the Hungarian economy which had direct consequences for many women. The introduction of a three-year paid child-care leave in 1967 and the economic changes of the New Economic Mechanism (NEM) in 1968 were of great importance in changing many women's everyday situations.

It is important to consider the background to these developments in terms of changes in paid employment. The impact of the policies associated with child-care is examined in the Chapter 4 in the context of domestic environments. The general economic situation in the mid-1960s was one in which the previous rapid annual growth of national income had slowed somewhat and signs of lower growth were apparent. Economists tended to view these changes as marking the end of a period of extensive growth (mainly based on the establishment of new workplaces and involving large numbers of those previously not employed) and they proposed structural change in the economy towards intensification of production. This was realised in the elaboration of the system of new economic management introduced in 1968. Essentially this system was designed to give greater autonomy to enterprises in deciding the details of activities within the framework of national planning so working towards more efficient production and better utilisation of labour power and capital by applying only indirect regulators.

It was also at this time that the fear of unemplyment began to be felt. Some economists thought that the NEM would result in some unemployment, and as full employment was a principal socialist value, several (economic, social–political and legal) safeguards were established, or strengthened, in an attempt to avoid unemployment. Such safeguards included regulations of the employment and income policy of the enterprise, incentives for on-the-job training, several forms of assisted adult education and one of the minimum guarantees – the right to free choice among workplaces.

So far as the child-care allowance (GYES) is concerned this can be viewed in similar vein. It is irrelevant here that later economic studies have shown an apparent labour shortage in Hungary in the 1970s. That all indicators were pointing towards a situation of surplus labour formed the basis upon which policies, including the child-care allowance, were created. Coupled with fears of unemployment was the knowledge that crèches and pre-schools are expensive to build, so it could be seen that paying women to stay at home to care for children was not only less expensive than investing in the provision of more services but also had the added bonus of flexibility – removing a section of women from the workforce for certain periods of time.

In a positive aspect, the child-care allowance offered a guarantee for young, often unskilled or semi-skilled women, to withdraw from the labour force without losing their jobs, after the birth of their child. In this way it safeguarded them from suffering disadvantages in the competition for workplaces because of caring for their young children. In this context, several mothers with whom I spoke who were at home on child-care leave, spoke of how important the job security aspect was to them:

> Oh, yes I really do miss my workplace. I would not just have left altogether and stayed at home. I know I can go back at the end of October when Zsuzsi is two or take another year. It isn't my work that I miss, punching cards, not at all, but I do miss the liveliness of the days and the jokes. I may go back in November (Olga: Corrin, 1986).

Women's rights and entitlements were preserved in connexion with labour-force participation, during the period of their drawing the grant. Here the crux of the ongoing debate concerned not only the aims of the introduction of this social-policy measure, but the consequential effects of withdrawing large numbers of women from direct labour-force participation and paying them much less than a low average wage, to work in the home for a period of up to three years (or longer if child-care allowance was claimed for a second or third child). Yet in one area at least, from the 1960s to the 1990s, girls and women in Hungary appeared to make great gains – in their educational progress.

WOMEN'S EDUCATIONAL OPPORTUNITIES

At the outset it is well to be clear that under the 'socialist' regime in power in Hungary educational policies were primarily geared towards economic and political needs and goals. In such a situation those pupils who did not aspire to university study were basically trained for unskilled or semi-skilled work. Such workers were useful in an economy which lacked modernisation in many areas and had developed little technical or technological innovation.

For women this policy of overemploying 'cheap labour' had wide-ranging consequences which basically meant that despite their education or training they could rarely expect to gain work which was suited to their qualifications or expectations. When a profession such as teaching or branches of the medical profession became dominated by women it also dropped to a low status and became a lowly paid profession.

Coupled with child-care provision, the need for women to have equal educational opportunities, became even more necessary with their full participation in production. In order to prepare women for entry into different occupations the aim was to set right the imbalance of education which disadvantaged women from the outset. Within the Hungarian context it was desirable that this should occur whilst educational levels were being raised more generally, for all sections of society. With the increasing level of educational attainment of the whole population, and a considerable enlargement of the educational framework, the relative position of women improved rapidly, as Table 3.6 shows.

It was not just the number of years of education that was important here but also the quality, in terms of direct training and vocational skills attained by women. Women tended, and still tend, to form the majority of the student population at the grammar-school type of secondary schools, which do not offer any

Table 3.6 Indices of schooling analysed by gender (to 1960)

	Percentage of population with:					
	8 yrs schooling completed among those aged 15+		*12 yrs schooling completed among those aged 18+*		*Degree or diploma in higher education aged 25+*	
	M	*F*	*M*	*F*	*M*	*F*
1941	16.1	14.1	7.0	1.0	2.8	0.4
1960	34.5	31.3	11.6	6.3	4.5	1.1

Source: Ferge, 1979, p. 107.

direct training or job qualifications. Although, by the 1960s, girls attending technical secondary schools, represented over 33 per cent of the students, they still tended to congregate in schools preparing for white-collar and service jobs. In higher education women tended to be over-represented in institutions of low academic prestige leading to relatively poor jobs. Of course, the other side to this was the under-representation of women in areas which prepare for higher-level administrative or managerial posts. By 1960 the percentages of women employed in engineering, economics and law remained well below those for men, whereas in such areas as education, which is low-status and lowly paid, and medicine, which is more sharply differentiated between general doctors and surgeons in 'socialist' societies, women are in the majority.

In terms of equality of opportunity to obtain basic education both boys and girls in Hungary attend compulsory schooling from the age of six to sixteen. At fourteen years of age pupils can either study further for university preparation in grammar schools (*gymnaziums*) or they can enter technical schools. Several types of vocational training centres and schools can be attended for a further three or four years. One 14-year-old girl explained to me why she wanted to go to university:

> I will study hard and go to university because I want to do things. I don't enjoy studying but that is because we have to do everything – I am not at all good at chemistry. I would like to become a writer or a poet and I know that I must study hard even at chemistry to be able to sit the entrance examinations [for university] (Eva: Corrin, 1987).

This young woman pinpointed an exceptionally difficult aspect of compulsory 'socialist' education – that of its rigidly structured nature. Even though changes are being made in educational instututions in the 1990s such changes are by their nature relatively slow, and young people still have a large amount of 'unlearning' that they must go through to be able to constantly think for themselves. This will be considered in more depth in Chapter 7.

The structure of undergraduate higher education includes 3-year colleges and 5-year universities, which are generally independent of each other, with few students continuing from college to university. In the early 1960s the colleges were started with the aim of training production engineers and are comparable to the post-secondary technician education (*fachhochschulen*) in Germany. The 5-year university programmes are generally specialised but without any emphasis on interdisciplinary work. Some universities have realised that a 3-year programme is sufficient to prepare students for their chosen career and have recently begun 3-year options within the 5-year programmes. Of those women students who do attend institutes of higher education the majority train in four or five basic areas.

As can be seen, health work and teaching are the primary sites of training followed by economics, law and public administration. In comparison with some Western educational and training prog-

Table 3.7 Women students attending full-time courses at institutes of higher education as percentage of total number of students in each speciality

	1981	*1987*
Teacher training	73.4	73.4
Medicine	56.8	54.4
Health work	92.0	96.3
Economics	61.5	64.6
Law and public administration	50.8	57.3
Engineering	17.6	15.3
Agriculture	28.3	31.2
Veterinary medicine	15.8	19.5
Total	50.1	51.7

Source: Eberhardt, 1991, p. 12.

rammes the Hungarian system appeared to enable girls to be more numerate and at ease with scientific subjects, yet it is the case that individual initiative and creativity are not encouraged within the highly formalised, cumbersome educational framework in Hungary. At the same week in June each year all potential university entrants sit their entrance exams. This is similar in Poland and other neighbouring ex-'socialist' countries. Such rigid centralisation could mean that a 15-year-old girl who failed a chemistry exam had to re-sit a whole year, regardless of whether she had any intention to use chemistry within her career. As in other areas of life, the element of choice is very much lacking in the present system of education.

TRAINING

In terms of training, the ratio of trained to skilled women is usually 3:1, whilst for men it is generally the reverse – i.e. more men become skilled rather than just receiving on-the-job training. Miklós Haraszti's comment is apposite here:

> The scene is peaceful; I walk past the semi-automatic machines from England and West Germany. Mainly women work here; every minute they take out a finished piece, replace it with a new one and press the starter button. A single worker sets three or four machines to turn out the same few types of work. My contact in maintenance says training these women operators doesn't take more than a quarter of an hour. Their wages are so low that no man would take the job (Haraszti, 1977, p. 117).

It remains the case that training is not only underdeveloped within Hungarian labour market policies but has actually been neglected over a long period. There is little recognition by some authorities that women workers cannot be 'retrained' if they were not actually trained initially. Table 3.8 gives an indication of the percentages of skilled women amongst skilled workers from the mid-1970s to the mid-1980s.

It is clear that the percentage of skilled women workers has remained relatively constant, rising from 20.4 in 1976 to 22.1 in 1984. The fact that in the 1980s women made up almost half of the workforce employed in industry yet only less than a quarter of *skilled* workers is significant. There is currently a definite lack of

Table 3.8 Number of employed women including skilled women: exluding employed pensioners (as at 31 December), 1976–84

Year	*Number*	*Employed women as % of all employed workers*	*Number*	*Skilled women as % of all skilled workers*
1976	773 094	44.8	126 325	20.4
1977	768 308	44.9	125 505	20.2
1978	763 178	45.1	125 831	20.3
1979	736 931	45.1	125 563	20.4
1980	724 310	44.9	124 461	20.5
1981	710 425	45.1	125 177	21.0
1982	689 326	45.2	123 538	21.3
1983	671 116	45.5	122 038	21.9
1984	664 562	45.5	122 212	22.1

Source: Statisztikai Évkönyv, 1984.

adaptable and skilled labour necessary to carry out the demands of the more market-oriented economy now developing in Hungary. With the support of the World Bank, the Hungarian government has initiated the development of Regional Adult Development Centres that will be operated by local boards under the general guidance of a new National Training Board. These centres aim to provide a more comprehensive and flexible adult training service than anything previously available, including small-business assistance, vocational training and contract-customised training for enterprises. Financial support comes from the community, enterprises that wish to obtain contracted services, individuals who pay for their own training, the National Training Board, and the Ministry of Labour which contracts for services for the unemployed through local labour offices. Yet given an environment of shortage – be that of jobs or of places on training/retraining schemes, women may once again lose out on the opportunities available unless some attention is paid to their particular skills and needs.

SKILL SEGREGATION

Of those branches in which skilled women actually predominate, the textile and clothing industry had the largest proportion in the

1980s, and 'handicrafts and homecrafts' was also high. These two industries can be seen as 'feminised' in that the majority of workers are women and pay and conditions have become lowered accordingly. Whilst some argue that they neatly parallel 'women's work' in the home, it is important to remember that textile work is amongst the 'heaviest' employment in terms of workload and physical stamina required on looms and equipment. It is perhaps surprising that the largest sector of women's activity is that of heavy industry (employing 315 032 women in 1985). That the ratio of women to men is much higher in heavy industry is partly caused by overstaffed offices. Yet many women do work in areas which are more physically demanding than the 'typically female' work such as textiles or food processing which, as has been noted, entail much physical work.

At this point is it well to note that the definition of 'what constitutes a skill' is of importance in terms of women's skills. There have been many disputes within industrial enterprises in Western countries concerning grading. As recently as 1984 some women sewing-machinists at Ford's main UK plants won their dispute and were regraded as 'skilled'.[3] These women sew together many pieces of material with great precision to make car seat covers. The men who cut the material were on a higher grade than the women machinists. This 'de-skilling' of women's work is a common feature of industry in many parts of the world – who decides what is skilful? Few similar decisions have been upheld in Britain concerning women's jobs being regraded so that parity with male counterparts is enforced. Such blatant discrimination as women office cleaners being paid much less than male 'industrial' cleaners – the only difference in their work being in the definitions used – is another example of this. Discrimination of

Table 3.9 Percentages of active wage-earners in physical jobs

	1 January 1981		*1 January 1988*	
	Men	*Women*	*Men*	*Women*
Skilled workers	57	22	59	25
Semi-skilled workers	30	50	30	51
Unskilled workers	13	28	11	24

Source: Ládó, 1990, p. 2.

this kind goes on within Hungarian factories and workplaces. Instances are occasionally reported in various newspapers and discussions on radio.

REASONS FOR INEQUALITY

As noted, despite women's ability and qualifications, inequalities of opportunity and employment have existed for Hungarian women right up to the present. As with neighbouring 'socialist' countries, the legal status of women in Hungary in terms of equality of work and earnings has long been recorded – since 1949. The Hungarian Constitution of 1972 stated that 'in the Hungarian People's Republic women enjoy equal rights with men' and that the 'quality of rights is safeguarded by the provision of work openings and conditions in an appropriate manner'. Article 70/B states that 'for equal work everyone, without difference, has the right to equal pay'. Yet several Regulations from the Ministry of Labour during the 1980s informed enterprises that women should be placed in appropriate leading positions according to their numerical ratio, just as they should be in the direction of their public life. Since the early 1970s the National Council of Hungarian Women and the Council of Ministers have monitored this principle of 'equal pay for equal work' to see how far it has been implemented. This was perhaps the one area in which the official Women's Council actually had some positive impact for certain groups of women workers. Discussion of these issues continued throughout the 1970s and 1980s.

EQUAL PAY

When considering how far equal pay principles have been implemented, it is apparent that women still receive less money than men – occasionally for the same work, generally for their less well-paid work. This is sometimes through lack of access to training to gain skills, or through limited promotion opportunities. There is a good deal of information available on women's earnings which shows a distinctly unfavourable pattern for women on both counts. Although pay differs according to qualifications, experience, length of service and people's actual positions within a firm, women consistently earn less than men. Enterprises typically pay 1 to 2 forints less per hour to young girls starting work, than to young boys in the same position. In the same context, the pay of women in leading positions, such as directors, is 18 per cent to 21 per cent lower than that of men.

There are other reasons besides non-implementation of equal payment. One is that women in leading positions often work for smaller enterprises. In addition, in the distribution of annual bonuses, premiums and similar sums, women are usually also in an unfavourable position because such payments are wage-related and as women earn less so their bonuses are lower. There are interesting sectoral differences in this pay gap as Table 3.10 shows.

The biggest gap is apparent in manual work such as construction and water works whilst it is gradually being closed in commercial work and transport. It is difficult though from such broad categories to gain a real sense of which jobs are most unequal in terms of pay. In 1987 the closest parity was achieved by women radio and television mechanics who earned 97 per cent of men's wages, whilst the greatest difference was for women working in water works and construction, earning only 65–69 per cent of men's wages (Eberhardt, 1991, p. 39). Given the vertical and horizontal segregation which women face within the work-

Table 3.10 Average monthly wage of women in manual jobs as percentage of men's average wage

	1982 %	*1987* %
Industry	70	73
Construction industry	65	69
Agriculture, forestry	69	70
Transport	74	71
Commerce	77	80
Water works	65	66

Source: Eberhardt, 1991, p. 38.

force it remains very difficult for women to gain promotion to better-paid jobs and positions.

WORKING CONDITIONS

It was clear from various government publications during the 1970s and 1980s that improvement in the situation of working women had not kept pace with the involvement of female workers in the national economy. As noted earlier, much of the work carried out by women in heavy industry is not skilled so these unskilled women workers are less well-paid than their skilled, male counterparts. This situation has not arisen because of any 'de-skilling' of women's work, but is due to the lack of priority given to teaching women various skills.

The majority of women workers work on assembly lines often carrying out simple, monotonous yet pressurised tasks. Women textile workers often operate several machines at a time and have to stand for most of their working day. Some workers walk as far as 15 to 20 kilometres between machines and in some brickyards women lift tons of bricks in 12-kilogram bundles. The harmful effect of unduly heavy and monotonous work is aggravated by bad working conditions. Often women's places of work are crowded and very noisy, the lighting is dim and the ventilating systems inefficient. In several places employing mainly women workers the air is filled with gas, smoke and dust.

Such conditions have increased the likelihood of early retirement for women, as is shown by the rising statistics for women workers retiring before the legal retirement age. Many women workers retire early, mainly because of damage to their nervous systems. The number of women receiving disability pensions was generally twice that of men during the 1980s, and in many enterprises up to 15 per cent of women workers can be assigned only to light jobs because of damage to their health from poor working conditions. Women often suffer worse working conditions than men. Unfortunately, because women's earnings are generally less than those of men on average (and women still sometimes receive less for doing the same job) many women choose to 'make up' their money by working night-shifts and holidays. Enterprises often take advantage of the fact that women are forced to do this and employ women to do extra overtime.

TRADE UNIONS

It was hoped during 1988 that with the founding of several new associations and some new independent trade unions that the monopoly and power of the old communist-led union structures would be broken up. As the political changes intensified the organisational developments within the independent unions slowed. This had much to do with the power of the formerly monopolistic National Council of Trade Unions (SZOT) which although it appeared challenged, in the face of 'competition', given the weight of numbers still involved in the 'official' unions and the lack of cohesion and numerical strength in the independent unions, the development of alternative networks to redress workers' grievances has been, and will continue to be, a slow process. Property relations alone, in terms of the trade-union homes and buildings owned by the 'official' unions are a complex web to untangle, even if the will to do so is present. It is clear that the old-style unions do not wish to speed the process of their own disintegration. As noted in Chapter 2, the new tripartite discussions between employees, employers and unions are still going ahead, but the introduction of new unions or indeed new employees and employers into this process is slow and less than fully democratic.

INCOME INEQUALITIES

Within the increasing moves toward a marketised economy with extensive wage differentials some discussion of income inequalities is appropriate. The cost of living has been rising steeply in Hungary throughout the 1980s, and dramatically since 1989, though some groups are less affected than others. For those on low and fixed incomes it is important that welfare payments are utilised to make up some of the deficit. In the 1980s between 10 per cent and 30 per cent of the population fell into the poverty category. This grouping was made up of those on low incomes (almost all Roma families and 50 per cent of pensioners), approximately 50 per cent of families with two children and up to 90 per cent of those with three or more children. These people have been the victims of the shortcomings of social policy, and no matter how they live they will remain poor. A second part of this group includes those with housing problems and those who are no longer capable of looking after themselves. There are undeniable differences in earnings between various groups in Hungary, and the possibilities now exist for certain people to earn a great deal of money. In this context, the first designer clothes show took place in Budapest in 1990 with average outfits selling for approximately £400 each.

In the first quarter of 1991 inflation reached over 30 per cent. This was complemented by a decline in industrial production, notably in heavy industry and mining. Studies on income inequalities have shown that whilst 37 per cent of income dispersal was explained by differences in occupational incomes, 63 per cent was explained by the family's demographic structure (Timár, 1977, p. 75). The double aim of Hungarian incomes policy then, was to have been mediated by an equalisation of family incomes, through social welfare policy. The two major elements of this strategy were the general pensions scheme and cash contributions to the upbringing of children. The system of child benefits including the child-care allowance (GYES) and family allowance is considered in Chapter 4. Despite an overall incomes policy approach to these problems, the existence and growth of the second economy, did make the gradual equalisation of incomes virtually impossible. Since the changes in 1989 the 'privatisation packages' on offer to Hungarian firms make any attempts to equalise incomes increasingly unlikely. Some of the consequences of privatisation in terms of income inequalities and unemployment are considered in Chapter 5 in terms of social policy. In the concluding section attitudes towards women working are considered.

ATTITUDES TOWARDS WOMEN WORKING

In a survey carried out by TARKI (Social Science Information Centre, Budapest) attitudes towards women having a job were questioned in various European countries – Hungary, Britain, Austria, West Germany, Italy, Ireland, the Netherlands and the USA. In the Hungarian section 1737 people were sampled, with two types of questionnaires. One questionnaire was concerned with the way that women's work fitted into family life-cyles and the other asked for opinions about certain statements regarding women and work. It is the latter which will now be considered.

There were eight statements made – four containing so-called 'traditional' attitudes and four containing so-called 'modern' ones.

The first 'traditional' statement, 'A job is all right, but what most women really want is a home and children' was accepted by 76 per cent of all Hungarians asked – 79 per cent of men and 75 per cent of women. There was no difference between older and younger respondents. Women with higher levels of educational attainment accepted the statement less, yet still 51 per cent of women with university degrees accepted it.

The second statement, 'A pre-school child is likely to suffer if his or her mother works' was again acceptable to a lot of Hungarians – 71 per cent of those questioned. The gender differentiation was more marked with 75 per cent of men and only 67 per cent of women approving it. One out of five Hungarian women rejected it, and again only 46 per cent of women with degrees accepted, compared with 76 per cent of men with similar educational backgrounds. The largest proportion of men and women rejecting this statement were those living alone.

On the third statement, 'All in all, family life suffers when the woman has a full-time job', Hungary was the country with the highest ratio of respondents accepting this opinion – 63 per cent. Whilst men and women have similar views on this, age differences were important as less than 50 per cent of the youngest people accepted it whilst in the oldest age group the ratio of acceptance was 74 per cent for women and 81 per cent for men.

The final 'traditional' statement, 'A husband's job is to earn money; a wife's job is to look after the home and family' was the only one to polarise respondents. Those accepting were in similar proportion to those rejecting – 44 per cent and 40 per cent. This statement was particularly rejected by women with university degrees – 75 per cent whereas men with similar qualification rejected it less – 56 per cent. A smaller percentage of younger women accepted this – 30 per cent – as did a smaller percentage of younger men – 41 per cent.

Moving to the 'modern' opinions, the most widely accepted statement was 'I would enjoy having a job even if I didn't need money'. This was again asked of both men and women. Overall 60 per cent of respondents accepted this opinion, which was an average across participating countries, yet in every category more men than women wanted to work. One in three women and one in five men in Hungary stated that they would not wish to work if their financial situation did not compel them to. The ratio of those wishing to work was highest amongst university-educated women and men (67 per cent and 79 per cent) and also unmarried women (69 per cent) and divorced men (76 per cent). Whereas more of the older men would wish to work, older women would prefer not to have to work.

The second 'modern' opinion, 'Having a job is the best way for a woman to be an independent person' was accepted by 55 per cent of respondents – small in comparison with Austria's 75 per cent or Ireland's 69 per cent. Men and women held similar views on this, with the exception of divorced women agreeing in higher numbers – 66 per cent.

When the third statement, 'A working mother can establish just as warm and secure a relationship with her children as a mother who does not work' was discussed, over half (52 per cent) of Hungarians accepted. This was the lowest of all countries. More Hungarian women (61 per cent) than men (41 per cent) accepted this, whereas the tendency for women rejecting is low – only 29 per cent of women think that a working mother cannot building as strong a relationship with her children as a non-working mother – and for men high – every second man rejected it. Educated men's opinions were as conservative as those of men with less education, and higher proportions of divorced men and women believed that working mothers could have warm relationships with their children. Interestingly perhaps, fewer married men believed this.

The final 'modern' statement, 'A woman and her family will all be happier if she goes out to work' found the smallest level of acceptance in all countries. Hungary and Italy were countries where relatively more people rejected it – 36 per cent and 48 per cent respectively. Of the youngest group, 55 per cent of women and 40 per cent of men agreed with the statement. Amongst unmarried and divorced women between 47 per cent and 49 per cent thought that everyone would be happier if women work, whereas of divorced men only 24 per cent could agree with it.

In her multivariate analysis Olga Toth notes as 'indisputable' the fact that people in Hungary hold more conservative views about the employment of women, than people in the other countries under consideration. She suggests that these views on women are connected to 'choice' in terms of the lack of choice for working women, responding as they were to economic pressure. Even those women who enjoy their work, who might even choose to work if there was less economic pressure, may still feel that work is not in itself valuable, this being 'propaganda' from the previous regime. Of those women wishing to remain in the home, the signs seem to show that this demand is short-lived in many cases. These aspects are considered in Chapter 4. Certainly, for women who choose to remain in the home caring for their young children, several of whom I spoke with at length, said they chose to return to work for reasons which were not solely financial.

Toth attempts to explain the men's opinions in terms of men not being able to 'digest the fact' that they cannot maintain a family by their own income – 'Men imagine a "petit-bourgeois"' old middle-class world, where they could carry the patriarchal role of the breadwinner' (Toth, 1991, p. 21). In such circumstances Hungarian men answering this survey could look forward only to a nostalgia for an 'idealised' past. There would certainly seem to be some substance to this in terms not only of the backlash against independent women's actions and Hungarian feminism, but in the confusion over just what 'progressive', modern values can/should be upheld by Hungarian men and women within their various domestic environments. This forms part of the subject of Chapter 4.

CONCLUSION

To understand why it is that many women in Hungary were forced into jobs and lifestyles which cannot be fulfilling, several factors are fundamental. Principally, it is important to recognise that the Hungarian 'socialist' authorities were attempting to change the economic imperatives but not the dominant, conservative, patriarchal values of the population. Women were recognised as workers and mothers, but their equal rights as citizens was actually restricted by the conflation of the two aspects of work which were often in conflict. It must be borne in mind that concrete aspects of the 'socialisation' of housework did not materialise within the Hungarian economy at the same time as millions of women were being introduced into paid work. These two areas seem to be the major stumbling blocks to the realisation of any form of full equality for women.

By working generally in low-paid, low-status jobs which are often quite boring and sometimes very dangerous for women's health, Hungarian women were officially recognised to be 'liberated'. However, as noted, the opportunity to remain in the home caring for young children does not appeal to all women, so that the 'poor compromise' of the child-care leave cannot become fully effective until it is based on *choice*. Indeed, choice and recognition are the key terms when considering women's work in Hungary.

Choice is essential in that many women may choose to be in paid work, rather than caring for small children, whereas some women may want to stay in the home and care for children. Yet these choices need to be not only recognised as a parental choice but fully utilised as such. Until men and women make decisions regarding paid work and unpaid domestic work on an equal footing there cannot be equality for women.

Recognition, is therefore important, in terms of recognising and assigning the true value to work within the domestic context so that it is not viewed as insignificant, or secondary, or 'non-productive'. At the present time in Hungary, however, there is little or no discussion of such matters regarding women's work. Child-care facilities are closing and unemployment is rising. These factors are considered in depth in Chapter 5. For the present, it is opportune to consider the domestic environment and family situations in Hungary, in order to reflect on the duality of women's work and despite many structural changes, the constant over-expectations placed upon women within Hungarian society.

4 Domestic Work and Family Considerations

INTRODUCTION

This section builds from the consideration of women's paid work to look at some of the other types of work which women do, the unpaid and generally undervalued work which women carry out in the home and in caring for their children and other family-members. Over the past few decades certain changes have taken place in Hungarian families – both in terms of structure, and of members' expectations. Some of the structural changes which occur when people meet, marry, have children, and divorce are considered. Although partially attempted, in terms of large laundries and catering/canteen facilities at workplaces, the socialisation of housework has not been successfully achieved in Hungary. Although most workplaces did have cheap canteens and there were many neighbourhood laundries, the major burden of domestic work, including cooking evening meals, cleaning, ironing, and mending clothes, fell to women. On the other hand, the need for socialised child-care services was recognised from the early 1950s. Rather than easing the burdens of working mothers, this debate was viewed in the overall context of labour efficiency prevalent at this time. The form which such services should take was unclear in the early days and began to be seriously debated within the context of the benefits or programmes debate which is considered in Chapter 5. Certainly, the introduction of the child-care allowance from 1967 changed the terms of reference.

Within this section it is important to bear in mind the notions of public and private work, and 'real' work. These fine, and not so fine, distinctions underlie much of the societal expectations regarding women's activities. As noted, to be 'only a housewife' in Hungary was to be a social parasite in certain terms, yet in others, to be able to be 'looked after' by a husband who earned enough, was definitely something good for many women. The blurring of distinctions between work in the home, within families, and outside paid work can be very harmful to women's situations unless there is a conscious, political drive towards recognising the true value of each type of work. Women cleaning one home for money and another for 'love' cannot be explained or logically supported in anything other than the patriarchal framework in which it has been taking place for centuries. Two apparent options are to make housework waged work or to ensure an equal gender division of tasks within the home. Neither are easy options nor straightforward, and neither have been fully debated within the Hungarian context. From a consideration of social relations in Hungary in terms of domestic environments, rural/urban distinctions, 'family' types, structural changes in terms of marriage, divorce, decreasing size of families, a picture is built up of the slowly changing processes within different Hungarian families, and what these processes have meant, and mean for women in Hungary today. Within this, aspects of what 'work' is, highlight the undervaluation of women's work in many spheres.

ASSESSING 'FAMILIES'

Much literature on 'the family' in Hungary, as elsewhere, is value-laden, with notions of an 'ideal' family to which everyone living in the society must aspire, even if they do not live in such a way. From 1948 in Hungary there was an apparent emphasis on the 'socialist' type of life towards which Hungarian policy-makers had supposedly been trying to move. Essentially there were four elements connected with the character of families which made formulation and implementation of any form of across-the-board 'family policies' difficult. In the first place 'the family' in Hungary was viewed as 'oversaturated' with religious context – the institution of the family was expected to contribute to this traditional religious aspect. Second, the traditional model of the 'bourgeois' family was not egalitarian, incorporating (in its Hungarian form at least) the domination of the husband, which permeated husband–wife relations as well as relations between the generations. The third consideration was that in the first years after 1948 a highly positive value was attached to activities taking place in the public sphere – in politics, reconstruction of the country, or productive work – so that 'the family', seen as a stronghold of private life and individualism, was considered as diverting attention and energy from public concerns and weakening the collective values. Finally, the most fundamental point, in terms of its long-documented history, is that of 'the family' as the most important mediator of social positions, thereby conserving social inequalities. In this context Ferge states:

> In the Hungary of the 1940s and 1950s it was obvious that the creation of a system of high-standard communal education was no immediate possibility, and that the institution of the family had to be safeguarded. But still, it could not be accepted with enthusiasm, and was inevitably considered as a necessity to be endured rather than as a value to be strengthened for its own sake (Ferge, 1979, p. 72).

Of course this was all the more true since it was not clear what would remain of family forms given the introduction of women into productive work, and the socialisation of housework and child-care, which included communal education. It was within this framework, with the marked absence of autonomous social policy, that the development of notions of 'the family' and 'family policies' emerged in Hungary.

Hungarian sociological theory in this area began to distinguish the 'socialist' family from its Western counterpart in terms of the collectivist, as opposed to individualist, values which informed the way of life within it. Here the situation of women remains centrally important – the question 'is there a form of family organisation in which women are not oppressed?' is significant. The extended-family model could be equally as oppressive to women as the nuclear-family model, and collectivist ideals can have similarly high (over)expectations of women, as those with a more individualist orientation.

HUNGARIAN FAMILY THEORY

Much of the debate amongst the early Bolshevik revolutionaries concerning the replacement of families by communal living was carried on in terms of 'socialist' consciousness – Kollantai arguing for collective responsibility for those in need, aimed at building an increased 'socialist' awareness among the people. Other prominent party members, including Trotsky, argued that 'socialist' awarenesss had to be developed first, because the state could not build new social institutions without cooperation from the masses. These discussions were all imbued with certain notions of strong protecting weak. The concern of social policy with *images of women* is a recurrent one, in terms of the way in which questions are framed explicitly affecting policy outcomes. In connexion with the family, notions such as 'a woman's place is in the home', or that 'women's primary roles are those of mothers not workers', radically affect the way that policies on housework and child-care are framed. In turn this often affects the outcome of such policies within society, in terms of changing (or not changing) certain adverse aspects of the conditions within which women work.

The main difference proposed between Hungarian family models and western equivalents was that within 'socialist' families, there was cooperation (in the extended family network and presumably between spouses) and that in Hungary the family as an economic unit was not exploited by the state, unlike under capitalism. Yet this notion of 'socialist' family was always somewhat nebulous and the benefits for women living in such 'socialist' families are rarely documented. In this connection my conversation with Anikó, who was aged twenty-four, had four children and lived on a large housing estate on the outskirts of Budapest, is revealing, regarding her views on 'socialist' ethics:

> Everybody says there are ideal socialist people but nobody knows what it really means. At school it is the same, they are always speaking about our ideal as the socialist type of man, but they don't say exactly what it is. I can speak only about my situation and as I didn't get anything good which showed me where, in what direction to go, neither at school nor in the family, which in my opinion is typical in Hungary, what I call the socialist type of family, that is why Catholicism meant a lot to me. It was good for me. Of course everyone must find something adequate for his or her own personality, but that was something I could use in my life (Anikó: Corrin, 1986).

Within the present changed climate in Hungary there are no longer defences of the 'socialist' type of lifestyle, yet certain ideas and values about family life are again fashionable. Current ideals concerning family life are being proposed by the leading party in government, the Hungarian Democratic Forum (MDF). In a long interview with the Head of the Women's Section in the MDF, Katalin Filó discussed women's 'choices' in Hungary:

> In Hungary women never had choice but economic constraints brought them away from home and forced them to take jobs. Therefore the MDF programme aims to restore the possibility of choice for women . . . Our idea is for one breadwinner per family so that women are not forced to take jobs (Filó, 1990).

On the face of it this could sound quite reasonable, except that the expectation is for a male 'breadwinner'. As has been noted the Christian–nationalist values of the governing coalition support two interrelated sets of ideals – those associated with the mythical nuclear or extended 'family' and those concerned with the 'good of the nation'. Within both sets of ideals there are obviously elements which appeal to a broad range of Hungarian citizens, yet within each also there are aspects which can be potentially very destructive for women's opportunities and the development of a new consciousness concerning women's activities and abilities within Hungarian society in the coming years.

Most obvious repercussions of the Christian–nationalist ideas and policies have been in the areas of contraception, childbirth and employment. Attacks on abortion from the Catholic Church and its supporters have increased with the Group *Igen* (Yes) becoming much more vocal and active. In terms of employment this revival of 'family' commitment affects women's situation in the labour market. Women are becoming reconfirmed as a flexible pool of labour. In the current climate, there are no job guarantees for women who remain in the home caring for children. Many of these women who may or may not 'choose' to remain home on child-care fees could face the bleak prospect of long-term unemployment. Of course women's opportunities to return to paid work vary according to qualifications, skill, experience, market demand and other factors discussed in Chapter 3.

On the subject of a 'family wage' which is also viewed as a popular aim by many women within Hungary, Katalin Filó noted that 'Men should be paid well enough to keep the whole family . . . We would like to encourage family enterprises and family jobs similar to Japanese models, so that women could work at home on some big enterprise if required.' There are echoes here of the disastrous home-working situations forced upon women throughout the world. Without any legal working conditions, union protection, minimum wages or statutory working rights, homeworking conditions can be some of the worst working conditions imaginable.

It is pertinent that it was only the MDF that had a women's section after the 1990 election, and that the only in-depth interview concentrating solely on women's issues was with Ms Filó. Yet, in 1991 it was claimed that only the Socialist Party had a policy for women. Why this was the case is considered further in Chapter 5.

For the present the recognition that an 'ideal type' of family was proposed under the 'socialist' administrations – that is, a family of the 'socialist' type consisting of mother, father and two or three children – is fundamental to understanding why so many Hungarian people felt that they had 'failed' if they did not live in such a way. It is the case that many people in Hungary do actually live in family situations similar to the so-called 'ideal', the point being that they do so for much shorter periods. Several women with whom I spoke told of their 'incompleteness' after divorce, even though they were relieved to be freed from the particular situations which were oppressing them:

> It is strange, but I know, I did feel somehow incomplete when we were here alone, just myself and the girls, after János left. In one way I could not have been more relieved not to have to face the rows and other upsets, but somehow 'being divorced' was almost like a stigma, a failure (Katalin, 1986).

In Hungarian society more generally, neither widows with children, nor unmarried mothers, nor a grandmother, daughter and granddaughter living together, nor two cousins choosing to bring up another relative's children, nor any number of other combinations, can be considered 'proper' families according to the above definitions. Such definitions when made socially acceptable/correct, can have quite an impact on people's perceptions of how they are living. This is further considered in Chapter 7 on women's identities and self-images.

HOUSEHOLD EQUALITY

Equality in the context of the allocation of tasks in the household is important. To what extent is this allocation sex-linked or neutral? So far as breast-feeding is concerned this can only be done by women, but there is no reason why bottle-feeding and other such skills needed for baby/child-care cannot be carried out by men as reliably as women. Some jobs requiring very great muscular effort are sometimes better left to men, if the men are stronger. Another area of family equality concerns the nature of decision-making – i.e. is it autocratic in that only the 'head of the family' decides, or democratic in that it is a matter of agreement between the couple with some input from the children? Closely related to this is the matter of where power lies within families. Although some amount of hierarchy is inevitable with adults and small children, there are no matters in which a man should dominate. In an unbalanced power situation equality can never be fully realised. A balance of power needs to be reached in which children have some say. For some women however, such changes are too dramatic to consider quickly:

> You must understand that these things would not work here in Hungary. I know families where women have been too aggressive, wanting to share all tasks 50:50 and these families have broken down. Change is very slow here in Hungary, it takes time (Ágnes, 1986).

FEMINIST THEORY ON FAMILY SITUATIONS

In contrast to much Hungarian work on family theories, feminist critiques view family situations as generally oppressive for women, whether in capitalist or in 'socialist' systems. In her feminist critique of the family, Gittins argues the controversial nature of claiming such an entity as 'the family':

> Childbearing, childrearing, and the construction of gender, allocation of resources, mating and marriage, sexuality and ageing, all loosely fit into our idea of family, and yet we have seen how all of them are variable over time, between cultures and between social sectors. The claim that 'the family' is universal has been especially problematic because of the failure by most to differentiate between how small groups of people live and work together, and what the ideology of appropriate behaviour for men, women and children within families has been (Gittins, 1985, p. 70).

So far as an ideology of appropriate behaviour for women is concerned, historically in sociological theory women within a family situation tend to have been viewed as very necessary to its survival and smooth-running. As such, women's position within families has been elevated (socially) into something to which women are expected to aspire. A cynical observer might say that because women's cheap labour in the home is vital to the reproduction of society, then it is in governmental authorities' interests to propagate the impression of what on the surface appears an unattractive method of working – isolated at home, no set hours so no overtime, no safeguards against exploitation, and so on – as an attractive, 'natural', 'fulfilling' and totally rewarding experience for women, as mothers or as child-carers (grandmothers and other women relatives). The old adage that 'marriage bribes housewives into thinking that they are householders' might be appropriate here. For some mothers not living up to the 'image' it is problematic:

> I think I did 'idealise' it [motherhood]. Perhaps I just expected too much, but after the the first few weeks of getting used to it all I started to feel drained of energy and in some ways a 'dependent' yet I was working harder than ever to show my husband and older boy what I could do. It seemed the more I did the less they took care. Now I think I have reached more of a balance, but I am looking forward to going back to work (Mária: Corrin, 1986).

Certain feminist emphases, in theorising familial relationships and the consequences of such relationships, centre on the importance of ideology and psychology in understanding women's situation and oppression. Some theorists see this aspect as fundamentally important, insisting that psychological determinants of human behaviour are at least partially independent of more general economic and political changes (see Millet, 1971, ch. 4; Mitchell, 1975; and Rowbotham, 1972, ch. 5, and 1973).

Much feminist criticism of the workings of the family as an economic and social unit in society has been in terms of production and reproduction, the domestic labour debate. One perspective is that by which 'wages for housework' is taken as a political perspective – the struggle for which 'is going to produce a revolution in our lives and in our social power as women' (Federici, 1982, p. 218). From this perspective, Federici argues that to ask for wages for housework will undermine the expectations that society has of women, and is a struggle against the essence of women's socialisation, against the social role of women as unwaged, slave labour in the home. In her work on this theme, Joan Landes argues that:

> The family conceptualised as a mode of production is actually a mode of production and reproduction of the working class as a class. It is a mode of production . . . of the housewife as a housewife as well as the reproduction of that same woman as a potential and often employed wage labourer (Landes, in Evans, 1982, p. 227).

In connexion with women's unpaid work under 'socialism', Judith Stiehm argues that one reason why male-oriented analysts of production have ignored the reproduction of labour and non-waged labour is because it is considered 'woman's work' – 'Women's work is something that men tend to know little about; moreover, it is to their interest to devalue it' (Stiehm, 1981). A second reason for overlooking them is that until recently women have provided 'enough' children and provided 'enough' domestic labour to service family life. Yet in Hungary (as in some neighbouring countries) birth-rates are falling and divorces are increasing. Official arguments about family policy in this context parallel the 'demographic crisis' arguments in the Soviet Union (Pilkington, in Corrin, 1992).

Most feminist critiques of the 'socialist' family make the point that in both types of family domestic labour is carried out mainly by women and is unpaid labour in the family. Women in almost all families organise the home and are responsible for the care of children. Currently, the shape and size of such families are similar – two adults and one or two children. When the adults work, children are cared for by other women in crèches, playgroups, and schools. Given these similarities feminists have argued that families play the same role in western and in eastern Europe. As the Women's Collective of Labour Focus on Eastern Europe pointed out:

> Many Western socialists have been sceptical of Eastern European claims to have discovered 'a socialist family' – after all . . . Kollantai argued that socialism meant changes in the family as well as economic life; socialisation of domestic labour

> and the encouragement of collective ways of living would lead to greater scope for the full development of the human personality. Western feminists today are hardly likely to accept that a social unit in which women are responsible for 80% of the work is egalitarian and unoppressive (*Labour Focus on Eastern Europe*, 1978, p. 18).

Yet the collective goes on to point out that given the many advantages that family units have for capitalism – using women as a flexible pool of labour, children are born and reared in the family and the workforce is serviced within it, property and propertylessness are transmitted from generation to generation, working-class loyalties are divided between struggles at the workplace and the need to support the family – some differences between Western and Eastern families may be apparent. Some sociologists in Hungary (including Ferge and Szalai) have argued that families in Hungary also had many advantages for the 'socialist' state, similar to the capitalist state – largely in terms of housework, child-care and employment of women. Yet family forms have been changing, and the authorities in Hungary began to rely upon propaganda, about the joys of family life, to bolster attachment to the 'ideal' family.

CHANGES IN HUNGARIAN FAMILIES

On a fundamental structural level, diminishing size of families – in numbers and generational terms – is perhaps the key feature of change within Hungarian families in the past fifty years. Since the 1940s there has been continuous decline in the size of the average family, indicating the breaking down of the three-generation family. The average number of children by families (accounted for in families with children) in 1949 still exceeded two, yet by 1970 it fell to 1.67, and by 1980 to 1.62 (Hegedüs, 1977, p. 165). The demographic ups and downs experienced in Hungary during the 1950s and 1960s led First Secretary János Kádár to comment in 1967 that:

> The question of whether there should be children or not should not be a matter of calculation. Of course, one must always calculate the cost of a pair of socks, a baby carriage, diapers,

> but we cannot be reduced to 'calculating' the cost of the existence of the next generation. We are aware of how difficult it is to assure a simple room for two young people to begin to lead their own lives. After obtaining that, we assume they are going to be all right but they then say, 'once we have another room we are going to have a child' (Volgyes, 1977, p. 154).

There is a hint of censure in these words – that couples who choose not to have large families or certainly those who do not have any children, are 'mean' or 'anti-social'. Bearing in mind a couple of major constraints on the development of large families in Hungary, primary amongst these are the lack of adequate housing and shortage of money.

Young people cannot marry and look about for a home as a matter of course. There is a chronic shortage of available living accommodation in Hungary (and in almost all other central/eastern European countries), and young childless couples come very low down on the 'list' in terms of priority for living space. Essentially, young couples tend to be forced into a situation in which they are living with one or other pair of 'in-laws' and often younger brothers and sisters as well. It is quite common for this situation to extend over many years with the couple's room being shared with their first child, who may well have to be kept quiet for the sake of the 'older people'. Cramped conditions, pressures of noise, cooking, cleaning and caring for a small child can combine with the lack of privacy experienced during this initial marital period to cause both the women and the men involved to 'rethink' their decisions – on marriage and on child-rearing. High divorce rates and low birth rates eloquently testify to the substance of such problems. Many women with whom I discussed this pointed out difficulties not solely in terms of overcrowding, as Judit noted:

> Unfortunately I am sleeping with János at the moment and my husband is sleeping in the other room with Zsolt. Normally my husband and I try to sleep in the other room but you see when the three children sleep together they wake each other and I am afraid to let any of them sleep on this top bunk as it is dangerous. So, every night, always when we are sleeping one of them comes in to us. My husband and I are always discussing this, it is very unpleasant as we really have a distance between us because of this not sleeping together (Judit, 1986).

Problems of over-crowding or women's isolation on large housing estates are common in urban centres in Hungary. To some extent these difficulties are less apparent in rural areas and there are different issues which concern families in rural areas.

RURAL/URBAN DISTINCTIONS

So far as the rural/urban distinction between family types is concerned, it is obvious that the village is still very much present within Hungarian family life. Many families still have ties to the villages, either in terms of origin, residence or place of work. The rural worker–peasant family, which is numerous in Hungarian society has, a simultaneous influence exerted upon it by urban models and by the accustomed peasant values. Their way of life supports and strengthens a 'traditionally developed family value-system concerning the position occupied in the family by the spouses and as regards the main content of family life' (Szanto, 1984, p. 284). Changes in patterns of living, and the gendered division of labour within the home have been very slow. Amongst the factors militating against change, external pressures and customs are viewed as determining. Yet with the political changes in the 1980s certain cultural patterns have been broken and young people are certainly experiencing influences different from those experienced by their parents.

YOUNG WOMEN

Young women are often amongst those who suffer the most blatant discrimination in terms of prevailing family ideology. 'Unmarried mothers' and 'illegitimate children' are considered outside the 'good' family framework in Hungary and such women and children suffer because of the social attitudes which prevent them forming an alternative family arrangement. Since 1974, the total number of abortions in Hungary had declined, yet abortion figures have risen steadily among women of the youngest age group – under the age of twenty. Under Hungarian law all women may marry at eighteen and those with a special permit can marry at sixteen. As official statistics make no distinction between induced abortion of married and unmarried women it is difficult to separate the two. Still, there is a good deal of evidence to suggest that a large number of the very young women who undergo induced abortion are attending their last years of primary school – i.e. they are aged between thirteen and sixteen. For this and other reasons, juvenile sex has become a subject of serious preoccupation among experts concerned with demographic questions. The current rules on teenagers' access to oral contraceptives leave them little choice of contraception.

There was discussion in the late 1970s and early 1980s of helping families and educators to develop a new code of 'socialist' standards of sexual ethics which would fill the gap left by the abandonment of the once-dominant religious ethics. So far as sex education goes, the government had been trying to solve what is seen as the problem – who should educate the youth of Hungary and by what means? As early as 1974 the Council of Ministers decided that all elementary schools had to include sex education in their curriculum. Yet as should have been expected, attitudes generally lagged behind legislation. Many teachers still either disapproved of talking to the students about sex or were simply too embarrassed to do so. As this subject was left to the 'home-room' teacher, who may specialise in geography or mathematics, it was rather optimistic to expect such an 'unqualified' teacher to have promising results. In the majority of interviews conducted with women who attended (or should have had thc opportunity to attend) such classes, it became clear that such lessons were either not availabe at their schools or that they had become general counselling sessions – valuable though such human relations sessions could potentially be, very little in the way of explicit sexual education took place in them.

Returning to the situation of under-age parents, as is generally the case, the full burden of responsibility falls upon the girl and her family. In many cases the girls are unable to support a baby, and their parents are unable (or unwilling) to adopt the child, so 70 per cent of the babies born to young women outside marriage are given up for state care. In certain intellectual circles in Hungary, it has become a sign of cnlightenment to give birth to an 'illegitimate' child. Yet in the villages social pressure is still very great on the unmarried mother.

Still, there are not enough facilities to give assistance to young mothers wishing to raise their children. In 1980 8 per cent of births were 'illegitimate' and a large number of them were born to mothers who were still legally regarded as children themselves (*Magyar Nemzet*, 10 November 1981). Such mothers would need adequate facilities to help them to adjust to their new family lives. Male attitudes towards their offspring in such situations are seen as generally irresponsible. The number of lawsuits to establish paternity increased steadily throughout the 1980s.

Women seem to have few 'rights' in such matters. At such hearings the public guardianship authority represents the child, whilst the mother is just a witness. It is notable that in many European societies the state has a very large 'say' in what happens to children. It is still solely the women who are considered irresponsible by Hungarian society (when they have a child outside marriage) yet many such mothers would willingly accept responsibility for their children if they received financial and moral support. The language by which women's experiences are written in newspapers is often crude and moralistic, as this quotation from *Magyar Nemzet* shows:

> The immature young men – if the position taken by the parents of the girl is not strong enough – leave their playmates in the lurch like a dishonest driver who fails to stop on the road after an accident. And because of the bind these girls get into, they throw away their children or give them to a government care centre (*Magyar Nemzet*, 25 November 1981).

In Hungary, as elsewhere in the world, young women are at risk because of social attitudes and lack of sexual education. When such young women become pregnant, again social attitudes and the women's legal position *vis-à-vis state* regulations, mean that they are unprotected and little is provided in the way of care for themselves, or for them to bring up their children. In such a situation, it is hardly surprising that many young women relinquish hopes or dreams of being able to raise their children independently, because clearly neither society nor the state authorities are prepared to acknowledge them as suitable 'families'. On the material side, shortage of money not only limits access to accommodation – there are many private apartments available in Hungary if the forints to pay for them are also available – but also increases the necessity for two wages so both parents need employment. Increases in pressures on the financial constraints of a family often mean that having more children can seem like a non-consideration in that the expense, in terms of loss of the woman's earnings for a period and the need for more living space, rules them out of the equation.

MARRIAGE AND DIVORCE

In their longitudinal marriage survey Kamarás, Oroszi and Bárány (1984) interviewed thousands of women at specific times within their married lives – before marriage, after six months, one year and so on – to find out their views on many aspects of their lives. Areas considered include expectations of marriage, housing problems, sexual satisfaction. Amongst the women interviewed many became divorced over the periods of the survey. These women gave various reasons for their divorces, and other 'causes which endangered the marriage' including factors such as alcoholism, violence, emotional deprivation and so on. How far such factors are the end-results of disappointed expectations is hard to tell. Although marriage is popular, the rate of divorce in Hungary has markedly increased since the end of the 1950s. Of course, deteriorating relationships do not always end in the legal dissolution of marriages. Given the shortage of housing space available in Hungary some couples decide that it is just not practicable to divorce – where would they live separately? Yet the new divorce law introduced within the family law makes this situation even more difficult for couples wishing to separate, as terms such as 'living apart' take on a different complexity when this could mean curtaining off a room, or boarding part of a flat off so that there is some privacy between the 'separated couple'. Still, the increases in divorce rates do show how many marriages finally reach legal dissolution (see Table 4.1).

In comparison with other European statistics Hungary receives a fairly 'prominent' place in the statistics on divorce rates. There are varying sets of figures on divorce in Europe and in each Hungary has a prominent position. Many Hungarian sociologists and policy-makers see the high divorce rates as a 'disintegration of the family' and as such the cause of other social problems – maladjusted children of divorced parents, alcoholism, housing problems. On the other hand one important point to note is that the entry of women into productive work has not brought about

Table 4.1 Number of marriages ending in divorce

Year	*Average age on marriage*		*Marriages ended per 1000 marriages, due to:*	
	male	*female*	*Death*	*Divorce*
1938	29.5	24.9	648.0	77.5
1948	28.8	24.5	429.6	113.2
1960	28.8	24.7	531.2	187.3
1970	27.1	23.6	600.5	236.4
1975	26.4	23.3	607.6	250.5
1980	27.2	24.2	876.7	346.0
1983	27.7	24.6	929.9	386.2
1985	27.8	24.6	931.6	400.2
1988	information changed in 1988 and details not available			

Source: *Statisztikai Évkönyv*, 1986 and 1988.

significant changes in the so-called 'traditional' family lifestyle. Certain historical and gendered family lifestyles appear to be preserved with the apparent willingess of the women and of other family members. Where women do skilled jobs involving qualifications, their employment can result in a transformation of the way of living, but in most families where women work in unskilled work, some historical patterns and gendered divisions of labour remain. This is being seen as a social problem in Hungary though not in 'emancipatory' terms. The tensions within Hungarian family life are resulting in strains being placed on women, men and children living together, so that 'broken families' have become a cause of social concern.

According to the longitudinal survey analysis (HCSO, 1984) in about 25 per cent of the marriages made in 1974 which ended in divorce, disaffection and lack of love and understanding contributed to the final break, with alcoholism causing the breakdown in another 25 per cent. After this, conflicts with parents and/or relatives are most frequent, then neglect of the family and financial problems. Although financial problems and jealousy are not often shown here as the primary reasons for divorce, there were indications in the survey material that they do put a great deal of stress on married lives, and can produce crises in relationships. Those women who indicated the husband's alcohol consumption, rough treatment, neglect of the family and financial problems were generally in families with the most children. Women who mentioned emotional, psychological problems or conflicts with relatives had far fewer children than average. Of course, reasons differ, and can be separated out only partially according to women's experiences, histories, ages, occupations, residences and/or educational levels. In rural families the excessive consumption of alcohol was observed more frequently than average. In the case of women who were non-manual workers, relations with parents, mothers- and fathers-in-law upset the stability of marriage more than anything else.

The various structural conditions affecting domestic environments should not be underestimated. The chronic housing shortage which can mean that it takes between ten and fifteen years for a couple to buy or build their own house or flat places great strains on people in terms of how little they see of their partner, and/or how little money is available for anything other than necessities. During the 1980s the decline in state-supported construction – less than 1 per cent of dwellings are state-financed now – coupled with increased costs meant that most newly married couples have to live with parents or in-laws, generally in very cramped conditions. An additional factor was that of participation in the second economy. Unlike almost all other full-time work which was for 'the state' and therefore not something with a strong pull in terms of interest or enthusiasm, much second-economy work was actually defined or controlled by those working within it.

Having such second or third jobs meant an extremely long working day of up to twelve hours and often people worked weekends and 'holidays' too. As has been noted, such conditions are not conducive to calm, supportive relations in the home because stress adds to other strains, such as economic or spatial difficulties, and everything becomes highly charged and tense, far away from any romantic notions that young people might have associated with married life.

WOMEN'S LIBERATION AND DIVORCE

Certain sociolgists and lawyers in Hungary suggest that one of the major causes of divorce is the 'liberation of women', claiming that it is within marriage that many women win equality. As has been noted, most women work and thus reasonably expect some sharing of home chores by their spouse. Many husbands actually refuse to do any work in the home. An article in the Patriotic People's Front daily, *Magyar Nemzet*, describes this situation:

> Our social adjustment to the working woman is a revolutionary process, during which the entire structure of the family changes not quietly, in peace, but rather with such commotion . . . counter-posing long-established social and moral standards against the vague or hardly established ones governing a new situation.[1]

Some Western sociologists had viewed the sexual equality policy in 'socialist' countries as being a possible factor in marital stress. David Lane comments 'there is evidence to suggest that the values of equality of sexes espoused by socialist ideology have created conflict between married partners' (Lane, 1982, p. 90). So far as Ferge and other Hungarian sociologists are concerned, whilst the facts are correct, in so far as divorce rates are high, the explanation is at best doubtful. Ferge suggests that:

> Divorce may occur not only because women 'aspire to independence' and 'engage in rivalry', but also because, having acquired some independence, they can no longer accept a relation which is in fact based on male domination and female subordination (Ferge, 1979, pp. 109–10).

The keeping of 'harmonious relations' within marriage is often achieved at the expense of one partner (the women more often than not), and working out ways to change relations between partners was one direction in which various 'family policies' in Hungary may have become channelled in the late 1980s had not the centre-right coalition gained power in 1989. As noted in the interview with Katalin Filó in Chapter 3, attitudes towards family situations are distinctly conservative in the Christian–nationalist atmosphere of the early 1990s. Given the interventionist nature of 'socialist' social policy and the need for women workers, decisions concerning population policy were made by policy-makers in a pro-natalist atmosphere. Propaganda concerning the diminishing size of the Hungarian nation was addressed to 'real' Hungarian women, to appeal to them to have more children, whilst the population policy measures attempted to reinforce such decisions.

POPULATION POLICY MEASURES

In the period after the war (late 1940s) the birth rate in Hungary stabilised at around 20–21 per thousand. By 1953/55, because of the strict measures limiting abortion, the first 'baby boom' occurred, reaching a peak in 1954 when the crude live birth rate rose to 23 per thousand. After this time, partly because of the after-effect of births in the 'boom' period and partly because the abortion restrictions were lifted (1956) the number and rate of births began to decrease. The lowest point was in 1962 when the crude birth rate was 12.9 per thousand, which meant that the number of live-born children was lower by over 48 per cent than in 1954 (ILO Report, 1984, ch.1). A slight increase in birth rates after 1966 was followed by another stagnation with fertility rates below replacement level until 1973. It was in 1973 that the extensive new population policy measures were adopted (see also Appendix II). The measures initially had the desired impact in terms of a new 'boom' which coincided with the fact that large cohorts of women who were born at the earlier stage (1953–5) were now giving birth to their own children. The number of births rose from 156 000 in 1973 to 194 000 in 1975, so that a maximum was reached in 1975 of 18.4 births per thousand (Szabody, 1979, p. 152).

Since this time though, a renewed decline has taken place and decreased fertility has lasted until the beginning of the 1990s. In part this was because both marriage and birth rates were determined by the small female cohorts born in the first half of the 1960s but attitudes towards larger families also play a part here. Given the difficulties facing young couples in setting up their own homes, the answer given to me by Judit regarding a third child is quite common:

> No. I know I won't. Some of my friends have only one child and are not sure if they will have a second. Now that I am lucky enough to have one of each, I know we will not have a third. We can barely afford shoes and clothing for Eszter and

András and I want to get back to work. GYES is not enough for us to manage on (Judit: Corrin, 1986).

WHY DO PEOPLE HAVE CHILDREN?

Most survey data in Hungary concerning children within families has focused upon the *number* of children couples would like to have or decide to have, there is little or no information available as to the reasons *why* people have children. Within the general guidance service provided by genetic counsellors operating under the Counselling Service for Women and the Family (never Men, Women and the Family?) there are twelve genetic clinics – seven in the provinces and five in Budapest. Each year about 4000 couples make use of the service, whose task is to improve family planning, in its broadest sense. Writing about the work of counsellors, Endre Czeizel discusses people's motives for having children. Czeizel notes that the stress often fell on the material advantages of having children – including the 3-year child-care leave, maintenance of seniority at work, priority in housing allocations, family allowances, exemption from military service, relief from night work, children's help in domestic work and later in supporting aged parents. Another group, though, placed emphasis on family and family ties, so they are noted as being:

> out to cement the marriage, to commit the man to his marriage or to keep the wife occupied; they want the family to survive, the family name to live on, and the family wealth to be passed down; or they may want a second child primarily as company for the first; they may want children of both sexes, etc. (Czeizel, 1980, p. 147).

It is women and men within this group who cited personality fulfilment as their main reason and speak of the flowering of the female personality, motherhood as an experience and an achievement and family responsibility as 'marking the attainment of adulthood'. Children are seen by such people as fulfillers of the parents' hopes and ambitions as well as someone to carry on the work and efforts of the parents. In the fourth group Czeizel notes people for whom social expectations and adherence to the 'family model' are all-important so that they have children because their parents, siblings, colleagues and their neighbours all have children – essentially, they wish to conform.

In terms of the economic reasons for having children a particular phrase came into common usage in Hungary in the early 1980s – that of 'the OTP children'. This names comes from the abbreviation of the Hungarian National Bank – *Országos Takaret Pénztar* (OTP) and since 1977 couples were able to acquire apartments at reduced costs providing that they had a certain number of children. Part of the price of their accommodation however, is children, who could perhaps become treated like economic commodities. According to an emotive and prejudicial report in *Népsava*, many couples are not suited for the role of parents:

> But why do these women accept the role of mother? Perhaps because they feel their lives would be unbearably empty without children? Or perhaps because, for many people, this is the relatively easy way of getting an apartment? In other words do they interpret the new life as a means of payment? (*Népsava*, 6 March 1981).

It is unfair to blame *mothers* who choose to take up the OTP offer of reducing housing costs when they generally have partners who are also involved in both the banking contracts and fathering the children. It is not untypical that Hungarian press reports accord primary responsibility towards children to mothers, and it is to them that all blame attaches when things go wrong. In this context Gittins notes that:

> Because fatherhood is always potentially unknown, and always politically contestable, it is therefore also always a social category. Motherhood, on the other hand, is always known. Yet apart from carrying and giving birth to a child, the biological base of motherhood stops there. The rest is socially constructed although it may be – and often is – attributed to biology or 'maternal instinct' (Gittins, 1985, p. 66).

Illustrative examples of this are found in various anthropological studies, including that of the situation of some women in Tahiti who give their children away to the care of others and so do not take up 'motherhood' despite having produced children (Endholm, in Whitelegg, 1982).

ABORTION AND CONTRACEPTION

Certainly up to the late-1970s abortion was quite 'common' in Hungary, because of the relative shortage of cheap, reliable and readily available methods of contraception. The number of induced abortions went down from 170 000 in 1973 to 96 000 in 1975. The decrease in induced abortion was almost twice as great as the increment in births. In this connection the severity in the authorisation of abortions, brought in with the 1973 regulations (effective 1974), played a role. Whilst the number of refused applications for legal abortions remained below 1 per cent in 1979 there have been indications, that illegal abortions have risen since 1974, especially for younger women.

It is clear that women are in a very weak position if they cannot defend their rights to abortion and contraception. Decisions concerning women's bodies and their future lives are taken by predominantly male groupings, in an almost 'anti-woman' environment, in which women 'count' primarily as workers and mothers, not as equal citizens with needs and desires outside their working and maternal environments. That women within Hungarian society have not been able to resist the various policy manoeuvres concerning abortion legislation at least since 1973 (see Chapter 7) shows that women within Hungarian society have been in a very weak position, and have had certain fundamental areas of their lives dictated by male policy-makers. How far this situation is comparable with that of women in other countries is considered in Chapter 8.

IMPACT OF WOMEN'S EMPLOYMENT ON FERTILITY

A report published by the International Labour Office, Geneva (ILO, 1984) shows the decrease in fertility amongst married women.

The proportion of babies delivered of employed mothers has increased (see Table 4.2), whilst those delivered of non-employed mothers has decreased. There is a very big increase between 1965 and 1970, presumably due in large measure to the introduction of the child-care allowance, in that women drawing the allowance will be listed as economically active. This transformation showing over 88 per cent of mothers as being economically active needs to

Table 4.2 Percentage distribution of live births analysed according to mother's economic activity status

Year	*Economically active*	*Dependent*
1960	33.7	66.3
1965	51.4	48.6
1970	74.5	25.5
1975	86.5	13.5
1980	88.6	11.4

Source: *Hungarian Demographic Yearbooks*, 1960–80.

be viewed within this framework – that is, of mothers remaining at home with their young children for up to three years. It is evident also from the figures that employed married women have a smaller number of children than those not employed. Here begins the theory that an increasing number of women who are economically active have come to consider that a two-child family is in many senses at least manageable, if not 'ideal'. Given earlier discussion of the fact that nuclear families, consisting of heterosexual parents plus 2.4 children, are in fact a minority family situation in many European countries, including Hungary, notions of 'ideal' often bring with them oppressive stereotypical myths.

PUBLIC OPINIONS ON DEMOGRAPHIC MEASURES

The public opinion research on demographic issues (Budapest, 1985/2) considered which measures were approved and accepted by public opinion and which met with opposition. It is a difficult area in which to examine 'opinions' – as with many other areas, the reception of demographic principles and practice depends also on the values and norms prevalent in respect of the areas in everyday life which the demographic policy wants to influence. The method chosen was a 'questionnaire' with fourteen statements which related, some in sharply contrasting manner, to the values and norms that contained the most characteristic demographic issues encountered in public opinion. Upon being read each statement respondents had to say whether or not they agreed with it.

Table 4.3 Responses to questionnaire on principles and practice in demographic policy

Items	*Agrees*	*Does not agree*	*Uncertain*	*Does not know*
1. Parents with children are not given as much respect and support as they deserve	34	48	13	5
2. People who have too many children irresponsibly ought not to be supported	46	40	11	3
3. It is a private affair how many children a person wants, the state may not interfere	83	9	6	2
4. The trouble is that women find their work today more important than having more children	42	28	19	4
5. Families do not have more children because of financial difficulties	61	18	17	3
6. The state has a right to determine how many children a woman may have	6	87	4	3
7. It would be good if women were paid a salary for bringing up their children and for housekeeping instead of having to go to work	51	35	10	3
8. The main reason why families break up is that our laws make divorce too easy	46	38	18	4
9. The state had better care for a higher living standard than for the number of new-born children	53	20	21	5
10. Young people should be allowed sex only with the person they marry	41	47	8	3
11. The family allowance today is practically not enough for anything	39	38	16	7
12. Young people nowadays start families irresponsibly because they are not brought up strictly enough	41	36	18	5
13. Each young married couple should have as many children as demanded by the interest of the country	23	62	10	5
14. The fact that somebody has a child should not entitle this person to receive benefits even in employment	15	74	7	4

Source: Public Opinion Research on Demographic Issues, CSO, 1985.

Many different aspects are covered in the fourteen questions. The first pair of questions that show an obvious and very striking correlation (questions 3 and 6) concern the role of the state intervention in child-bearing. Those who agree that having children is a private affair are the highest percentage – 83 per cent, whilst those disagreeing that the state has a right to determine how many children a women may have are the highest in that column – 87 per cent. There is firm agreement that the state has no rights in determining the numbers of children women may wish to have. Nevertheless, the state/society divide is somewhat blurred in terms of providing for children. So far as child benefits are concerned a high proportion (74 per cent) of people believe that parents should receive benefits, even when in employment. Whilst opinion is fairly evenly divided on whether the family allowance is a reasonable sum, there is strong agreement that families do not have more children because of financial difficulties. In this context more than half of the respondents felt that the state should be more concerned with raising living standards, than with raising the birth-rate. Again, more than half of those questioned felt that it would be a positive move if women were to be paid a salary for bringing up their children and for housekeeping (instead of going out to work). Unfortunately, there was not an equivalent father/parent question – the responses would have been very interesting.

In this sense the question concerning women finding their work more important than having more children is a central one. If women were to achieve their 'liberation' through work, then it was imperative that they find their work important despite this being seen as a 'trouble'. Considering the 'responsibility' factor, it appears to be commonplace to put a certain amount of blame on large families, considering those parents of many children 'irresponsible'.

It would seem that many people feel that it is each individual's private affair to have children, and that they do so on their own account. In other words, whilst the state has no right to a say in how many children people have, so too the state (or society) cannot be expected to bear the ensuing burden. As is often the case opinions have complex roots and ingredients so that this particular group of questions involves various motivations. Perhaps the major general opinion is that 'people should only have as many children as they can provide for adequately, or well', so that prejudices against large families (such as some of the large Roma families) become apparent. The other aspect is that of aversion to 'state handouts' which are available to families with children as it offends the sense of 'fairness' of those for whom such benefits are not available (any more). Such people feel that they actually suffer disadvantages from those who have children – in respect of receiving flats, cheap vacation possibilities, work assignments and such like. So far as divorce is concerned a fairly high percentage of the respondents (46 per cent) felt that Hungarian laws made divorce too easy. Since the survey, of course, divorce laws have been made more stringent. A general trend has emerged from this consideration in that smaller families are becoming the accepted 'norm' and state responsibility towards caring for such smaller families is expected. Opinions differ on the ways in which state assistance should be given to families, regarding child-care and child-rearing.

What does all this mean for the changes we have seen in family structures and in policy changes towards childbirth and child-rearing? It seems from the survey material that there has been a marked influence of social policy upon certain social groups and areas of activity. Given the increase in economically active women the basis for marriage appears to have shifted from an economic motive (in terms of financial security for women) to an emotional/social basis in which certain emotional needs are expected to be satisfied and certain social roles fulfilled. The general information available on reasons for divorce show that to a large extent dissonance between expectations and reality was a common cause for dissatisfaction. Still, where the root cause of these dashed expectations lies – in underestimating economic pressures say, or undervaluing the changes in women's lives in terms of paid employment – is an extremely complex question.

WORK IN THE HOME

It is obvious that employment in areas such as child-care assistance in crèches and kindergartens is extremely lowly-paid, seen to be of low-status and therefore few women are actually keen to do it. When this same job is carried out in the home, without pay but with the extra duties of caring for the home, shopping and cooking for the child(ren) and a partner as well as perhaps, parents, then this is certainly viewed by society generally as a job that women should be keen to do. Having considered 'ideal' notions about 'the family', it is worthwhile to look briefly at the 'ideal' woman – or 'superwoman'. As mentioned earlier there is a totally unreasonable belief, rarely stated but 'hovering' in many people's conversations, that women should aspire to being or becoming, 'superwomen'. By this is meant that women are expected to be wonderful mothers, cooks and cleaners all day, then teachers in the early evening and adorable sex creatures at night! This is a theme which crops up again and again in many different ways – just how much is expected of the successful woman. It would seem that for many women in Hungary such a complex set of social expectations is a massive pressure to bear and the ways in which this comes out can be manifold, including strains on women's health, decisions about not having more children, or getting divorced. This is not to say that there are not many other reasons for divorce, for limiting the number of children within families, nor that most women's health problems are necessarily directly stress-related, yet such social overexpectations cannot be ignored.

'Work' is obviously a central feature of life in Hungary (and other countries) in many ways which at first are not apparent. By 'work' people generally mean paid employment and there are obvious benefits from such work – money, which guarantees some standard of living, and personal social contact (rather than isolation), as well as status, in terms of 'non-workers'. Very often people ask questions like 'What are you?', or 'What do you do?', signifying that people are often categorised by the type of work they do – many researchers do this. For 'non-workers' in Hungary, that is, those not in paid employment, life is very different from that of workers – economically, socially and psychologically. In this context, the full-employment policies in 'socialist' countries had obvious advantages for citizens over the market-oriented systems, in which people can be unemployed for years at a time and consequently can feel 'useless' and 'lost' in their (usually poverty-stricken) 'non-working' lives. One of the major tasks of 'socialist' societal policy in Hungary was to reduce the most obvious gaps between workers and 'non-workers' in economic terms and in social terms. For women, social/psychological differences can include the value of working in the home, which is currently quite low, and an increased recognition of the valuable role of parents, men as well as women, so that motherhood is seen within a social framework of parenting, which is accorded high status.

One basic difference for working women in 'socialist' countries was that they were rarely given an opportunity to describe themselves as 'housewives', unlike many women with young children in capitalist countries – who are in large measure economically dependent upon their husbands – although with new employment structures emerging in various parts of Britain, this too is beginning to change. In Hungary being a housewife is generally a secondary occupation to paid employment. It is apparent that it is mainly women who undertake the majority of domestic tasks which are largely unrewarded. Yet in some ways, as the survey responses at the end of Chapter 3 showed, many men seemed to prefer to have their wives at home, and would 'help' more with housework, which seems contradictory:

> Before, when I was here [at home on child-care leave] I was sometimes getting a nice surprise from my husband – he would offer to help me with the cleaning and tidy the children's room. More than once he would help with the pots and bathe the children. Now that I am back [at work] it is strange. He never seems to bathe the children now and I have to ask him to tidy their room (Ágnes: Corrin, 1986).

Perhaps this is tied in with the old images of 'man the breadwinner' and so long as he is able to play this role, then he is also able to be magnanimous enough to 'help' in the home. The lack of recognition for women's unpaid work within the home could be a major factor in the response to demographic survey questions showing more than half of the respondents in favour of women being paid a wage to care for children and carry out household work (HCSO, 1980). This would certainly be in line with many campaigns, such as the Wages for Housework Campaign, which propose that work in the home should be waged, whoever performs it. In this connexion Hilary Land writes that:

> Central to the position of women today is the interpretation of female labour as an inferior version of male labour . . . These stereotypes apply both to female household labour and to women's labour in paid occupations. Thus it is normative to regard the employment work of women as an activity inter-

> rupted by domesticity, and to view housework as an intermittent (and interruptable) rather than continuous activity; to reinforce the poverty (in relation to the male norm) of women's monetary rewards for paid work by the total lack of remuneration attached to housework; to see both housework and women's paid work as marginal contributions to the national economy (Land, 1980, p. 67).

Fundamental to this debate is that housework is not regarded as real 'work' at all, so it is seen as unnecessary to pay houseworkers. Furthermore, as housework is not viewed as requiring skills or being physically demanding then housework can be carried out in addition to other forms of work. On balance it would appear that if household work were to become waged, then this would be a positive step, provided that some form of educational campaign accompanied such legislation to provide alternative models to 'women in the home' images which are currently prevalent in Hungary and elsewhere.

Of all the women interviewed in connection with this work, almost everyone mentioned that work outside the home for women should be a *choice*. This question of choice is important, as most women in Hungary have not had a choice concerning paid employment, then certain options become all the more attractive. Some felt that certain choices should apply to husbands – if a wife wanted to work outside the home then her husband could choose to do child-care work.

In her work on women and leisure Katalin Sulyok (1975) touches upon some of the disadvantages for women at home on child-care leave. Often this 'decision' to be at home and care for children is actually the only option open to women, as places in crèches are so limited and not everyone has access to a relative, neighbour or willing (and inexpensive) child-minder who will help with child-care. Of the questions concerning 'spare-time' activities, the answer to the question 'What do you do with your daily spare time?' was answered in a fairly 'typical' way by a 22-year-old woman on leave with child-care allowance:

> God, I'm fed up with all this free time! I'll wait another two months and then put the baby into the crèche. One and a half years at home has been enough. I'll be able to work at last! (Sulyok, 1975, p. 131).

Given that working women had to become 'speedy' in their household tasks when they were in paid employment, and given that many young children do sleep for several hours each day, there are possibilities that many women at home with young children feel bored and isolated, and long to return to the social and busy environment of their workplaces – even if their actual jobs were not satisfying. In reply to questions about 'What would you do if you had more free time?' the reply, again not untypical, from one mother was 'I'd be bored to death'.

So far as activities for young mothers on child-care leave are concerned very little is actually available for them to become involved in on a regular basis. Not every woman enjoys cooking, needlework or indeed playing with children for hours at a time. Given this, some sort of 'self-help' or activity groups would seem a good idea. In some of her writings Ferge has touched upon the desirability of some form of social work taking place in communities such as large housing estates. In this context those students entering the first social-work courses at Eötvös Lorand University in September 1990 may well take up positions such as community workers when they qualify in 1994/5. Trained social and community workers can initiate and coordinate various activities which would not necessarily entail great economic outlay. On some of the large estates around Budapest and other large towns, women at home have grouped together from time to time and organised group child-care so that the others may see a film, or visit a local exhibition or some such activity. Yet such joint activities often highlight tensions between women in terms of how to care for children:

> Often women would feel dissatisfied with the standard of cleanliness of some houses. Sometimes intellectual women would have untidy houses and would feed the children 'snack-type' food that some of the other women thought was not very nutritious (Iren: Corrin, 1986).

Problems of differing expectations are not easily overcome and given that institutionalised child-care is scarce, the idea of 'supported' group activities may help to ease worries some women have concerning differing methods of child-care. It could become a good forum within which women could confidently air their differing views.

SOCIALISATION OF HOUSEWORK

There are many, varied aspects which feed into perceptions of 'the family'. As we know, it was changes in the structure and attitudes towards the family which Engels expected to initiate social change towards emancipating women, in terms of the socialisation of housework and the public participation of women in the workforce. It is also clear that the Marxian ideal of socialising the chores associated with nuclear family life in order to free women for public participation within society has not been achieved, in Hungary or elsewhere. Attempts have been made in Hungary from the 1950s onwards to provide subsidised eating-places, yet the various factory dining-rooms, although relatively inexpensive to provide and maintain, were very poor in quality and the available choice was very limited. Whilst most new factories do have dining provision it is not on the scale nor of the quality originally envisaged by planners in the early 1960s. Other dining provision such as the option to buy subsidised restaurant food proved difficult to implement and also expensive to maintain.

Such 'socialised' services fall into two categories. The first is the network of child-care services, and the second is the provision of the services involved in 'making public' the tasks carried out in the home. The latter services are variable in quality and those areas which would be most useful to women, such as inexpensive but efficient laundries, have proved expensive to maintain at good standards. In addition, having to take laundry and collect it can prove difficult to fit into an already-packed day, unlike putting it into the machine at home at midnight! Despite apparently good intentions, the revolutionary changes needed to free women from the double burden of work outside and inside the home have not been implemented to anything like the necessary extent.

In terms of actual household work this is not made easier by handy equipment such as squeezy mops or spray cleansers. Most floor-cleaning is done with a form of headless brush around which a cloth is draped, and many of the cleaning products available are below average quality for speedy cleaning. There are problems with equipment, such as washing-machines (which invariably leak) and vacuum cleaners. Of the two main types of vacuum cleaners available at affordable prices in the 1980s, one was Czechoslovakian and spare parts were extremely hard to obtain, whilst the other, Russian, machine, seemed much less reliable but appeared relatively easier to repair. If someone in the household in Hungary does not become a reliable home-repair person the costs of sending equipment into workshops would definitely be prohibitive for most people.

Added to the fact that it is women who perform the majority of these household tasks is the necessity of giving schoolchildren some time with their homework – generally this involves helping the children to understand what is required of them, rather than executing the tasks with them. Often, especially if the man in the household has a second job, this task also falls to women. Once again there are echoes of the need to be 'superwoman' to be a successful working mother in Hungary, as in other parts of the world.

CONCLUSION

In concluding this consideration of certain aspects of Hungarian domestic situations, and the changes which families have undergone, it is clear that women play a central part in domestic life from various persectives. Just as 'the family' is by no means a straightforward unit nor can it be analysed as such, so women's lives within different domestic environments differ in a multiplicity of ways. Some crude distinctions can be drawn in terms of unskilled working mothers and intellectual mothers. Yet some of the unskilled women with whom I spoke really enjoyed motherhood as something of a vocation, whereas others were bored being 'caged' up in the tiny flats. Some intellectual women find all sorts of other pursuits to follow whilst at home, whereas others feared that they were losing their professional skills and would be shy and nervous when they returned to work. What is clear though is that societal, 'family' and often personal expectations of working mothers do centre on expectations that women are not only able to carry out a multiplicity of tasks but enjoy doing so and do not feel pressured by some of the more blatant, overexpectations, especially in terms of domestic budgeting.

It also seems quite clear that the changeover from the 'socialist' administration to the multiparty democracy now in place in Hungary will not much affect the overexpectations placed on women, except in so far as the outlook of many leading politicians from the governing coalition favours a 'return to traditional family life'. Given that this 'tradition' is nowhere clearly expounded, and that as we have seen the nuclear model of family life in late-twentieth century Hungarian society is but an ideal, it is difficult to gauge at this stage the longer-term effects of the newly emerging Hungarian policy-makers' attitudes towards women's 'appropriate roles' within the more market-oriented society. Discussion of a 'family wage' has long been present in Hungary. It does generally appear that many Hungarian women believe men should earn enough to 'keep' a family so that women are not forced into low-paying, low-status jobs just to help to pay the rent. Obviously, in this area there is often a contradiction between the emancipatory needs of women and their 'family' interests.

One legacy from the 'socialist' period has been the continuation of the interventionist nature of 'family policies' and within this family ideologies. These are very much complicated by the conflicting beliefs of what 'the family' is, or is expected to become, in terms of it being the bedrock, or base social unit, as well as being a safe, unique haven from the cares of 'society'. The difficult contradiction within 'socialist' societies between the personal/public dimensions of people's lives was nowhere more apparent than within the domestic environment. It is quite possible that one factor militating against the discussion and adoption of communal living plans from the 1950s onwards was that many Hungarians felt that their 'state' already encroached too much upon their lives, and that small, nuclear families were the 'safest haven' from the intervening arms of such powerful state forces.

Family patterns in Hungary have changed over the decades, with fewer children, fewer extended-family networks, and whilst many people do still experience a two-parent, two-children life, the period in which families exist in this form has become much shorter. So far as changes within families are concerned, the assertion which certain writers make concerning the steady development of modern, democratic families in which women and men share tasks equally and make decisions jointly seems premature at the present time. Much of the evidence from talks and interviews made by the author runs directly counter to such notions.

This is not to say that change is not occurring, but is merely to emphasise not only the slowness of such change but also the often contradictory nature of people's expectations. New patterns of living, including the new ways of thinking about aspects of everyday life, take time to evolve. Yet, as will be seen in Chapters 7 and 8, there is evidence that young women in Hungary are reacting against what they see as the 'bleakness' of their mothers' lives. In practical terms the rural character of much of Hungarian life cannot be ignored. As the statistics on rural and urban residence show, the extent of the village lifestyle is significant in contemporary Hungarian society. This is an added factor in the current administration's favouring of rural, 'traditional' domestic values. That prominent politicians are favouring a return to some idyllic, if mythical and unrealistic past, of large families where women remain at home caring for all, does not augur well for independent women's initiatives and campaigns. When this family ideology is coupled with restrictions concerning abortion and contraception, in an atmosphere of economic instability and unemployment, recognising the importance of domestic work in financial, emotional and psychological terms becomes imperative. When women can build upon the knowledge of the importance of the domestic sphere and the fundamental needs for equality within it, they are generally in a better position to start to change those aspects of domestic life which are oppressive. In Chapter 5 some of these policy options concerning child-care and child-rearing and the debates which have arisen from their implementation are considered.

5 Social Policy Developments

INTRODUCTION

It is clear that the attempted 'socialist' transformations regarding some equalisation of living standards from 1948 were not realised in Hungary. In the early period war losses and general poverty meant that standards remained very low. Given the various regime priorities in the economic spheres mentioned in Chapter 2, social policy measures remained in a dependent, secondary relationship. From 1990 other transformations have been attempted, but in major areas of social policy many of the changes are at best 'double-edged' and at worst divisive and discriminatory. It was an enormously important achievement to generate multiparty elections and empower new governmental structures, but the newly elected politicians inherited a very uneven, 'patchworked' institutional and legal legacy, within a shaky economic framework. In the 1990s fundamental priorities will need to shift so that the focus extends from the narrow concentration on the way that benefits and services will be funded towards an overview of the workings of the different actors and agencies involved. Currently decisions and proposals emerge from a form of 'power game' involving backstage struggles between various Ministries and the Social Insurance Institutes. There are echoes here of the former way of doing things.

This chapter focuses on aspects of 'socialist' social policy goals and achievements and on those changes, questions and decisions now being raised with respect to social policy developments in the new political democracy. By considering the aims and strategies of the 'socialist' period it is possible to assess the legacy that the new politicians and policy-makers have inherited. Within this, potential options for change and the ways in which certain social policy developments will affect women's situation can be outlined. One major focus is on the benefits/services debate in terms of caring for children. Western observers often considered Hungarian women 'liberated' as they were generally in paid full-time work and had some access to state child-care services. The double-edged nature of such a situation in which women had to be 'superwomen' has been outlined in Chapters 3 and 4. For the purposes of this chapter the actual debates which took place at the time regarding the impact upon women's situations are assessed.

Poverty has been a major feature of life in Hungary for several groups for many decades. There have always been income inequalities in Hungary but official policy claimed to be attempting to reduce such inequalities by direct intervention in terms of pensions and family benefits. Currently in Hungary income inequalities are an everyday reality and the efforts of policy-makers in terms of ameliorating the situation of vulnerable groups is not so clear. In the modern period the situations of Roma people, older people, members of large families (three or more children), and single parents have remained consistently impoverished.

In recognising the poor situation for many Roma people, who most definitely form an impoverished and marginalised group in Hungary, it is the case that there is much less open debate on their situation. There are often racist overtones to discussions concerning Roma people in everyday phrases which highlight the fact that some Hungarians think that 'the gypsies get what they deserve'. There are connotations underlying certain attitudes which show that some Hungarian citizens view Roma people as lazy and not 'deserving' of a decent standard of living. As noted elsewhere, my lack of detailed knowledge in this area of Hungarian reality is such that no concentrated focus can be given. Yet it becomes apparent when attitudes are considered that part of the recent racist attacks on Roma people has been fuelled by Hungarian society's traditional lack of acceptance of the Roma's strikingly different approach to sexuality and children.

SOCIAL WELFARE SERVICES

It is apparent that late twentieth-century Hungarian society is extremely complex so that interventionist policies run the risk of not succeeding, for many reasons. Primary amongst these is that attempts to obtain a total picture of needs/wishes within a complex society is well-nigh impossible. As is also apparent, there can be contradictory needs within a society so that information about such social matters is rarely unbiased or 'objective' in any sense. The implementation of social policies involves at least a tension between value clashes in terms of short- and long-term policy goals and expectations, between economic and social objectives and between groups with something to 'gain' and those who may feel that they are (relative) losers. Such tensions have an impact upon the 'success/failure' of social policy interventions and the consequent checks and balances required in their operation.

A major difference between the practice of social welfare institutions in Hungary and that of many Western countries is that in Hungary there has not been a voluntary sector. Changes are beginning to take place in terms of charitable efforts to help poor people, and within health care. The absence of a nationwide welfare service in the form of paid professional social/care workers highlights the fundamental differences between the welfare situation in Hungary and that existing in the UK. Not only are there no trained and well-staffed social welfare departments – no social workers, community workers, children's workers or care workers – but there are no 'voluntary' workers such as those women who work in women's refuges, on rape crisis help lines or lesbian lines. This is beginning to change, as will be seen in Chapter 8, but this development is very much at an embryonic stage. The state provision of social welfare services is also developing within Hungary, with the first social work students being admitted to Eötvös Loránd University in 1990 on 4-year and 5-year courses. Other shorter courses are also being supported, but it is to be hoped that these will not create a two-tier system of professional carers and underpaid assistants. The recognition of social work as a profession is important in aiming to prevent it becoming 'feminised' into a lowly paid, undervalued type of work. In 1990 several 'family centres' also opened with specialist help available for family members – children's specialists, psychologists – and some play-group activities. There is still very little of this in smaller, rural areas.

AIMS OF 'SOCIALIST' SOCIAL POLICY

After the Second World War the main principles of 'socialist' change – the establishment of egalitarian goals laid down in the constitution – proved difficult to realise. Hungary's 'defeat' left the country devasted and there were high levels of poverty throughout society. Some egalitarian intention in the social policy legislation can be noted from the fact that the basis of the later benefits structure was laid down in the immediate post-war period. Few of these benefits had anything much in common with pre-war policy and some had no Hungarian parallel at all. Most of the means-tested benefits were abolished and universal benefits were introduced, many of which were flat-rate. A marked feature was the high share of benefits in kind, which were also seen as capable of reducing inequalities, as their existence guaranteed some standard consumption for those entitled to benefit. There was also a good deal of simplification made to the financing and administration of the benefits, as the majority were covered either within the framework of social security or straight from the state budget.

As all social policy is dependent in large measure on the ideological commitment of its creators, social policy in 'socialist' societies was supposedly a different entity to that in capitalist systems. In her work on social policy Zsuzsa Ferge makes the important distinction between social and societal policy. Societal policy implies a project of deliberately changing a society, of altering basic social, human relations – economic, cultural and power-related elements alike (Ferge, 1979, p. 44). The existence of societal policy did not mean that the activities of corrective or palliative social policy were no longer necessary, but that there was a need for the two to coexist. A clearly defined societal policy would give a new orientation to social policy. In 'socialist' societies policy-makers were supposedly seeking to intervene directly in society with policies aimed at directing social change, be it idealistically in terms of bringing about more egalitarian social relations or realistically by concentrating power over the productive process.

SOCIAL SECURITY BENEFITS

Given the 'socialist' basis upon which social security was established in Hungary, benefits were a basic right of Hungarian citizens, noted in the Constitution in Article 70/E. This states that 'All citizens of the Hungarian Republic have the right to social security; people in old age, sickness, invalidity, widowhood and if they become unemployed (involuntarily) they are entitled to an allowance to live on.' Within the rigidly structured economic development in Hungary during the 1950s a centralised pattern was set for the development and direction of social security. The principal defenders of citizens' interests in this area became the communist-directed trades unions. In such a situation actual defence of people's interests was tied in with the Party–state bureaucracies and in such a situation neither individual workers nor groups of workers were adequately represented or protected. Vulnerable groups such as the elderly, those within large families, Roma people and young people beginning their working lives, found themselves in increasingly unfavourable situations.

In 1980 the political leadership took an unusual step by commissioning the Institute of Sociology to elaborate over a period of five years a long-term uniform welfare policy conception. This uniform welfare policy stood little chance of 'success' given the power-political relations then in place, so that the forecasts were not taken seriously and no effective preventive measures were taken. From 1988 new measures were introduced which aggravated an already bad economic situation – state subsidies were ended, a personal income tax and value added tax were introduced and at the same time a virtual wage-freeze was also imposed. With continuing inflation the vulnerability of the low-income groups was confirmed.

POVERTY RESEARCH

One distinct aspect of Hungarian policy and that of other 'socialist' societies was that poverty had long been regarded as a feature of the 'capitalist' past. This meant, of course, that all those who argued about its actual existence were considered anti-government. It was partly because of 'unauthorised' research into poverty that scholars such as István Kemény had to go into exile in the 1970s. Since the 1981 Hungarian Sociological Society conference, the 'taboo' nature of poverty research has been removed. At the conference researchers considered groups of people at multiple disadvantage from various aspects.[1] Rudolf Andorka notes that this conference was important in that it considered other factors than low income as relating to poverty – poor housing, underdeveloped environments (small villages), low education, illness, social adaptation difficulties (one family-member being alcoholic)(Andorka, 1989, p. 135). One striking factor in terms of poverty research is that it was not until 1987 that poverty was considered to have actually increased, and that the ratio of people living below the comparable limit of poverty was much larger in 1967. Despite falls in real wages and a considerable increase in prices between 1978 and 1987, poverty was not considered to have grown considerably.

Andorka emphasises three major factors in the connexion:

(i) most households compensated by undertaking 'second economy' work;
(ii) the number of dependents per hundred households has decreased – recent reduction in the number of children; and
(iii) ratio of social incomes (primarily pensions) has grown within total household incomes

Yet these explanations do not change the fact that over a million people in Hungary in 1987 were forced to live on incomes lower than those necessary for their minimum existence, with up to 1.5 million people whose incomes did not reach the socially acceptable income level.

Over the years, the composition of poor groups has changed in that the proportion of very poor people in rural areas has fallen – from 74 per cent in 1962 to 53 per cent in 1987 whereas the proportion living in Budapest rose from 6 to 11 per cent. Members of agricultural physical labouring households made up 35 per cent of the very poor in 1962 (earning below 400 forints) yet by 1987 this percentage (earning below 2600 forints) had fallen to 11 per cent. In contrast the ratio of members of semi-skilled and auxiliary worker's households had increased from 35 to 38 per cent (Andorka, 1989, p. 142). This has meant that poverty has become more visible in its shift from small villages to large cities. It was not uncommon in the late 1980s to see elderly women searching for food in public refuse bins.

INCOME INEQUALITIES

The double aim of Hungarian incomes policy then, was to have mediated an equalisation of family incomes, through social welfare policy. The two major elements of this strategy were the general pensions scheme and cash contributions to the upbringing of children. Despite an overall incomes policy approach to these problems, the existence and growth of the second economy did make the gradual equalisation of incomes virtually impossible. Since the changes in 1989 the political will to concentrate efforts on attempts to equalise incomes is unlikely to emerge, but there is recognition in governing circles that many aspects of social welfare policies in Hungary need dramatic reappraisal.

Within the increasing moves toward a marketised economy with extensive wage differentials discussion of income inequalities is fundamental. The cost of living has been rising steeply in Hungary throughout the 1980s, and dramatically since 1989, though some groups are less affected than others. For those on low and fixed incomes it has always been considered important that welfare payments should be utilised to make up some of the deficit. In the 1980s between 10 per cent and 30 per cent of the population fell into the poverty category.[2] This grouping was made up of those on low incomes (almost all Roma families and 50 per cent of pensioners), approximately 50 per cent of families with two children and up to 90 per cent of those with three or more children. These people have been the victims of the shortcomings of social policy, and no matter how they live they will remain poor. A second part of this group includes those with housing problems and those who are no longer capable of looking after themselves. There are undeniable differences in earnings between various groups in Hungary, and the possibilities now exist for certain people to earn a great deal of money. In this context, the first designer clothes show took place in Budapest in 1990 with average outfits selling for approximately £400 each. By the end of 1991 inflation reached 38 per cent. This was complemented by a decline in industrial production, notably in heavy industry and mining.

CONTEXT AND ILLUSION REGARDING WOMEN'S INCOME

Questions of income maintenance, lessening the gap between the waged and the non-waged, between 'earners' and 'dependants' were obviously important for women's lives. As has been shown in Chapters 3 and 4, it was in the early period that women were experiencing their 'liberation' through waged labour, that is, as workers who could be manipulated by governmental policies. As noted in Chapter 3, women consistently earned less than men, received less training and promotion opportunities and carried out the bulk of the work in the home. Throughout the 1950s women who had believed in the 'emancipation' which was being offered to them were consistently disappointed not only in family life but also in paid work, public life or everyday situations. The reality certainly did not match up with the official rhetoric.

It is important to remember that the allocation of social policy measures was usually based on conditions of employment, rather than made available as a civic right. This had important repercussions, not just in policy-making circles but also for those who fell outside the 'relevant categories' for welfare. To be 'just' a housewife was to be a parasite on society. To be an old 'housewife' was to be disregarded altogether. Some medical treatments, such as compulsory cancer screening, were connected with employment entitlement, so those not in employment had to pay 50 per cent of the costs. The social insurance reform carried out between 1971 and 1975, which widened the scope of coverage, did not deal with elderly women who had not previously been in employment.

Given this attitude to women who had constantly worked in the home, by the mid-1980s 13 per cent of the elderly – all of them women – did not receive either a pension or any other regular income from the state because they had not been in employment for a sufficient period or at all (Széman, 1990, p. 9). The gaps were being created between older women and younger women, between those women with children who also had paid work (the majority) and those women who did not have paid work. It is in light of this, with benefits tied to paid work and with the state wanting women in public work and bearing children, that child-care provision must be viewed, certainly in terms of the services/benefits debate. It proved more 'economical' to pay women to care for their own children than to provide child-care services in crèches or kindergartens. As domestic budgeters and home-makers the caring roles which women also played meant that poorer women certainly bore the brunt of coping with their poverty.

BACKGROUND TO PENSIONABLE BENEFITS

Pensioners make up a large group in Hungary – around two million people (19 per cent of the population) in 1990 were aged over 60 years. The proportion of women pensioners is high – over 60 per cent. Women retire at 55 and men at 60 but there have been various discussions about change.[3] With steep price increases since the mid-1980s many fixed-income pensioners have become amongst the poorest people in Hungarian society. For financial reasons many older people reaching pensionable age cannot cease work and accordingly many pensioners remain economically active. The monthly pensions for the over-70 age group represents only between 45 and 50 per cent of the average monthly income. Their poor economic situation arises primarily from the fact that pensions do not reflect the achievements of people who have worked all of their lives, as it is only a person's income during the last five years or so and not over the whole working period, which serve as the basis for determining pensions. In addition pensions have only increased by 2 per cent annually which has not been covering the rising living costs – inflation averaged 5 per cent in 1985, 7 per cent in 1986, 9 per cent in 1987 and 14 per cent in 1988 (Széman, 1990, p. 10). Given that pensions have not been index-linked, except recently for the over-70 group, the average pension amounted to approximately 65 per cent of average monthly incomes, with pensions for the over-70 groups representing only between 40 and 50 per cent of this average income (Eberhardt, 1991, p. 43). On 1 April 1991 the official minimum monthly wage was agreed at 7000 forints. Many older people live on less than this minimum, below 'the poverty line', especially those who have failed through their work record to gain a state pension. Although they can apply for residual social aid schemes, these vary from region to region. In Budapest they are available only to women over 60 years and men over 70 years – that is, ten years after the standard retirement ages.

SITUATION OF ELDERLY WOMEN

Elderly women could definitely be seen as one of the most vulnerable groups within Hungarian society, historically and today. Given that they could not provide the 'socialist' state with the two requirements – public paid work and children – for which younger women were 'rewarded', then this group of Hungarian women was treated very badly. As noted, women who had previously not worked or had not worked for long enough, were not included within the 1975 reforms. In this context, it must be remembered that there are no pensions in Hungary to which people are automatically entitled. Provisions such as those within the Family Law meant that if elderly people had relatives, whether or not there were good connexions or relationships, they were then not entitled to State help. Some women are supported by their elderly husbands. For couples such as these, where only the husband receives a pension, many were virtually starving. In such a situation the authorities intervened with a very paternalistic 'solution' by giving the husbands a supplementary sum. Those women who were widows received a widow's pension, approximately 50 per cent of the pension received by deceased spouses, which often meant that these pensions were around the level of the minimum pension. The extent of the problem is highlighted by the developments in terms of means-tested emergency aid which was originally intended as a supplement for those in dire need but which came to play a major role. In 1975 the number of cases of emergency welfare aid reached barely 100 000, whereas by 1986–7 over 350 000 people were involved, mainly elderly women (Széman, 1990, p. 10). It is not surprising that the over-70 age group were the most disadvantaged, as their secondary work on household plots, which involved a large group (61 per cent), did not count towards their pensionable income. Between 1985 and 1988 pensions were indexed for those over 70, as their pensions were more or less their only income. As the pensions had already lost their values at this time, these changes and those associated with increasing widows' pensions caused only a slight slowing down in the loss of the real value of pensions.

This bad situation was highlighted in a study which gave attention to suicide rates and attempts (Somnor, 1982).[4] In 1980, 5108 people committed suicide. Approximately 40 per cent of male suicides and 55–59 per cent of female suicides were committed by elderly people. In an attempt to clarify the reasons why so many older people decided upon suicide, Somnor decided to visit elderly people who had survived suicide attempts. Common threads emerged in the situations she researched.

Many older people had reached the point where they found they were unable to get out of their flats to visit shops, friends, relatives or the local council, to apply for emergency aid or any help. Despite regular emergency social allowances given by the local councils, many people were living on starvation diets under appalling conditions. To be eligible for 'meals-on-wheels' types of help, people have to be absolutely bedridden, as the waiting-lists are very long. When people are unable to get help for themselves there is nothing that can be done for many of them.

In a very shocking report,[5] Katalin Peto tells of conditions in the Eighth district of Budapest where she was working:

> I found unimaginable misery. I saw people vegetating half frozen in dirt, in the cold, among vermin. I would never have thought it possible to find life under such conditions . . . I found small dirty holes that I would not even call emergency housing . . . I saw an old lady, whom I did not notice at first since the place was dark and there was only a small pile on the bed . . . she weighed only 30 kilos. She had been sent home from the hospital only the day before having been told that 'it is not a hotel', and she was left in front of her door by the driver of the ambulance (Peto, 1982).

Peto goes on to relate the frustrations involved in attempting to get help for such people. If they had money and could mainly look after themselves then they could have an official care worker to visit them and help, once a week. Yet it was impossible to get daily help. For elderly women hunger is a very real phenomenon and Széman notes from survey material that between 1987 and 1989 their situation deteriorated markedly. By 1989 the number of those eating three times a day had drastically declined and many more pensioners were involved in gardening work. In 1987 most of the elderly respondents felt that their food intake was sufficient, but by 1989 this opinion changed when half of the sample did not eat as much as they would have liked (Széman, 1990, p. 14).

It seems also that as long as the present housing shortage exists in Hungary the problems of older people will still be related to their financial well-being. Having a flat to exchange for a room in a retirement home means a great deal. A number of older people living alone also make contracts with young people. The young people – often single women or young couples – agree to care for the older person, often cleaning, shopping, cooking and sometimes physically caring for ill pensioners in return for an agreement whereby they 'inherit' the flat in which the older person is living. Given that certain benefits are only available to older people without relatives, there seems to be an assumption that relatives have a responsibility towards helping older family-members. Yet because many young relatives have neither the money nor a great deal of time to give adequate support, this situation places great strain on relationships. In this context the experience of those in large families forms a case study comparable to that of elderly people.

According to a 1983 survey (HCSO, 1983) families with two children had between 75 per cent and 80 per cent of the income levels of those households without dependents, those with three children, 66 per cent, and larger families, 50 per cent. It was noted that lack of education and cultural disadvantages amongst the 'larger families' group perpetuated disadvantages in other areas of life. Often young people from larger families were unable to learn a profession, and so performed heavy manual labour which endangered their health, and they were often pensioned off early or became casual workers. As a result 'the role of the disadvantaged on the job market is similar to that of the guest workers in Western Europe. They take on jobs that others will not accept' (*Magyar Hirlap*, 24 October 1986).

Roma families are also amongst the most disadvantaged groups. At least 66 per cent of Roma families are in a 'multiple disadvantaged' situation and live in destitution in camps and hovels. There is apparent racism against Roma people in Hungary. As with other minority groups elsewhere in the world, disadvantages arising from unequal access to education, housing, jobs, benefits and other basic rights combine to depress still further their living standards and life chances.

POLICIES FOR ASSISTING FAMILIES WITH CHILDREN

In her work on benefits and programmes for early child-care (Szalai, 1978, p. 76) Julia Szalai points out that there are at least three functions in common from the early period, and the post-war basis of benefits and programmes, connected with child-care and child-rearing:

1. Stimulating women's participation in the labour force.
2. The need to express and to realise the responsibility of society towards new generations.
3. The reduction or elimination of the previously marked social inequalities apparent in families in different social groups with regard to rearing children. The ratio of universal, flat-rate and in-kind benefits was higher in this field of social policy than in others.

Of the benefits accorded to families with children, maternity benefit and family allowance are the two major elements available to all. Maternity benefit is a cash benefit offered to mothers, once a child is born. The precondition for becoming eligible for maternity benefit is to have a certificate of at least three consultations (visits to the doctor) during the pregnancy, or one if the baby is born prematurely. This certificate is called the 'booklet of the pregnant woman' and contains important information about the woman's health. After the birth this certificate becomes the basic document entitling the woman to several benefits.

Family allowance is a universal, flat-rate benefit generally paid to men in families. It is well to note here how the state tends to relate to women economically through men. Why is it that men receive the family allowance? Perhaps the traditional assumptions of 'family' wages, and men 'protecting' women and children are present here. The first noticeable increase in family allowance was in 1959 – for families with three or more children. Subsequent modifications extended this in 1965 to families with two children, and in 1966 and 1971 modifications (also for large families) reinforced the universal nature of the measure, covering a larger proportion of the population, including peasants (members of cooperatives). Since the end of the 1950s there was a steady tendency to reduce the gap between the level of allowance received by industrial workers and that of 'peasants' – members of the agricultural cooperatives. Yet it was not until the 1970s that the members of agricultural cooperatives became fully integrated into overall benefit schemes. In 1974 and 1975 modifications were introduced which reduced the gap, bringing the two more into line with each other. The benefit is not now tied to paid work, in that it is also available to occasional labourers, industrial apprentices, students in higher education and home workers.

Table 5.1 gives an indication of how the family allowance system operates and the numbers involved in it. It can be seen from the differences between 1980 and 1988 that the numbers of families receiving the allowances for two children have dropped as have those in all further categories – those with three, four, five and six children.

Another type of statutory benefit available in Hungary is the special housing allowance in terms of giving priority to families with children. Given that housing is a major problem, housing allowances enable families with children to have a dwelling and to assume their priorities in buying houses as well as in building new flats by their own efforts. There are three major areas of housing allowance, the first being a form of price reduction (introduced in 1971) on some forms of purchase, mainly in cities where the shortage is most pressing. A couple may make a contract with the National Savings Office (granting credits for purchase). The terms of such a contract mean that the family should have one child within three years, or two children within

Table 5.1 Numbers receiving family allowance (half year average)

Those receiving family allowance	*1980*	*1984*	*1988*
For one child:			
single parents	130 060	133 870	147 000
families	206 540	242 750	248 000
For two children:			
single parents	45 490	55 300	63 000
families	581 450	599 900	554 000
Families with:			
three children	114 700	117 150	114 000
four children	22 020	20 380	20 000
five children	7 410	6 060	6 000
six or more children	5 310	3 830	4 000

Note: Families with one child receive family allowance if they earlier received allowance for two or more children and in the meanwhile these children reached the age limit and therefore were not entitled to it any more.

Source: Special run of HCSO, 1985; *Statisztikai Évkönyv*, 1989.

six years. For this contract they get a reduction of about 8–10 per cent or 16–20 per cent (respectively) off the total price of the flat. Here can be seen the dual interest of stimulating childbirth and providing housing. The negative effects of such policies are clear in terms of young couples 'committing' themselves to having a certain number of children regardless of various eventualities which can and do arise. Such a pressure to have children in order to keep one's home seems at best problematic and at worst very destructive to developing good relations between women, men and children.

A second form is in the allocation of state-owned flats (administered by the local councils) where families with three children get top priority. Since waiting-lists are extremely long, this priority extended to families with children in the mid-1970s, still often meant several years of waiting. Attention is now given to the debates surrounding child-care policies in Hungary. The introduction of the child-care grant in 1967 was to have major repercussions for women in Hungary and for Hungarian society generally. The various angles of this debate are considered here in terms of the benefits/losses for women themselves.

CHANGES IN CHILD-CARE ALLOWANCE

The child-care allowance is payable after maternity leave has expired. In 1985 the maternity leave was extended to 24 weeks (from 20 weeks) so that the mother receives payment in accordance with her previous year's salary for these 24 weeks. If, after the maternity leave expires, the mother wants to stay at home with her child (up to her child's third birthday) she can get child-care allowance (GYES), or from 1985, one year's child-care fee (GYED). From 1985 the allowance was gradually replaced by a fee so that by 1989 women could claim fee for two years and allowance for the third. The fee is higher than the allowance, because like the sickness benefit, it will be 75 per cent of the mother's/parent's average salary. The analogy with sickness benefit is not a positive one in terms of attempting to raise the status of child-care and domestic work.

This allowance is now a parental right so that after the child's first birthday the father can also choose to be on child-care leave. From when the child is eighteen months old whoever is staying at home can work four hours daily, and at the same time get the child-care allowance; s/he can be employed either by her/his previous employer or a new one, without losing the right of employment by the original one. Until 1991, jobs were safeguarded while people were on child-care leave, and s/he was usually given the salary rises which others received so that when s/he returned to work s/he would not be at a disadvantage. The changing employment situation in 1991 has been such that jobs are no longer necessarily guaranteed. These changes are considered in the concluding section on unemployment. The years spent on child-care leave are considered full working years at retirement. Where the management and the working community were good, the young parent was given a bonus with other colleagues, and the argument goes that this was because s/he was seen to be doing a useful job in bringing up a child. Some employers made more effort than others to keep in touch with parents on child-care leave by visiting them in the home and inviting them to functions at the company or factory.

DEBATES SURROUNDING THE IMPLEMENTATION OF THE CHILD-CARE ALLOWANCE

Since the child-care allowance was introduced in 1967 there have been discussions concerning its place in Hungarian social policy in terms of adequacy/efficacy, and how such an allowance is seen to be changing certain structures within society, what it means for families and particularly for women. This grant rapidly became 'popular' and the majority of mothers availed themselves of this opportunity for at least one year. Yet despite this popularity, the grant had mixed consequences from the point of view of women's emancipation. Ferge stated a belief that the grant 'cheapened the value of the female labour force, and hindered the modification of traditional sex roles' (Ferge, 1986, p. 5).

It was understandable that such a policy change would engender much discussion about whether or not it was a good idea for women to stay at home with young children. In an interview with Judit Sas, in June 1986, she noted that there had never before been an ideology amongst doctors which questioned whether babies needed crèches in their first years of life, but with the introduction of GYES, discussion points centred upon children's needs in terms of the socialisation of the crèche and pre-school.

There were essentially two sets of arguments – those in favour of home care and those in favour of group care. Of the former the main concern was that as children build up their first, and decisive, patterns of emotional life and personality in their early years, home care was seen as the most suitable. Those favouring this line of argument saw the precondition of a well-grounded pattern as the opportunity to establish a constant and close relationship with the person who concentrated love and attention on the child. It was maintained that the chances for realising a stable connection with one person (generally the mother) were higher in a family than even in the best group care. These arguments were held mainly by psychologists and trained paediatricians, and child psychologists, and they held that for children under the age of three.group care should be put off as long as possible. There have been several investigations of crèches in comparison with home care, with observations on the general mental, physical and emotional development of the two groups.

On the other side of the debate were the arguments in favour of group care which are held mainly by doctors not trained in psychology and also by district nurses. Those preferring group care stressed the better facilities, equipment and hygienic conditions provided by crèches. It was also argued that the very young infant does not show signs of conflict and disappointment when going to crèches, so that young children may be better able to become accustomed to radical change, more easily adapting to the separation from the mother and home surroundings.

CHILD-CARE PROVISION – BENEFITS OR PROGRAMMES?

Nevertheless, waiting-lists for attendance at crèches and pre-schools have consistently remained long and there has always been a perceived shortage of places. In this context much of the increased percentage of children looked after by mothers on the allowance could be accounted for by either:

(a) fewer children looked after by mothers without payment; or
(b) fewer children cared for by grandparents;

In other words, the child-care allowance has not greatly reduced the percentage of children attending crèches and kindergartens or day-time homes. It is apparent that the introduction of the allowance prevented any increase in institutional care which might otherwise have taken place.

Although official statements favoured the further development of both benefits and programmes during the 1970s and 1980s the relative standard and diversity of the range of benefits available has become better developed since 1967 than that of services such as crèches, kindergartens and pre-schools. Statistical analyses of the situation vary somewhat, but the overall picture shows a steady demand for the provision of more child-care institutions. Apart from the health and psychological reasons given for children under three years to remain at home with a parent, the obvious high costs of investment and maintenance of crèches were important considerations. In the decade 1975–85 new places in crèches did not markedly increase. It is the situation with regard to pre-schools that is much more emphasised in the literature of institutional child-care. Child care outside the home had been accorded a priority with policy-makers until the introduction of the child-care leave. Table 5.2 illustrates the different ways in which children were cared for between 1960 and 1987.

A year before starting to attend school, at the age of 6, all children are admitted to pre-schools or to school preparatory courses. Single-parent families and families on low incomes are accorded priorities in access to institutional child-care. Table 5.3 shows something of the range of access for different family situations.

Table 5.2 Percentage of those caring for children up to the age of two

	1970	*1980*	*1987*
Mothers on maternity leave	8.5	10.2	12.2
Mothers on child-care leave	37.9	58.6	61.0
Crèches	9.5	15.9	13.8
No socially organised care is granted	44.1	15.3	13.0

Source: *Women in Present-day Hungarian Society* (Hungarian Women's Council, 1989) p. 21.

Table 5.3 Access to crèche and nursery places, 1983.

	Total number of crèche-goers as % of age group		*Total number of nursery-goers as % of age group*	
	Single parents	*Families*	*Single parents*	*Families*
Budapest	18.21	31.05	85.80	87.92
Towns	69.21	20.20	89.81	84.52
Large villages	10.07	7.16	86.34	79.30
National totals	37.84	16.04	87.71	82.70

Source: Special run of HCSO, 1985 input (Ferge, n.d.).

Some interpretation of these figures is required, as the picture is a complex one. It can be seen that both in Budapest and in the large villages the proportion of single parents placing their children in créches is significantly lower than the level of national totals. This may be explained in part by the fact that most single parents are women, who choose to take child-care allowance, and have increased benefits as single parents. In addition, the pressures of running a home, caring for children and earning a wage outside the home would be excessive for most single people. Yet for single people in the towns the proportion of those with children in crèches is significantly higher than the national totals In part, this may be due to the shorter waiting-lists in the towns for admission to créches, but it is also possible that single parents living in towns have less of an extended family network available to them for child-care – unlike many single parents living in the countryside. In both social and economic policy since the mid-1970s, benefits and child-care arrangements have been designed to ease the burden of single-parent families. In the case of the family allowance system, single parents receive in-cash supplements to ensure some equality of income (although single parents remain in the lowest income brackets).

In the 1990s the figures of children cared for outside the home have begun to decline drastically, due to closures of many workplace nurseries (the main reasons given are 'cost-cutting'and 'streamlining' for privatisation) and a reduction in the availability of community-based and centrally funded child-care places. The changing, and confused, property relations in Hungary since 1990 have hit local child-care facilities. The rates of closure are higher amongst child-care institutions than other communal services such as health-care centres. Whilst 'financial' arguments for closure are generally given, the lack of protection of women's interests is particularly acute in this respect. Despite the apparent inadequacy of some child-care services in Hungary both qualitatively and quantitatively, this is one 'gain' of 'socialism' that most women would wish to retain, but few women have the resources, abilities or energies to be able adequately to resist these piecemeal closures.

CONSEQUENCES OF CHILD-CARE ALLOWANCE FOR WOMEN'S 'LIBERATION'

When considering the benefits or otherwise, of the child-care allowance system for women's self-realisation, it is interesting to see just how positions have changed over time. In the early days, in the late 1960s and early 1970s, it was apparent that the stand taken on this issue by the Hungarian Women's Council was that paying women to stay in the home was necessarily a retrogressive step for women's emancipation. Essentially, the argument was that women on GYES are seen to be of low status and that despite all the safeguards within the system, women would tend to lose out in terms of career prospects – if for no other reason than lack of motivation. Now this attitude ties in with the belief that women's major means of achieving liberation is through paid work outside the home. Yet by 1985 the leaflet produced by the Hungarian Women's Council stated that:

> Altogether 220,000 parents were on child-care allowance and fee in 1985. These significant benefits have eased the rearing of children and positively affected demographic growth. For example, in 1985, 130,000 children were born – five thousand more than in 1984. The ratio of births increased from 11.8/1000 in 1984 to 12.2/1000 in 1985 (*Women in Hungary*, Hungarian Women's Council, 1986).

Rather than arguing against the enforced domesticity implicit within the child-care leave for women, the Council began to argue about how women benefit from spending a period at home with their children with their jobs being fully protected. This change of orientation has much to do with the total change in structure of this Council. It was never an active women's forum, but much work was done in terms of 'education' of working-class women in such areas as hygiene, health care, family planning and domestic science. In the mid-1980s this Council was recognised by the majority of women as a 'paper organisation' which did not even have local councils (since 1970) nor workplace representatives with any potential for working on behalf of the women they were supposed to represent. Yet this was the only official voice of women generally within Hungarian society that was consulted on every policy measure which affected women. Given its close links with governmental forces this body tended to follow the general 'line' of argument which viewed women in terms of their usefulness in production within a pro-natalist framework.

The system of child-care leave introduced in Hungary was seen very much as a compromise. The so-called middle strata of families were seen to suffer most from a form of 'identity crisis' in which both husband and wife were aware of the prevailing view that men should 'help' in the home, yet given the circumstances in which the woman was being paid GYES to remain in the home, lack of money often meant that the men took second jobs to cover the loss of earnings. It quite often seemed that the only option was for the women to do the vast majority of household chores, thus returning to the historical, gendered, division of labour within the home. This highlights a problem which recurs again and again – that of attitudes and how they may be changed.

It is the attitude of 'man-the-breadwinner' which re-emerges here. When a young child is introduced into a couple's lives then there is a massive social push towards the roles of mother-the-nestbuilder and father-the-earner, and GYES is seen as compounding this situation. According to Ferge the policy-makers were aware of the possible negative effects of the child-care allowance on women's and 'family' lives, so that the building of crèches and kindergartens was not slowed down (in theory) and steps were taken to lessen the mothers' isolation and of course, GYES then became a parental right. In her consideration of this question, Ferge pinpoints the specifics of the compromise:

> In general, the child-care grant, in the form in which it was introduced in Hungary, is a compromise between two conflicting aims: the immediate well-being of young children and mothers, and the long-term goal of equality between the sexes (Ferge, 1979, p. 104).

In her argument, Ferge notes that the child-care allowance is more like maternity leave than payment for housework, and as such there is often an emphasis placed on the biological and psychological specifities of motherhood, rather than the social aspect of parenthood. Once the allowance was opened to both parents, at least aspects of the gendered problem were recognised, but the question of how to change attitudes towards the value of work in the home, and child-rearing, remains a difficult one.

UNOFFICIAL ACTIVITIES TO ASSIST DISADVANTAGED GROUPS

In 1980 a private organisation was formed without government authorisation. This organisation, called the Foundation for the Assistance of the Poor (SZETA), was formed by a group of intellectuals committed to helping the poor by collecting money, distributing various goods and providing counselling. Some Roma families are excluded from benefits purely because they are unable to fill in the relevant forms, or to find out which forms to complete. Quite often children from Roma families are taken into state care because adequate structural support is not provided for the family, in terms of adequate housing, schooling for children, support for mothers. Although SZETA caused great embarrassment within 'socialist' Hungary and its members were harassed by the authorities, it continued to exist. When speaking with Ottilia Solt, a founder member of SZETA, in 1986 it was clear that 'demand' far outstripped what this group was able to do for the millions of poor people in Hungary. The slightly better-off families who had given a little money each month and clothing, could no longer afford to do this and as more and more people heard of SZETA and stated their claims, the situation was becoming desperate.

A new situation has now arisen in that state forces now actually welcome this kind of help, and in 1988 the Church began to take on some of the organisational work of helping poor people. Yet the problems of the poor and socially disadvantaged are so great in Hungary today that no kind of charity organisation can deal with them.

As a political organisation, though, SZETA was of great importance, as the consequences of political and economic changes were analysed by some of its members. Publications appeared regularly in *samizdat* publications (such as *Beszélő – The Talker*). Their main topic was police harassment of poor people, which remains very much a taboo subject in Hungary. Not even the most 'liberal-minded' press people touch upon this problem. So SZETA published in *samizdat* about this area of human rights, believing that one of its most important activities was to collect facts and observe events in order to record and publish details to more and more people. One group which will form some of the 'new poor' will be those without work.

UNEMPLOYMENT

The acceptance of some measures of unemployment pre-dated the removal from power of the communists and the setting up of a multiparty, democratic system. Since mid-1986 a certain amount of attention has been paid to unemployment issues. The legal framework has been in place in Hungary since September 1986 as part of the Bankruptcy Law. The 1987 state budget allocated 3000 million forints under 'Enterprise Reorganisation' to cover unemployment and retraining benefits (relocation support). Relocation support (basically unemployment allowance) was to be paid when a worker lost her/his job through reorganisation or the liquidation of an enterprise and also if ten or more people were laid off for disciplinary reasons (undocumented absenteeism, alcohol abuse) or because of the new market conditions. This support was for 15 months maximum and public works projects attempted to absorb some unemployed workers. Some miners who were laid off were 'allowed' to retire early.

Iván Berend, Chairman of the Hungarian Academy of Sciences, stated in June 1987 that:

> the idea of total employment used to be an untouchable principle, but the situation has now changed and the Government believes that structural unemployment is inevitable . . . It will only exist for a transitional period, which may last for some years but not forever (*Magyar Nemzet,* 27 June 1987).

A national network of 400 employment offices was set up to provide retraining. State funding paid for 70 per cent of new public works projects which were sponsored by local councils, e.g.

sewage pipe maintenance and cleaning, rubbish collection and road works. Participation was voluntary for unskilled workers who could not find jobs because of prison records, lay-offs or lack of skills. People who took such jobs were given preference when other work came up.

The preamble to Act IV of 1991 on Employment Promotion and Provision for Unemployed Persons states that:

> The Constitution of the Republic of Hungary guarantees the right of all to free choice of job and employment. With a view to promoting exercise of these rights, easing employment strains and making provision for the unemployed the National Assembly has passed the following Act (Ministry of Labour, 1991).

In many ways this Act compares favourably with similar legislation in Western Europe. Its major thrust is in terms of 'active' labour-market policies tied in with the Fund for Employment – a separate fund to promote not only training and retraining but some job-creation. An unemployment benefit insurance scheme is detailed, with consideration given to previously neglected groups, such as unemployed school-leavers. For those with special needs there is allowance for affirmative action and the Act set outs organisational principles within the labour market, for collective bargaining with an emphasis on the tripartite negotiations mentioned in Chapter 2.

There are various negative aspects to the Act including the fact that as the unemployment insurance covers only sections of those unemployed, there is no provision for those not entitled to the insurance. The period covered by the unemployment is from 180 days to two years at most – in the case of four insured years. One major problem highlighted by Zsuzsa Ferge is the low level of the unemployment benefit. As benefit is earnings-related, it amounts to 70 per cent initially, then drops to 50 per cent of the last wage gained. As Ferge notes: 'These rates are comparable to those applied in Western countries. The catch is that the wages are not' (Ferge, 1991, p. 3).

In order to give a broad overview of the current situation of unemployment it would be helpful to have some general statistics. In Hungary at the present time gathering such information is incredibly difficult as old statist statistical bureaux are in the process of changing their working patterns and resources for regional research into unemployment are limited. Problems associated with numbers, of people officially registered as unemployed and not officially registered but actually looking for work, are general to most industrialised countries. In Hungary, though, statistics are rarely gendered so it is difficult to look specifically at women's unemployment. Tables 5.4 and 5.5 show official figures for April 1991 so they do not include those who were not registered. As we can see from Table 5.4 figures unemp-

Table 5.4 Overall unemployment rates for men and women in April 1991

	Men	*Women*	
Manual workers			
Skilled	32 789	7 099	
Semi-skilled	16 899	17 216	
Unskilled	27 892	39 351	
Non-manual workers			
Upper-level managers	168	27	
Managers	2 115	795	
Technical managers	1 923	523	
Administrators	3 393	5 428	
Administrative assistants	1 884	7 137	
Totals	87 063	53 261	140 324

Note: Official registrations figures only.
Source: Nationwide Centre for Labour-Market (Országos Munkaeropiaci Központ).

Table 5.5 Proportion of unemployed population analysed by educational level (per cent)

Compulsory school (8 years or less)	40.6
Vocational training, technical school	39.6
Gymnasium (grammar school)	8.2
College, university	4.2

Note: Official registrations figures only.
Source: Nationwide Centre for Labour-Market (Országos Munkaeropiaci Központ).

loyed women are highly represented amongst unskilled workers and administrators and administrative assistants. In April 1991 there were 16 463 job facilities available. Out of this 4426 were open to either men or women, 7097 were for men only and 4940 were for women only. The first wave of industrial closures affected mainly the heavy industrial concerns such as mining and the iron and steel industries in which a majority of men were employed, although many women did staff the offices. It is expected that the second wave of closures which began in late-1991, will affect the textile industries, which are prime employers of women, and also educational institutions, such as schools, because of the demographic decline – the demographic peak has ended. In this situation there are three distinct groups of women who will be available for work as a result of the restructuring:

(i) largely non-skilled women from the textile industries and mining and steel industries;
(ii) professional educators and health workers – mainly school teachers and some doctors; and
(iii) young women school-leavers.

For many women who are unskilled or semi-skilled there is a definite need for some training schemes or retraining courses. As the overall responsibility for adult training is now primarily with the Ministry of Labour, it is important that training policies recognise the needs of women. Several very large training centres based on Swedish models have recently been opened in Hungary. Within these centres it would be useful to create some courses specially for women to deal with the specific needs of certain groups. Given the pitfalls of large-scale centralised training it is important for specific needs to be targeted.

Some of the courses currently available to school-leavers are at best rather general, and tend towards encouraging gendered outlooks within the workplace. Whereas many young male school-leavers who are without a job choose to enter a course in basic electronics, many young women are faced with the prospect of taking a general home economics or 'housewife' course. Something more creative, imaginative and challenging is needed in training, if young women, and men, are to be able to fill the gaps in a labour market which is now becoming geared towards efficiency and entrepreneurship to meet the needs of modern markets.

RURAL UNEMPLOYMENT

For those living in rural areas the dangers of falling into the unemployment trap and becoming involved in 'closed markets' are becoming a reality. In his work, particularly with regard to what he terms the 'rural socialist middle-class society', András Tóth notes the dangers of these country-dwellers falling into the unemployment trap. These dangers include:

- their industrial and employees skills will slowly become worn out;
- their social net will be tightened, they will slowly lose their acquaintances who could pave the way to a new job for them; and
- they are likely to take up deviant behaviour

Whereas for the market economy, those developments which lead to unemployed rural populations being squeezed out of relatively highly-paid urban workplaces into closed low-waged labour markets could have up to four consequences:

- broadening gap between prices and money incomes of broad strata of rural society will result in those people being unable to partake in the so-called consuming society;
- the lack of purchasing power will limit the trade and business turnover and several forms of self-subsistence and 'reciprocal' trade will exist;
- black-market activities and work-chains with kinships would tie the people into paternalistic ties and hinder the evolution of a 'civil society'; and
- some of the goods produced through private production by 'illegal' workers will appear mainly on the black market thus resulting not only in tax-free revenues but in the development of closed markets (see András Tóth, 1992, p. 13).

Within all of the above changes in rural communities women stand to suffer most, not only because they have long been considered the 'expendable' workforce with fewer skills and opportunities than men, but also because women remain in charge of household budgeting. This will mean that in times of severe economic hardship the challenges facing poor rural women to feed and clothe their families will dramatically increase.

OPINIONS ON STATE SUPPORT

Before turning to the actual finanacial situation so far as the redistribution of resources in Hungary is concerned, it is interesting to consider briefly what citizens' opinions are so far as state support is concerned. Table 5.6 shows opinions on state support. Whilst not giving any concrete data on which to base analysis – what is meant by 'deserving in terms of work and conduct', which social groups were included in this survey, this table does indicate that many Hungarian people seem to have become used to a strong, protective state. The opinions of those interviewed have steadily moved towards more state support for those who live in worse conditions, with a little less support expected for others in terms of work and conduct. Yet certainly in some communities the heavy reliance on the second economy, which has increasingly turned into a reliance on the 'shadow/illegal economy' since 1990–1, may change citizens' perceptions of 'who deserves what' and indeed on how actually to make a living within the changing Hungarian economic situation.

In a sense Table 5.6 crystallises one of the big dilemmas which the Hungarian authorities face with regard to the provision of social services. In the 'socialist' period the Party was theoretically committed to its egalitarian policy principles, yet the fact has to

Table 5.6 Opinions concerning whom the state should support (per cent)

	1978	*1980*	*1982*
'Those who live in poorer, worse circumstances'	33	38	47
'Those who deserve it on account of their work and conduct'	50	45	40
'Nobody'	17	17	13

Source: Heinrich, 1986, p. 96

be acknowledged that it was the underfunding and under capitalisation of the health service during the 'socialist' period which underlies the present crisis. The most probable solution lies within the realm of a duality of public and private resources, or market and non-market remedies.

RESOURCES

The budget for social security has always been an important item of state spending. Contributions from men and women are calculated by the same method, so that no gender differentiation is involved. There is differentiation as noted in terms of when women and men draw their old-age pensions. Perhaps the most notable feature of the system at the moment is that of the crisis management apparent in recent years. The present social security system in Hungary is in dire need of urgent reform. Since 1989 the government has started to face this problem. To keep the outdated system 'ticking over' would mean putting more and more public spending into welfare. With a budget deficit in the region of 78 billion forints and inflation at 38 per cent in the last quarter of 1991 this was not, in reality, an option.

The Németh administration attempted to tackle social security problems in 1988, and a new social insurance scheme was passed in December 1988. This provided for all social security monies to be placed in a fund which was separate from the public spending system, so that they could be invested and managed carefully in order to protect their value. This attempt at transforming Hungarian social security into a Western-style system was only partially implemented. As Hungarian legislation is enacted first by decisions of principle by Parliament, and then through the enabling acts and orders this seems to leave room for misunderstanding or misinterpretation.

In the case of social security a certain measure of relative independence was gained in 1989 and an extra 30 billion forints were generated, but there was a fundamental reversal at the end of 1989. One of the last acts of the old Parliament was to include placing the funding of the Health Service within the social insurance fund. In exchange it was proposed that the payment of family allowances would be included within public expenditure.

Such an 'exchange' was hardly an equitable one, given that family allowance costs could be approximately calculated whereas health-service funding, as has been noted, in times of over 35 per cent inflation, represented an immense outflow from the social security system. Predictably the system suffered a liquidity crisis, as the final budget spending for 1991 illustates (see Table 5.7), heightened by late contribution payments from state-owned firms and institutions, whose debt to the fund reached 20 billion forints. Added to such difficulties was the negative sense in which the funds of the social security system

Table 5.7 Public spending (in million forints)

Destination	*1990 estimated spending*	*1991 budget proposal*	*1991 final budget*
Presidency	82.7	123.6	80.7
Parliament	2 712.5	2 716.7	3 216.7
Constitutional Court	92.4	161.0	161.0
Supreme Court	178.1	236.2	236.2
Public Prosecutor's Office	943.5	1 785.2	1 765.2
State Auditor's Office	390.3	388.8	388.8
Prime Minister's Department	5 886.8	28 214.9	27 703.5
Interior Ministry	119 270.8	225 676.7	229 488.3
Int'l Economic Reltns Min.	6 080.1	10 199.3	8 684.6
Welfare Ministry	78 897.2	132 939.6	132 634.9
Justice Ministry	7 395.3	10 110.2	10 070.6
Trans./Telecom/Water Min.	28 874.9	21 903.4	30 684.4
Foreign Ministry	3 973.0	5 552.9	5 318.7
Agriculture Ministry	18 227.2	18 303.8	17 284.1
Labour Ministry	9 251.8	13 891.3	22 644.7
Finance Ministry	222 720.4	191 528.3	182 908.7
Culture and Education Min.	30 402.0	33 832.9	33 779.0
Industry and Trade Ministry	15 054.4	19 238.1	17 397.7
Environment Ministry	12 146.3	12 055.7	3 291.3
Academy of Sciences	7 419.4	8 437.0	8 433.9
MTI News Agency	1 642.4	1 458.7	1 458.7
Radio	2 655.2	2 377.0	2 377.0
Television	6 791.2	6 843.1	7 854.1
International Settlements	18 240.0	19 973.0	19 273.0
Domestic National Debt	67 700.0	110 100.0	110 100.0

Source: *Világgazdaság* (*Hungarian Economic Daily*) in *Hungarian Observer*, March 1991, p. 26.

were still viewed in 1990, in terms of a form of 'welfare reserve' from which other budgetary shortfalls of social expenditure could be funded as the need arose. Some optimism was given when Mihály Kupa took over as Finance Minister in December 1990 as he has consistently advocated separating social insurance from public spending.

The Solidarity Fund which was set up to cope with problems of restructuring and which is paid out of the state budget but separately administered will also need more and more funding. There will continue to be spending cuts but it is uncertain which groups these will most affect. Certainly in terms of unemployment benefit this is going to become an increasing area of expenditure. There have been various changes to the benefit schemes since 1989, the most far-reaching to date were concerned with unemployment benefits.

The new unemployment scheme passed in Spring 1991 differs from the 1989 scheme in several important ways. First, that benefit is not related to parental incomes means that the principle by which it was relatives' duty to support others has been eroded. Whilst the 1989 scheme offered no support if a person had not had 18 months' employment history in the previous three years, the 1991 scheme reduced this to one year in the previous four. On the negative side though, the total of two years entitlement previously provided by unemployment benefit and temporary allowance is only available under the 1991 scheme to those with continuous work history in the previous four years. Table 5.8 gives some indication of the levels of unemployment compensation paid in practice.

In terms of comparisons and 'incentives to work' Micklewright (1992) points out that 50 per cent of all unemployment payments and the vast majority of all temporary payments were below the minimum (gross) wage so that it would seem that many unemployed people were provided with only a modest standard of living.

CONCLUSION

Concerning the ways in which increased opportunities and better conditions for women could be achieved, there is less likelihood of this occurring within a framework of strengthening family values

Table 5.8 Amounts of unemployment compensation paid: all spells of benefit receipt during 1990

Forints per month (gross)	*Unemployment benefit Number of payments*	*Temporary allowance Number of payments*
Up to 3000	2 531	304
3000–5000	40 721	2 965
5001–8000	26 593	373
8001–12000	10 897	121
12001 and over	4 766	6
Total	5 508	3 769
Men	51 131	2 245
Women	34 377	1 524
Average gross monthly payment (in forints)		
Men	6 542	4 367
Women	4 959	3 845
All	5 889	4 156

Source: Micklewright, 1992, p. 30.

and paying women to work in the home. Yet, as is shown in the concluding sections of this book, new initiatives are emerging in Hungarian society which could lead the way to new networks of support being created for women's autonomous organisation.

In her work on women and the welfare state Elizabeth Wilson notes that:

> What feminists, socialists, and all those who desire to see constructive changes in social relations, should seek are ways whereby social welfare care, instead of trying desperately to shore up the family in its present inadequacies, would extend the possibility of social relations that are more successfully supportive and nurturant. We should actively seek in the present to work for the kinds of social change that points towards a truly equal society, one in which women and children are truly equal with men (Wilson, 1977, p. 137).

So far as Hungarian society in the 1990s is concerned a fundamental stumbling-block to any emergent social change is the nature of political 'power games' in both decision-making and policy formulation. Definite changes would need to take place in terms of proposals actually being worked out with the involvement of the representatives of the main actors concerned. New ways of making policy are needed. In this context though, one set of actors, the trade unions, both old and new, are still divided and to some extent disorganised. Within this context, the ideological framework of policy choice is a major factor. The move away from dependence upon relatives in terms of downgrading the importance of parental income for unemployment benefit is an important direction, yet much social welfare policy discussion is carried on within the framework of focusing on women as 'carers'. Questions concerning the overall aims of current policy-makers in Hungary are vital here in terms of the way that women in society are perceived and the primary goals of future social policy initiatives in Hungary. Moves away from full employment are obviously fundamental in deciding certain social-policy decisions and will have dramatic impacts upon people's everyday lives, not only in material terms but the psychological effects of feeling 'useless' will take their toll on those without paid work. Will the 'flexible pool' of female labour be returned to the home in vast numbers? This is unlikely to fit in with the requirements of Hungary's market-oriented and increasing specialised economy in the 1990s. Yet it may well be the case that many women will feel the heavy impact of a return to a very closed and constrained rural environment in which their choices are extremely limited, not only in terms of paid work but in terms of affordable goods and services. To some extent, the nature of the Health Service, considered in Chapter 6 is a prime area of concern within the changing Hungarian social welfare system.

6 Hungarian Health Care: Women's Health

INTRODUCTION

From the general background on the provision of health care in Hungary it is possible to consider the many health needs and problems which can and do arise for women. In this connexion close attention is paid to the interrelated areas of psychological and physical health needs. Many of the health needs and illnesses which women experience are related to their ability to give birth. There are branches of illnesses associated with menstruation and ovulation, with contraception (generally women are expected to deal with this), and with conception, pregnancy and childbirth. Some of the psychological disorders suffered by women have to do with the problems they face as child-carers in terms of isolation and the responsibility of being with children constantly. Evaluating the relevant weight of ideological and socio-economic factors in the way that women's health concerns are regarded and treated is important here. Two areas of women's lives which are generally controlled by men are those of their sexuality and their reproductive capacity. Some professional men, such as qualified medical practitioners and specialists, exercise more control over women's bodies than women themselves. In this area there is obviously room for manipulation, by the professionals and in terms of institutionalisation of certain practices and areas of judgement. Women's stress-related diseases, in terms of concrete problems they are facing, are considered and the various treatments of such illnesses are assessed to view the likelihood of any positive changes occurring in this area of health care.

HEALTH CARE IN HUNGARY

So far as social medical policy is concerned, there has been little clarity in this area as to any specific long-term social goals or aims. As with other areas of social policy, economic solutions were proposed to problems within health care so that as Julia Szalai points out, the pressures of expanded demand were postponed for over twenty years:

> The consequences show in an extraordinary and lasting over use of the system, that does not permit any improvement in standards. The main current problem is a double one: the quality of the services offered is deteriorating, while indices show an intensive and continuous growth of use; on the other hand the basic goal of the health services, equal treatment for all, is in danger (Szalai, 1981, p. 152).

Here Szalai lays out the basic problem facing the health service in Hungary – the present administration of health-care cannot adequately service the demand quantitatively, organisationally or qualitatively. Arising from this there are inequalities of access and treatment.

In April 1972 the Hungarian National Assembly passed a law which confirmed that medical services are a civic right: citizens became entitled to 'free medical examination and any necessary treatment including hospital care, maternity services and ambulance transportation'.[1] This entitlement was confirmed and brought into practice with 100 per cent coverage of free and universal health services by the Social Security Act of 1975. In theory, everyone in Hungary can receive free medical treatment whatever their needs. In practice, though, as is often the case in countries operating a universal health-care system, there are discrepancies between supply of service and demand. Demand is far higher both quantitatively and organisationally, than the medical network has capacity to cope with. The number of people with a right to free medical services has increased rapidly since the 1950s and despite varying amounts of money being made available demand has consistently outstripped resources.

The whole health system in Hungary is in desperate need of overhauling. Almost 75 per cent of the hospital buildings are over fifty years old and, according to Halay, 33 per cent of these buildings need to be demolished and rebuilt (Halay, 1980, p. 49). Most of the hospitals use outdated technical equipment. Bad management is also a problem in that the authorities rarely actually ask the doctors what kind of equipment they need. An unfortunate example of mismanagement was apparent in the provision of expensive electrocardiographs, which many doctors have, but just do not have time to use, as they are expected to see between 80 and 120 patients per day. If the necessary time was spent on each patient, obviously such high caseloads would have to be halved at least. The rising costs and consequent need for capital input has meant that urgent discussions have been taking place on how the health service can be revitalised. These deficiencies in the medical services have been apparent for a long time, but in the new era the crisis can no longer be ignored. As noted in Chapter 5, at the end of 1988 the Németh administration attempted to tackle some of the anomolies of the social security and health systems, but these plans were waylaid by the 'overburdening' of the social insurance fund with health-service funding. Table 6.1 gives an aggregated overview of general aspects of health care in Hungary.

As Eva Orosz has pointed out, the trends in life expectancy and mortality between advanced Western countries and Hungary have diverged from the mid-1960s onwards. For men, life expectancy is currently identical with that in the late 1950s and mortality rates from 1965 have increased in every adult male group, except that over 80 years. For women between 40 and 60 years, the mortality rates from 1965 have increased and from 1975 onwards increases have also ocurred in the 30–40 age group. Orosz notes that:

> This diverging trend is accompanied in Hungary by growing social and regional inequalities. Deterioration of the population's health status and increasing inequality in health must be understood as a part of the exploitation of human and natural resources by the state-socialist political and economic system (Orosz, 1992, p. 159).

A 'vicious circle' can be seen to have developed in that these serious social and health problems are creating obstacles to establishing more flexible and efficient economic relations in Hungary.

DANGERS TO HEALTH

Obviously, the dangers to the Hungarian population are apparent in terms of the discrepancies in the provision of health care. In

Table 6.1 Health care in Hungary, 1989 (population 10 588 600)

	Male	*Female*
Life expectancy (adults)	65.4	73.8
Infant mortality (per thousands)	15.7	8.1
Number of deaths	76 521	68 174
Death rate per 100 000 inhabitants	1 500	1 244

Most frequent causes of death	*Totals*		*Per 100 000 inhabitants*	
	Male	*Female*	*Male*	*Female*
Circulatory disorders				
Heart attacks	8 461	5 710	165.9	104.2
Strokes	9 588	11 539	188.0	210.7
Malignant tumours	17 307	13 527	339.3	246.9

	Total	*Per 100 000 inhabitants*
Number of active physicians	31 537	29.8
Number of hospital beds	104 479	98.5

Medical equipment	
Computer tomographs	7
Ultrasonic diagnostic equipment	413
Dialysators	176
Laser instruments	73
Number of days sick-leave per employee	25
Average duration of hospital care per patient (days)	14.9
Number of in-patient clinics and hospitals	148

Source: Adapted from *Hungarian Observer*, vol.4, no.3, 1991.

the area of children's health serious misgivings are being discussed in terms of the high number of premature births (often, it was suggested, caused by the mothers' previous use of abortion) and increasing childhood neurosis. In comparison with other industrialised countries that have developed health systems, the infant mortality level in Hungary is one of the highest. As noted, this is mainly due to the high proportion of premature births (10 per cent), that is, children born weighing less than 2,500 grams. The majority of infant deaths occur within the first seven days following birth. In 1980 these deaths represented about 66 per cent of total infant deaths. Newborn infants weighing less than 2500 grams had a mortality rate of 152.7 per thousand, in comparison with infants weighing more, where the rate was 8.2 per thousand. Of those newborn infants weighing less than 1000 grams 90.9 per cent had died (ILO Report, 19984, p. 14). Antenatal health care begins with the confirmation of pregnancy and regular check-ups are given to pregnant women. Many women, especially in rural areas, are found to be severely anaemic when they have their first check-ups; this is generally associated with poor and inadequate diets.

The equipment necessary to make ultrasonic examinations is in very short supply – there are about 200 such scanners in Hungary at the moment. As this type of equipment has to be imported for hard currency, there is a shortage of some very basic instruments. Because of the lack of sophisticated equipment, complicated operations very often have to be carried out abroad. In 1984 when Siamese twins were born in Hungary they had to go to West Germany to be separated, and the German surgeon appealed for financial donations from German sources. Obviously in some cases the money is just not available (either from the Hungarian authorities or from the patient) so sometimes a life-saving operation cannot be performed.

It has been noted that there has been an increase in childhood neurosis. The health service aims to ensure medical and preventive treatment for children until the age of fourteen years. In the cities, this is carried out by district pediatricians whereas in smaller settlements children are treated by the district doctors. Schoolchildren have regular medical and dental check-ups and special medical care is offered by the school medical officers.

WOMEN'S HEALTH NEEDS

The physical health needs arising from women's ability to reproduce can be analysed roughly as contraception, pregnancy and childbirth. Here we are considering those issues arising from contraceptive practices and those concerning childbirth. Until the January 1974 regulations, free abortion on demand was available to every woman in Hungary. Given the current shortages of personnel, equipment and facilities generally within the health service, it is hard to imagine that Hungarian women would regularly undergo abortions as a form of birth control if given a choice of other options. This area is one in which there has been a notable lag between legislation and attitudes, which an effective public education campaign could have eased.

It is not only this lag which is apparent, but a contradiction between the legislative policy of the Hungarian authorities and the actual provision of contraceptive information and equipment. Although the 1956 regulations stated that contraceptives should be placed on sale without restriction at low prices, manufacture of birth-control pills was not authorised until 1967. From 1967, many urban women particularly were urged to make use of these pills, yet only one oral contraceptive, *Infecundin*, was easily available on the market, and this obviously would not suit every woman's needs. It was not until the early 1970s that oral contraceptives were made easily accessible. Until September 1973 it was only gynaecologists who were authorised to prescribe them and purchasers had to pay the full price, which obviously meant that women on low incomes would be disadvantaged, if not prohibited, from using this form of birth control. From 1 October 1973 district and company doctors were allowed to prescribe contraceptive pills and the pills were placed in the same category as other medicines. This meant that purchasers pay only 15 per cent of the list price. It was around this time, in late 1973, that Health Minister, Zoltán Szabo, announced and described in detail the limitations that would be placed on induced abortions after January 1974. There were ten reasons for which pregnant women could get permission to obtain an abortion (see Appendix II).

With the introduction of the 1974 regulations came the realisation by the authorities that the zig-zagging, push-and-pull policies of the Rákosi era in 1953 and in 1956 must be avoided. Such deliberate measures which fundamentally affect people's lives in both the short and the long-term would have to be carefully planned and monitored in order to avoid the worst pitfalls, and unintended consequences. It was clear both to the Hungarian authorities and to the general public that the government could not institute a campaign to solve what the authorities chose to see as a 'demographic problem'. As with many of the population policy measures the 1970s regulations on abortion were dual purpose. On the one hand there was an underlying desire in these measures, if not to encourage births, then to discourage young couples from deciding to terminate a healthy pregnancy. There was another less-calculating aspect to these regulations and that has to do with the general health of Hungarian women. In gradually eliminating abortion as a method of family planning the authorities aimed to encourage the use of the more refined, efficient and apparently 'harmless' birth control pills.

In this context though, one of the safest forms of birth control – the diaphragm – is not advertised in Hungary. One woman with whom I spoke stated:

> I think the most natural and simple things to use are mechanical contraceptives – *pezzarium* – a cap. It is very cheap and reliable but few women use it. I can never understand why they don't let people know about it. But in Hungary they never do things rationally. They made lots of propaganda about pills, which are not without danger (Anna: Corrin, 1986).

In 1989 the availability of diaphragms became restricted in Hungary for 'hygienic' reasons which remain incomprehensible to this day. So it is the oral contraceptive pill that many women use, even those who are older than thrity-five, when the risks of thrombosis and other complications increase. As noted, young women are not eligible to obtain the pill. With the exception of women who have already had a pregnancy, women under 18 have not been eligible for medical prescriptions for contraceptives, on the grounds that the regular use of pills might upset their hormonal equilibrium. Because of increased teenage sexual experience, and the lack of reasonably well-informed literature or discussion on birth control specially for teenagers, one direct effect of the 1974 regulations may well have been an increase in illegal abortions, on which there is no available statistical evidence at present.

Oral contraceptives are still more popular with young women than with older women, and they are used more by women in the capital than by those living in provincial towns or rural areas, where the use of intra-uterine devices is more widespread. Table 6.2 shows that 'natural' contraceptive methods – *Ogino Kanus*, *coitus interruptus*, vaginal irrigation – are still most frequently used by older women, those having lower educational attainment, agricultural workers and the rural population.

These changes in methods of birth control can be interpreted in different ways. In terms of women undertaking a much greater role in contraception than men, the authors of the above study see this as women becoming 'more emancipated':

Table 6.2 Distribution of the main method of contraception used three years after marriage by age groups of users

Age group	*Coitus interruptus*	*Condom*	*Loop, spiral IUD*	*Oral*	*Other*
	Main method of contraception				
In 1969, people married in 1966					
at 1.1.1970					
17–22	48.5	11.5	0.9	26.3	12.8
23–27	40.4	14.4	0.8	25.6	18.8
28–32	42.6	11.4	0.6	17.7	27.7
33–37	46.0	6.9	–	19.5	27.6
Overall total	43.2	12.8	0.8	24.7	18.5
In 1977, couples married in 1974					
at 1.1.1978					
17–22	7.2	3.4	14.6	72.8	2.0
23–27	6.9	3.1	15.1	72.1	2.8
28–32	10.0	3.1	19.3	59.9	7.7
33–37	16.0	2.7	14.7	58.7	7.9
Overall total	7.5	3.2	15.3	70.9	3.1

Source: *Longitudinal Marriage Surveys in Hungary* (HCSO, 1984).

If coitus interruptus and condoms are categorised as men's methods of contraception, rhythm method however, as a joint one, then in the past it used to be primarily the men who practised contraception against women's pregnancy mostly not with great success. Today on the contrary it is the case that in 89 out of 100 spouses using contraception it is the women who apply some kind of contraception (HCSO, 1984, p. 57).

It appeared to be the case that when men took some responsibility for avoiding unwanted pregnancies the success rate was very low. When this responsibility was placed more upon women the avoidance of pregnancy became much more successful. This situation is by no means unique to Hungary yet with the spread of AIDS throughout many societies it may be that effective, efficient condoms can be produced and the distaste which many men have for wearing them may well be overcome. Despite some early discussion on AIDS-testing equipment to be manufactured jointly with Czechoslovakian firms, there is little or no information available in Hungary on AIDS or on safe sex.

CHILDBIRTH

Pregnant women have regular check-ups until the time of the birth draws near. When women are admitted to their local hospital it is often a question of chance whether or not their doctor is available. The personal choice of doctors is a complex situation, and it is good to detail here what generally happens in such cases. The allocation of housing via the centralised redistributive system is applicable in similar vein to health resources. Here Ferge suggests that:

> The allocation of scarce resources which are in great demand does not follow the predefined pattern of centralised redistribution nor is it operated by pure market forces. Both forms have been replaced by some kind of 'hidden' distribution, regulated partly by personal contacts and good 'connections': better situated groups have better access to scarce resources (council flats or places in kindergarten) because they have more contacts (Ferge, 1979, p. 256).

This touches upon one of the major contradictions in the provision of services by the state in Hungary, that of access. Of course everyone is supposedly entitled to the same high, or not so high, level of medical care in Hungary. In practice though, overworked and underpaid doctors and nurses can be influenced by offers of gifts or provision of other goods/services that are in demand. Such 'gratitude' money often amounts to several times their official salaries. A duality of market and non-market mechanisms are semi-officially allowed to operate within the health service, in that whilst all doctors and dentists must have a full-time job within the health service, many also have some private, paying, patients. As Orosz points out this 'taken-for-granted' practice of 'gratitude' money is a serious obstacle to reforming health care and as it amounts to a fee-for-service system its existence also shapes the nature of the proposed reforms.

Certain forms of private treatment are accepted to a large extent because they help to avoid some of the queueing and complement the basic or more expensive treatments. In the area of childbirth this practice has meant that women almost always decide to pay their doctor at the going rate. This is true of almost all hospital treatment but the potential health risks involved in childbirth make it appear more of a necessity for women to tip, or they may not get the care that they desire or need. One of the best ways to gain an insight into the various problems that can arise for Hungarian women during childbirth is from the personal accounts of several mothers. Of the women with whom this was discussed only a couple did not pay their doctors – primarily because they could not afford to do so – but one also felt that it should not be a necessity. For the other mothers it was apparent that paying for the safe delivery of their children was quite usual and acceptable. One young mother explained the payments involved with her four children:

> Yes, I paid the doctors. The first doctor didn't take anything as he knew we were both students. The other two accepted money and the fourth one was a friend of the family and we gave him presents. I gave the second doctor 1000 forints, then the third between 2000 and 3000 forints (Mária: Corrin, 1986).

Of course, the rate of payment varies and this woman paid less than the average at the time. The average payment in 1975 was 1000 forints, when an average monthly wage was roughly 3000. By 1982 it was approximately 3000 and in 1991 it varied between 5000 and 8000 on average, although there are stories that some women pay up to 20 000 or more. In 1990 an average monthly income was assessed at 13205 gross or 9960 nett and on 1 April 1991 the official minimum monthly wage was set at 7000 forints, approximately US $100.

In 1989 Hungary's first private out-patients' clinic was set up in Pomáz just outside Budapest, employing eleven doctors and six nurses. This is effectively a 'joint agreement' between Dr Sándor Karsay, a general practitioner with fifteen years' experience, and the Swiss MEDEC who agreed to equip the clinic in return for monitoring the therapy treatments. In its short existence the clinic has no shortage of patients, who must write or call for an appointment well in advance as the capacity of 100 examinations or treatments each day is readily filled. During 1990 and 1991 several other clinics were established with their most attractive feature being that all tests and therapies are given in the same place so patients do not need to 'make the round' of doctors which is required under the health service. Some clinics base their prices on that of foreign citizens' fees in the state medical service. Yet the question of demand remains. Whilst millions of Hungarians want a better health service, few have the means to pay the prices which private clinics are charging.

So far as the general standard of care is concerned childbirth has become an area monopolised by professionals, generally men, in which the patient is often thought to have no competence to judge the situation. This is the case throughout most of the industrialised world. In Hungary there are no 'radical midwives' offering full, supportive care at home to women. Almost all births – 99 per cent – take place in hospitals, which is understandable given the poor state of the Hungarian telephone system and the difficulties arising from non-availability of ambulances. In this context a ministerial decree of January 1990 allowed privately-run ambulance services to operate but the relationship between privately-run and nationwide services, which are free of charge, is complex. Most of the women who participated in this research had very little good to say of the environments within which they gave birth:

> Zoltán was a very big child and it was a dangerous birth. His life was in danger when he was born. He was 4 kilos which was big in comparison to me, not on his own. Zoltán was born with the care of a man who didn't know much about birth and pain. He was quite rude and yelling at me when I said I was in pain. This was a doctor who we had asked to work for us and we paid him too (Ildikó, 1986).

There were several instances in which women arrived at hospitals at night and the 'wrong' doctor was on duty. Cases such as this can mean that women undergo very long, painful labour without any help, often because the other staff do not want to wake the doctor at night. This could be because there was no way of getting messages through (even doctors can wait up to ten years for a telephone in Hungary) or because the doctors had already worked for ten hours and so they expected to gain some rest at night. Waiting for the 'right' doctor can sometimes be dangerous:

> They left me to walk up and down the corridor and at 7 o'clock in the morning my doctor came and examined me and in my water was 'meconium' which is a sign that the child is in danger – the excrement of the baby was in my water so the child was not getting enough oxygen. I was frightened because I knew it was a dangerous situation – almost too late (Kati: Corrin, 1986).

One doctor who was interviewed did not receive particularly good medical care, which is surprising as generally other doctors, or daughters of doctors, receive a bit of extra attention:

> I am a doctor and I had my child at the very same hospital at which I worked, so I wasn't unknown, for instance, to the nurses. The doctor put me on some kind of injection after the birth, and after the fifth day I said to the nurse 'Now, I think you had better give it to me because the doctor will ask about it', and then I gave her some tip and she gave the injection to me and I am a doctor . . . if I wanted to have not just something extra but say I wanted to have my temperature taken, I have to tip the nurses, yet they know me and they knew that I was a doctor . . . on the other hand their work is terrible and they are not paid well, so there are two sides to the whole question (Zsuzsa: Corrin, 1986).

Generally, the situation has been getting worse into the 1980s, as medical salaries have not increased significantly, nor has there been any significant capital input to improve the hospital premises. These premises are often dirty, lacking in medical provisions and do not generally inspire confidence in terms of satisfactory health care.

GENDER DIVISIONS IN MEDICINE

Within the Hungarian health system appears a phenomenon which seems generally universal in the industrialised world – that of the professionalisation of certain aspects of physical change. Such natural processes as menstruation, conception and childbirth can be viewed within the feminist critique of their 'medicalisation':

> Critics argue that phenomena that are often socially determined rather than pathologically based, and which, in the case of menstruation, conception and childbirth, are wholly natural events for women, have been colonised by doctors who see these human milestones as providing rich pickings in terms of financial gain and professional power (Ungerson, 1985, p. 150).

This comment refers explicitly to the British and American medical professions yet it seems that such criticism can be levelled implicitly at the Hungarian gynaecologists and obstetricians.

From Table 6.3 (on the following page) the most shocking gender segregation appears for surgeons in 1979 – 2095 men and only 206 women. In addition, in 1989, 1504 of the gynaecologists and obstetricians are men, compared with only 132 women and of specialists in general medical science there are 1091 men yet only 267 women. This ratio is reversed however, for paediatricians with many more women than men – 1946 to 712. It is also the case that the majority of professional medical staff are men and it is mainly women who are nurses, orderlies and radiographers. In her discussion of the division of labour within health-care systems Ungerson notes that this replicates the sexual division of labour in other areas of life:

> doctors are predominantly male, in authority and endowed with scientifically based propensities to cure and thus forestall mortality; in contrast, nurses are predominantly female, subordinate, and endowed with no special properties other than those of nurturing which anyway come 'naturally' to women (Gamarnikow, 1978) and which, far from magically forestalling mortality, simply make the paths towards death or recovery more wholesome and comfortable (Ungerson, 1985, p. 150).

It seems then, that the medical world is one in which sex-role stereotyping not only exists but is emphasised in this duality between the 'scientific' work and the 'caring' work. In drawing this conclusion, Jeff Hearn points to the well-noted observation that the paid work undertaken by women is often seen to mirror their unpaid work in the home in terms of cleaning, food preparation, and textile work. He goes on to draw the parallel:

> between the social emotional domestic tasks and the semi-professional areas of specialisation. This element of sex role

Table 6.3 Physicians by speciality and gender

Medical speciality	*1970*	*1980*	*1989*	*Men*	*Women*
Interns	2 255	3 391	4 374	2 193	2 181
Surgeons	1 549	1 983	2 301	2 095	206
Obstetricians and gynaecologists	1 214	1 533	1 636	1 504	132
Pediatricians	1 611	2 444	2 658	712	1 946
Pulmonary	877	942	962	441	521
Dermatologists and venereologists	378	462	508	155	353
Rhino-otologists and laryngologists	438	556	717	354	363
Urologists	205	315	501	471	30
Dentists and dental surgeons	2 008	2 884	3 453	1 557	1 896
Psychiatrists and neurologists	625	979	1 415	595	820
Ophthalmologists	472	603	752	173	579
Radiologists	578	825	1 133	515	618
Specialists in laboratory analysis	828	1 053	876	306	570
Prosectors and pathologic histology	248	324	374	230	144
Orthopedists	120	160	200	152	48
Rheumatics and physiotherapists	202	343	548	211	337
Public health specialists	464	595	634	228	406
Factory medical consultants	216	338	639	228	411
Sports physicians	55	67	135	94	41
Specialists of social medical science	259	429	635	454	181
Specialists of general medical science	–	1 161	1 358	1 091	267
Other medical specialists	232	438	1 660	921	739
General practitioners without special qualification	7 962	8 286	8 287	4 216	4 069

Source: *Statisztikai Evkönyv*, 1989.

> specialisation I refer to as the patriarchal feminine as it conforms to the feminine, 'caring' stereotype; patriarchal because in doing so it complements and thereby reinforces the masculine stereotype of specialisation. In this way the ideology of femininity is central to patriarchy in general and the semi-professions in particular (Hearn, in Ungerson, 1985, p. 198).

In the same way that women are generally relegated to the 'caring' non-professional work within the health service, so their ability to reproduce, or rather the expectation of their caring for children is used, often blatantly, to discriminate against them.

Several women in discussion with the author said that after they had had children and returned to work, their work was not appreciated in the same way, although they were doing exactly the same job or sometimes had even taken on more responsibility. Even if mothers never have time off with their children despite being entitled to sick leave, they are still not relied on in the same way. Most women explained it as a subjective thing, the fact that their bosses treated them as less reliable/useful when they had children. There is no evidence whatsoever to suggest that fathers are treated in this way. Men are not expected to take time off work when their children are ill nor do their bosses appear to feel that fathers become less reliable workers. This additional responsibility placed on women, as 'carers' as well as earners, can undoubtedly lead to women suffering from various stress-related illnesses. It is to this area of women's health that I now turn in considering the quality and availability of medical assistance.

PSYCHOLOGICAL HEALTH

It is not enough to say that because women are expected to care for children *and* to hold down paid employment they often become ill. There are different reasons why some women feel these pressures more strongly than other women and also why some react in certain ways to such pressures. To analyse how various types of neurotic disorders are treated within the Hungarian health system it is important to remember that in the early 1950s in most socialist countries, including Hungary, the teachings of Freud were rejected. Psychoanalysis and in some cases psychology came under attack. It was not until 1980 that the Hungarian Psychiatric Association was founded with the first meeting of its section for psychotherapy being held in 1984. It was around this time that articles began to be published describing the psychological anomalies of the population. A rise in the incidence of neuroses (and alcoholism) was not only apparent within Hungarian towns and cities but could also be seen to be increasing within rural Hungary as well. Heinrich points out that:

> While the number of neurotics among the population over sixteen grew from 30.1 per cent (1961) to 42.2 per cent (1971), 25.8 per cent of the village dwellers (42.2 per cent of the adult population!) were categorised as neurotics during the second half of the seventies. The figures were highest for two Budapest workers' districts (54.1 per cent and 57.4 per cent). The incidence of mental disorders is significantly higher in Hungary than in other capitalist or socialist societies (Heinrich, 1986, p. 134).

It has been recorded that the highest number of workers on sick leave because of psychological disorders was noted in the printing industry, followed by the public transport sector, news agencies, the paper industry and the textile and steel sectors (Radio Free Europe (RFE) SR/6 27 May 1986, p. 23). In each of these sectors the work involves a high level of stress and/or the use of primitive machinery in comparison with more advanced Western technological production of the same goods. It is in the 'feminised' textile industries that many women work. Both the stress and the effective length of the working day for the women workers are quite often increased by the considerable amount of time spent travelling to and from the factories which are in the cities. Indeed many older women who are unable to survive on their state pensions tend to look for work in textiles but the stress is often too much for them. Those factories employing psychologists say that they are booked up for weeks in advance. Stress through long working hours, long hours spent travelling and returning home to several hours housework/child-care is bound to make women feel harassed, anxious and in some cases desperate.

Something which became known as the 'GYES disease', or the 'child-care-allowance neurosis' was viewed as a particular problem for women. In her book, *A Gyestöl a Gyedig* (*From the child-care allowance to the child-care benefit*) Sándorné Dr Horváth Erika cites the research of the Research Institute of Trade Unions on women who were at home claiming the child-care allowance. This research discovered the problem that a significant proportion of those who are claiming the allowance suffer from neurotic illnesses. Some lack of inner balance drives them to taking sedatives, unlimited smoking and often to drinking alcohol. In the cities it has been shown that the primary reasons given include the lack of any company, the narrowing of living possibilities and simply wanting a job. In villages these symptoms were not as apparent. Dr András Veer wrote a series in *Nök Lapja* (*Women's Journal*) called 'Betegseg, amelynek szaz arca van' (A disease that has a manifold face). Dr Veer, principal assistant of the neurosis department of the Psychiatric Clinic, thinks that the allowance period is a critical time in a woman's life, when women are taken out of their regular environment – the rhythm of their lives – and often they are isolated in a way that they can scarcely bear. They become anxious and have phobias. According to Dr Mária Szilagyi, a psychologist working with neurosis patients in the VIIIth district of Budapest, young women getting the allowance 'are not alcoholics, they only congregate together, they get nervous because they cannot fulfil the desired purpose for which they get the allowance' (Horváth, 1982, p. 62).

In her book *Egy ország gyesen* (*A country getting the allowance*) Katalin Sulyok also describes how a proportion of women can 'hardly tolerate' being on the allowance, they become upset and are ill because of it. According to the conclusions of various research work carried out among women living in high-rise apartments in cities and other urban environments, in villages and settlements, it has been shown that the symptoms of the neurosis for women on the allowance occur principally in those groups of women for whom being at home receiving the child-care allowance means the greatest change in lifestyle.

One detailed research study undertaken by Emma C. Molnár among the working women of the Csepel Iron and Metal Works who were claiming the allowance has shown that among 200 mothers needing the allowance eighty-four were neurotic, forty-three showed neurotic dispositions, and only seventy-three of them were registered as being fully healthy. Still, the data of the three groups involved were often contradictory so that the conclusion formed was that a woman's nuerosis cannot be purely from the basis of being at home and receiving child-care allowance. Whilst this may be the primary reason, other secondary factors played important roles. Such secondary reasons include growing up in a 'non-harmonious' family, negative identification with the role of being a mother, a less-feminine quality or role and the 'womanly' identity or role. In this framework, the formation of neurosis symptoms is viewed as interrelated with the woman's relationship to motherhood, and fulfilling certain 'roles' within the home or not feeling able to do so.

There is something here of the superwoman complex mentioned in Chapter 3. Within this complex, women may come to believe (whether or not their families/husbands do expect such things) that they should be wonderful mothers, cooks and cleaners all day; then teachers in the early evening; hostesses to their husband and his friends in the late evening and adorable sex creatures at night! This is a theme which seems to crop up again and again in many different ways – that is, just how much is expected of the 'successful' woman. It would seem that for many women in Hungary such a complex set of societal expectations is too much pressure to bear – the ways in which this comes out can be manifold from decisions to divorce, to questioning having more than one child, to various stress-related health problems. This is not to say that there are not many other reasons for divorce, for limiting the number of children within families and of course, that many women's health problems are not directly stress-related. So far as women claiming the child-care allowance are concerned it is true that the pattern of their lives is upset, but they also face the sets of problems which many young people in Hungary face when starting their families – obtaining apartments, creating homes, not feeling fulfilled in their expectations of married life.

Regarding the steps which can be taken to help to ease this situation for women who suffer from such neuroses, one suggestion is that the prediction of their neurosis danger should be included in the care given to pregnant women. In addition, since screenings and tests proved the fact that the women tending towards, or suffering from, neurosis are less willing to give birth to more children, Molnár suggests that a new system could be designed to prevent the recurrence of neurotic symptoms. Such a new system would combine teaching and group therapy. Another possible way of easing the situation would be to have community workers working in certain relatively deprived communities – such as large housing estates. Such community workers could provide a central community focal point for women at home caring for their children. The People's Patriotic Front did attempt to provide something along these lines in certain areas but many people were suspicious of 'Party' interference in their lives.[2] The PPF provided classes which women could attend whilst their children were cared for in the crèche. Yet this way of providing for young mothers was in no way systematised and seemed to operate more readily in the countryside than in the towns and cities. Also the People's Patriotic Front was generally associated with dull, politicised state events and many young people were not prepared to join in with such activities. The barrier against either education and group therapy as part of the basic medical care for pregnant women or the idea of social/community workers creating joint projects, is largely a financial one. As we have seen the health service in Hungary is already overburdened, the same is true of most branches of social services, so that whilst the intention may be there to implement new measures aimed at eliminating some of the sources of neurosis which many young mothers face, the means of supporting and financing such measures is not currently available.

ALCOHOLISM AND ALCOHOL-RELATED ILLNESS

Another disturbing area so far as women's health is concerned, is that of alcoholism and alcohol-related illness. From January 1978 the sale of alcoholic drinks became restricted by a decree of the Ministry of Domestic Trade (No. 19/1977). No alcohol was supposed to be sold in kiosks or buffets, at railway and shipping stations or at bus terminals. Neither bars, wine shops nor other spirit-selling stores could be opened within a 200-metre radius of factories and offices employing more than a hundred people. In addition, restaurants were to have more non-alcoholic drinks available. Yet it is obvious to those spending time in Hungary that although apparently well-intentioned, these regulations had very little, if any, effect on the ease with which alcoholic beverages may be bought, and indeed are bought. A more significant factor in reducing consumption may be price rises, so that people cannot afford to buy as much alcohol.

Whilst every effort is made to systematise the collection of data on alcoholism it is a difficult area in which to achieve any precision. As Hungary is a wine producing country, the thousands of bottles bought and sold from private vineyards around the country (e.g. Balaton, Eger) cannot be accounted for. When we ask, 'Who is drinking and how much?' – again it is difficult to be specific. Estimates have differed, but generally analysts agree that the higher proportion of alcoholism was in the villages, where more than 12 per cent of the adult population were classified as alcoholics. Yet social drinking has also become a feature of white-collar workers' lifestyles. Heinrich points out that:

> The groups that seem to be specifically predisposed to developing regular drinking habits are skilled workers and young urban professionals with a rural background, i.e. people of humble social origins with pronounced career ambitions (Andorka, 1985) (Heinrich, 1986, p. 135).

So far as women drinking heavily is concerned, several recent studies have highlighted the upward trend that is apparent amongst many women drinkers. One such book called *Miért isznak a nök?* (Why do women drink?) attempts to discover the complex roots of women's alcoholism. At the outset though, Valkai proposes that 'it would be incorrect to come to a general conclusion that would explain the alcoholism of all women' (Valkai, 1986, p. 131). Valkai outlines the positive motivation for some drinkers – 'because it gives me pleasure', 'because then I feel I can get everything'; the negative motivations, trying to forget through alcohol – 'because without alcohol I don't feel good about myself'. 'I only take alcoholic beverages to forget about my problems'; and the neutral option – 'because everybody drinks around me'. According to various studies the neutral motivation occurs most often, as almost half of the people drinking too much alcohol argue in that way. So according to Valkai, half of the alcoholics in Hungary are simply following a social example – they do what they experience in their everyday environment.

Considering the statistics it is apparent that amongst women who are in paid employment, of those that seek official help (for psychiatry, detoxification, or other help), 17 per cent are in the 21–29 years age-group, while 83 per cent of them, in the statistics signifying problems close to alcoholism, are among the 30–49 years age-group. Experience has shown that those who are included in the statistics would have had a history of drinking for several years. Age, then seems to be a factor. So far as women working in paid employment and those not, the differences between those receiving help seems negligible. Of the six female classes of the Nervous and Mental Asylum over a period of six months, 54.5 per cent of women being treated for alcoholism were in paid employment and 45.5 per cent of them were not.

Considering the high proportion of women in Hungary who can earn money, the difference is not too great. In considering the causes of women drinking it is certain that women never drink simply because of one reason. The most frequently occurring factors given are: lack of self-confidence; hurt or unrealistic self-esteem; stress, inherited and environmental influences, defective 'socialisation' process; hurt feelings and social and cultural influences. Many alcoholics can be seen to have medical disorders such as neurosis, suicidal tendencies, or psychosomatic disorders.

In trying to decide which seems to be the major motivating factors which push women towards alcoholism, it can be seen that many of these women suffer from a lack of self-esteem. In outlining this Valkai suggests that:

> We all have critical or heavy times, mainly when things do not happen as we would like them to. None the less it is possible that we women doubt a lot in ourselves, we blame ourselves because of being unlucky, more times than men do, because we are expected to have a sexual role by our cultural traditions, a woman can only feel herself fully well, not when she is a self-developed independent being, but when she lives with a man in a relationship of dependency (Valkai, 1986, p. 137).

These sentiments speak volumes about the hidden pressures under which women in Hungary, and almost everywhere else in the world, have to live. This notion of the 'sexual role' is by no means a new one, yet has always escaped any definition or codification. That women who live alone or with other women and children, without men, cannot feel good about themselves, as if they are leading incomplete lives, is something that can only change with a definite change in attitudes towards women as independent beings. Many women in various countries do choose to live without men. Some of these women have men as lovers and some have women lovers, yet even whilst it is generally socially acceptable to their peers that they live independently, there are often misunderstandings and misgivings with relatives or colleagues.

In Hungary, whilst neither lesbianism nor homosexual sex between two men is illegal, it is a subject which is talked about very infrequently. Section 199 of the Penal Code provides for a higher age of consent (18) for lesbians and gay men, than for heterosexuals (14) (Section 201). Prison terms for violation of Section 199 are up to three years. Typical comments concerning homosexuality include: 'I know what one is but I certainly am not acquainted with any' or 'I think he is one but I could never mention it'.

There are obvious dangers in attitudes that imply that women living alone have something missing in their lives or something wrong with them – 'can't get a man', 'hates men', 'seems to prefer women'. Such comments can be said in a cutting way to make women choosing a single life feel inadequate and isolated. Still, there are are many women who find themselves living alone who would dearly wish not to be alone – women who are widowed, divorced or who have never become close enough to develop longer-term relationships. It can be seen that women are often viewed (and view themselves) in relation to men. As such, women are seen as the 'second sex'. This is a subject to be considered, but for the present it is definitely something to be borne in mind when considering why women turn to drink.

The socio-economic conditions under which many women have to attempt to construct some form of harmonious life for themselves and their partners, children, parents, or relatives cannot be ignored when considering the incidence of alcoholism. In a sociological report published in *Mühely* by Éva Csoregh which deals with the drabness of life in high-rise flats, she notes that:

> The lack of personal contact in the housing developments is well-known, 'boxing oneself up' attitude restricts information gathering and thus the disclosure of danger is difficult and slow process. In other words, the situation might possibly be far worse than shown in the records (RFE HSR/19, 22 December 1981, p. 13).

Here Csoregh is primarily concerned with the increasing problems of youth welfare, some of which are to be found in the habits of the inhabitants of the housing developments – alcoholism and criminality. In this connexion several of the women interviewed by the author spoke of other young mothers whom they knew who were drinking too much. Most of these young mothers had recently moved into a new flat on large housing estates and were finding it very difficult to manage financially, as well as to 'settle in' socially. The payments made to women claiming the child-care allowance were by no means equal to their salaries. Generally their husbands took on a second or even a third job to help to pay the bills. This is when trouble very often begins as the man is out of the home for the vast majority of the waking hours, coming home just an hour or so before it is time to sleep.

Many of these women spoke of being caged up 'in little boxes just like everyone else's and feeling that they had no adult company, and were just alone with babies who wanted feeding, or needed nappies changing'.[3] Some of the women who kept up sporadic contact with workers at their workplace realised that they had already become 'out of touch', and had little to talk of when they visited. In such instances it is not difficult to see how some women may just come to see themselves as 'useless' – both in terms of not engaging in productive work, so not helping to pay the bills, nor having a role or place outside the home so becoming 'part of the furniture', also in terms of believing themselves to be 'bad mothers' for no apparent reasons. In such a situation when women do have some drink it is primarily to 'forget' – all their troubles and their own bad self-image – but of course, later when they have drunk something the vicious circle is complete because they are fulfilling their own worst fears of themselves as 'unfit' mothers or bad people. This theme is considered further in the study of women's self-images. For the present, another aspect of a stressful life is examined, that of suicide.

SUICIDE

For the past quarter of a century Hungary has had one of the highest suicide rates in the world, according to the data collected through the World Health Organisation (WHO). Yet comparing suicide rates is generally accepted as having little value as the differences seen are almost purely the product of reporting procedures. Variations in definition are very wide. In Hungary though, suicide has generally been seen as one (relatively acceptable) solution to what are felt by the persons involved to be insurmountable problems. Yet, in Britain for example, suicide cases are generally seen to be an embarrassment to friends and families concerned and there is often some indefinable 'shame' attached to the act of taking one's life. Despite the dubious value of comparing suicide rates, we can see from Table 6.4 that over a 65-year span the incidence of suicide has risen more or less steadily. It is well to remember that suicide attempts, which do not result in death, are between four and eight times higher than the suicide rate itself. That suicide attempts and deaths by suicide have been an increasing aspect of Hungarian life has long given cause for serious worry within Hungary. Yet in a radio interview in 1980 a well-known psychiatrist, Béla Buda, stated his negative opinion of what was being done to counteract this trend:

> the appropriate quarters have every right to be ashamed . . . for a decade nearly every country has developed a number of regulations and institutions to reduce the problem and to treat and save potential suicide victims. One can say that Hungary is in the worst position in the world in this respect: there is no true research on suicide, little attention is paid to the problem, and

Table 6.4 Incidence of suicide in Hungarian society, 1920–85

Year	*Number of suicides or yearly average*	*Per 100 000 inhabitants*
1920–21	2 017	25.2
1930–31	2 840	32.7
1938	2 684	29.3
1941	2 522	27.0
1948–49	2 196	23.9
1959–60	2 527	25.4
1969–70	3 503	33.9
1978	4 610	43.1
1979	4 770	44.6
1980	4 809	44.9
1984	4 900	45.9
1985	4 725	44.4

Source: *Demográfia Évkönyv*, 1985; *Statisztikai Évkönyv*, 1980.

> there are no institutions where these people could be treated. Until recently, psychiatry and clinical psychology have been comparatively undeveloped and suicide-prevention clinics non-existent. There are only two suicide prevention telephone services in operation in the country (RFE HSR/4, 17 March 1982, p. 3).

Whilst the trends illustrate that just under half as many women as men took their lives in the period 1960–75, in the following decade between 1975–85 the difference was increasing with the number of women committing suicide being slightly more than one-third the number of male suicides. Some sociologists place the explanation of this gendered differential within women's 'caring' situation, in that women are often held back from taking this drastic solution by thoughts of how it would affect their children and other relatives. The evidence on this subject, for Hungarian society, is at best very sketchy and no firm conclusions can be drawn or inferred. Some suggestions for coping with this problem have been put forward, but as is so often the case, the financial support for this area of health care is lacking. Yet in the case of suicide attempts it would also appear to be the case that the social and political will is absent as it is seen by the Hungarian health authorities as of very low priority. In an article in *Mozgó Világ* in January 1982, Dr Samu notes that:

> if the problem is ever openly discussed, the institutions shove it along to their neighbour's desk; while today the megalopolis of suicides, of dead souls, is already increasing by close to 5,000 every year. Those who commit suicide are only a very small part of those people who are in a mental crisis. There are probably several hundred thousand in our country who would need some speedy help and 'first aid' but have nowhere to turn (*Mozgó Világ*, 1982, vol.1, no. 48).

By considering comparative data on health care for various types of suicide problems (see World Health Organisation Reports and Moscow statistics) it does appear that the Hungarian infrastructure is less well-prepared, to handle the growing number of suicide problems. It has fewer social homes, fewer neurological consulting hours and less social-policy campaigns aiming to help the affected groups. In this situation, the remedies proposed are similar to those which psychologists and research workers put forward in the case of women suffering from the 'child-care-allowance syndrome'. Primarily, these include the need to create a system of various psychological counselling and education campaigns aimed at specific groups. In addition, there is a need to increase those internal medicine wards which specialise in emergency cases. At present those available have to release their patients too soon, often when the patients are still dependent upon drugs. Resources are not yet available for these people to have the psychological treatment that they need.

DRUG TAKING

Since the mid-1980s more and more illegal 'hard' drugs have become available in Hungary. Despite serious problems with glue-sniffing and raids on pharmacies for anything from cough medicine to amphetamines the availablity of so-called hard drugs in Hungary is relatively recent. In June 1991 several large caches of heroin (over 1 kilo) and cocaine (over 5 kilos) were seized by customs authorities in Budapest. Whereas the heroin may well have been 'in transit' the cocaine was definitely marked for domestic use within Hungary. Yet whilst imported hashish, cocaine and LSD are now available on the streets in Hungary, specialists in Szeged noted in August 1991 that most of Hungary's drug-addicts are 'a home-grown breed', using opium. Zsuzsa Gal, a founder of the pioneering Drug Outpatient Centre established in Szeged in 1987 spoke of the battle not only for money but for acceptance: 'We wanted to break through the walls of traditional health services, and the authorities were totally against this. Political change has helped a lot in this. The government is actually appreciative now' (*Budapest Week*, August 1991). The drug clinic offers clean syringes to avoid possibilities of users spreading AIDS. At the end of 1989 there had been a total of forty-nine cases of AIDS reported in Hungary, of which twenty-seven were fatal. In 1990 seventeen new cases were reported.

Despite various withdrawal programmes including substitute drugs and psychological therapy, the staff in Szeged are unhappy with their 'success' rate. With the unstable economic situation it may be that young people will be even less able to achieve their goals and may turn to drug-use as a withdrawal from difficulties. Other drug-treatment centres have now opened – two in Budapest, one in Pécs and one in Györ.

ENVIRONMENTAL DANGERS

Pollution in Hungary does not just affect the quality of people's lives, it can also put their lives at risk. In 1990 one in seventeen deaths in Budapest was related to air pollution, and oxygen booths have been set up. Some industrial plants are closed during smog alerts. The air in various cities is monitored and at certain times parents are advised not to take their children into particular parts of cities. Certainly children in push-chairs are at exactly the level to inhale the lethal carbon monoxide fumes from the increasing numbers of cars be they Trabbants or Mercedes, crowding city roads.

Even the much-admired Duna (Danube) which elegantly separates Buda from Pest is now full of oil, mercury, iron and ammonia, not to mention untreated sewage. Over one million cubic metres of untreated human waste are discharged into the Danube each day, and 20 per cent of the city's drinking water comes from the river. Whilst swimming in the Duna is banned, fishing is allowed. Air-quality statistics are regularly announced, and as Table 6.5 shows, certain areas of Budapest are 'lethal':

Table 6.5 Lead concentration reading taken Budapest, June 1991

	District	*Lead concentration (mg/cu. m)*	*Health limit excess*
I	Clark Adám tér	4.80	16 times
II	Mártirok utja	3.12	10 times
III	Lajos utca	4.56	15 times
V	Kossuth Lajos utca	5.75	19 times
VIII	Rákóczi ut	8.15	27 times
IX	Ferenc körut	6.83	13 times
XI	Bocskai ut	3.14	10 times

Source: *Budapest Week*, 10 April 1991, p. 3.

There is now something of a realisation within Hungary of the high environmental cost of socialism. According to the Ministry of Environment, the damage to the environment will cost society in the neighbourhood of 100 billion forints a year, or 8 per cent of the gross domestic product (GDP), in terms of medical expenses, deteriorated resources and industrial corrosion.

TRANSITIONAL DEBATES

It is clear that Hungary is in urgent need of effective and flexible health policies, yet no single actor has primary responsibility regarding the state of Hungarian health. As Eva Orosz notes:

> Rather, the state is primarily interested in reducing expenditures, and health-care professionals in serving the highest possible number of patients. Meanwhile strata of the population struggle to maintain their living standards at the expense of their health (Orosz, 1992, p. 159).

In terms of instituting a system of compulsory insurance it remains unclear whether everyone, or only certain groups, would be included in such a scheme. In turn, questions concerning how to reduce or eliminate the extensive role of the state authorities in financing and service provision remain unanswered. In practice, in 1990–2 there was much confusion, with churches claiming back previously-owned property including hospitals and schools. The operation of foreign capital in the health market was not regulated in any way. It is clear that changes in the political system have not entailed changes in policy-making processes within the health-care sector.

CONCLUSION

'What does this mean for women's health?' So far as the specific physical aspects of women's health, such as contraception, pregnancy and childbirth are concerned, the potential for change is varied. With increased drug prices the costs of oral contraceptives are increasing rapidly. Health care during pregnancy is at present less than adequate, and is not advanced as far as scanning procedures and screening for abnormalities in the unborn infants. Yet in the field of childbirth it would seem unlikely that any positive changes will come about in the near future. Buying modern medical equipment, renovating decaying hospitals, employing more medical staff at decent rates of pay and providing first-class medical facilities and medicines is likely to be a very slow and complex process. Provision of sympathetic and supportive medical care from staff who have the time and willingness to listen, and attend to women's needs and wishes can only come when such staff are not so overworked, under-resourced and underpaid. That the new government is considering restricting abortion rights is considered in Chapter 8.

When considering the psychological health of women in Hungary, it seems that the negative effects of the crisis in the health service are readily apparent. Overcrowding in many mental wards has reached such proportions that patients actually take turns to sleep in the same bed. Hungary is by no means alone in relegating nervous and mental disorders to a lowly position. Britain certainly does not have a good record in this sort of care. Perhaps one reason for this is that the majority of patients classified as 'insane' lose most, if not all, of their legal rights and so are not in a position to complain about their treatment. In Hungary some patients with mental disorders are placed in 'welfare homes' which are viewed as long-term-care institutions and lack the requisite specialists. Those patients admitted to these 'homes' lose all rights to their apartments and these 'homes' are generally situated in remote areas.

So far as women becoming alcholic is concerned, this is a subject which will be considered again in terms of women's images of themselves, which often have a great deal to do with the way that women have to deal with difficult situations and crises. to some extent the images which women have of themselves are socially created, and in the case of Hungary, women often received very contradictory and conflicting signals as to what being 'woman' entailed, or what she should be able to achieve in modern Hungarian society. In the context of financial constraints, any proposals concerning group therapy and educationals for young mothers, to help them to deal with the feelings of isolation and 'uselessness' which some experience, seem unlikely to be implemented in the near future. For those elderly women who cannot manage alone, financially or physically, the option of staying in hospital may not have been readily chosen, but it seems that life will certainly become much more difficult for this very vulnerable group in the future.

For those with money nowadays in Hungary, private care may increasingly be viewed as their preferred option. It remains to be seen whether or not the 'feminised' aspects of the health care, and the workers within these areas, benefit to the same degree from any changes in legislation, as the 'prestige' and profitable areas. For the majority of women in Hungary today, key areas of health care, such as childbearing and caring for others, are made more vulnerable in situations of increased pressures from unstable economic situations. As 'homemakers' and domestic carers and budgeters, women certainly shoulder some very heavy responsibilities. In Chapter 7 consideration is given to these strains in connexion with women's images of themselves and some of the attitudes in Hungary towards sexuality, women's liberation and feminism.

7 Attitudes in Transition

INTRODUCTION

This chapter concentrates on issues concerning women's autonomy and societal images of women. These two arenas highlight the gendered aspects of everyday life in terms of the control of women's bodies coupled with societal images of 'good' and 'bad' women in the context of certain social and political attitudes within Hungarian society. As has been noted, cultural change in Hungary is very slow and certainly control of the media and educational propaganda is something which does not seem to be open to less-gendered approaches in the early 1990s. Relevant questions include:

- How are images of women changing in the 1990s?
- Are linkages being made between increased availability of pornography and increasing violence against women?
- With more women working in the sex industries are attitudes changing towards these type of activities?
- How have Hungarian women been able to construct their identities within society and how have 'state' and societal forces intervened and shaped this process?[1]

Consideration is given to some of the particular pressures currently faced by women in Hungary in terms of the debate structured around the 'good' and 'bad' aspects of women gaining a measure of equality, that is, of gains/losses for women and men, and the 'relative deprivation' which some argue men have suffered.

During the 'socialist' period, the state authorities and policy-makers intervened directly in the process of basic material provision, allowing women access to the fundamental preconditions for entry into the public sphere. Given that for the generation of post-war women the disappearance of patterns of rigid, underdeveloped peasant–feudal society in Hungary did very materially mean a liberation of sorts it is important to consider the costs, for subsequent generations of women, of the rigidity of so-called 'socialist' development. Women as paid workers, domestic workers, child-bearers and child-carers are at the heart of social relations, yet so far as decision-making in these spheres is concerned women are seen to have a negligible part. In terms of attitudes about and towards women, and women's autonomy and sexuality, it would seem that changes in this area are occurring but often in contradictory manners. The 'virgin/whore' divide is becoming even more ridiculous within some situations such as economic necessity driving women to work in the sex industry.

PERSONAL AND POLITICAL ATTITUDES

Whilst there is evidence that a good deal of attitude formation takes place within the home environment, it is also the case that in Hungary for about forty years (between 1948 and 1988), people's ideas and beliefs were shaped in the public arenas of education and social activity, and from the various media – television, radio, magazines and newspapers. There are areas of contrast with Western societies, yet of course there are similarities. Perhaps the one area of direct contrast has been that of the 'public' and 'private' spheres of existence. In many Western societies it has been the politicisation of the so-called 'private' world that has been important for women's realisation and articulation of the contradictions within their everyday lives. This 'personal is political' which was so important in feminist politics generally, has been absent from Hungarian women's reality.

It is commonly accepted in Hungary, that most citizens feel that, historically, state forces entered too openly into the 'personal' area of citizen's lives and there is a marked reluctance to open up 'personal' areas to any aspect of politicisation. There is evidence that many parents 'protected' their children from 'external' politics to a very large degree, inculcating a distinct process of distancing from the political arena. If this is still the case within the more open political situation, this could have direct bearing on young people's attitudes towards any form of political group pressing for particular demands. Something of these attitudes may underlie some Hungarians' perceptions of feminist groups in other societies, and of women's activities within Hungary.

YOUNG PEOPLE'S ATTITUDES TOWARDS THE FUTURE

It is useful to consider something of the development of young people's attitudes and beliefs in connexion with education and within the wider social framework. Young people's views were often seen to be underpinned by official propaganda, in areas where parents and other family-members and friends are silent, or do not wish to intervene. Yet in terms of sex-role stereotyping within family situations, it is often actions which speak louder than words. Children watch what their parents do and often absorb ideas of their future lives from what they see around them. Three studies of young people are considered here – one in the 1970s, another in the 1980s and a third in the 1990s.

In her study about the aspirations of young people for the future Judit Sas surveyed 800 girls and boys aged between fourteen and twenty-four living in different parts of Hungary. These young people were attending primary schools, vocational schools, universities and colleges. They were asked to write essays about how they imagined their lives would be in ten years' time. When listing the family activities in which they would expect to take part, it is evident that the girls, despite the fact that they wished to work outside the home, saw most of the household tasks as their own, whilst boys not only registered the household tasks less, but rarely regarded them as tasks for themselves (see Table 7.1).

Table 7.1 Attitudes of boys and girls to family tasks (the essay-writer states whether s/he will do the task)

	Boy	*Girl*
Washing	0.0	77.0
Preparing dinner	10.7	71.5
Cleaning	33.5	74.5
Shopping	52.3	76.4
Taking children to crèche	22.0	43.4
Changing nappies	33.3	74.5
Playing with children, telling them stories	24.3	14.3

Source: Sas, 1977, p. 295.

It is evident from Table 7.1 that these young people's perceptions of life took account of the unequal social opportunities for the sexes, so far as the positions and professions open to them are concerned. In reality the young people were talking more of their present lives than the future. So far as the family goals are concerned, the imagined family remains basically an economic alliance. In their experience, after bringing children into the world and educating them, the main goal is securing the financial conditions for a good flat, furniture, a car and a comfortable environment. These are regarded as fundamental needs in Hungary in the second half of the twentieth century. In order to gain what is seen as the requisite economic security it is understandable that young girls expect to work, yet it is by no means consequential that they should expect to gain less good jobs than their spouses, nor to have less of a 'career' because of the family duties that may fall to them. In this context the counselling and training in schools could be improved, above all by abolishing the prejudices which see women as less-capable workers.

POLITICAL EDUCATION

It is not just within schools and families that young people develop their beliefs and attitudes regarding their potential futures and their expectations of those around them. The media have a strong influence in Hungary, as elsewhere. Some of the survey material available on certain aspects of media influence on children, primarily in the form of television, highlights aspects of what has been referred to as 'political socialisation'. Whilst family-members were generally considered as primary transmitters of information to children about events experienced in everyday life, the role of the television tended to dominate in those areas which have some political aspects. As is noted in Chapter 8, the political openings did bring changes in the various media. There was also a realisation of the important political messages voiced. Much media attention in 1991–2 was focused on the attempts by the ruling coalition to replace key media figures with 'loyal' political supporters.

In 1982 two researchers at the Mass Communications Research Centre working with a group of older children investigated the role that television plays in determining the political knowledge which children gained. Twenty-six concepts were put to the children and for seventeen of them over 50 per cent of the children said that they heard the most about the particular concept from television. Only twice was the family mentioned to a greater extent, and as the source of seven concepts more than half of the children claimed to have heard most about them from school. Table 7.2 shows the breakdown of this association of concepts.

An average of 62 per cent pointed to television as their primary source of comprehension of certain concepts, and 25 per cent

Table 7.2 Source of political concepts (percentage)

	Television	*School*	*At home*	*Friends*	*Not known*
Minister	96	2	1	1	–
Demonstration	95	2	–	1	2
Parliament	94	3	1	–	2
Strike	93	5	1	1	–
Politician	93	2	3	1	1
Politics	93	3	2	1	
Party secretary	86	6	6	1	1
Council chairman	86	6	4	–	4
Trade union	81	7	9	1	2
Party	81	11	6	1	1
Army	74	7	11	7	1
Socialism	72	23	3	–	2
Police	72	11	6	10	1
Capitalism	69	21	2	3	5
Working class	67	25	4	1	3
Parade	60	25	8	7	–
Revolution	59	29	2	2	7
Pioneer's scarf	1	93	1	5	–
Voluntary work	12	75	6	7	–
National anthem	24	68	6	1	1
Tricolour flag	28	68	4	2	1
Festive speech	35	62	–	2	1
Red flag	41	55	2	1	1
King	35	53	1	6	5
Money	39	4	47	10	–
God	14	11	29	19	27

Source: Fedító Szabó and György Csepeli, *The Public of the Future*, Jel Kep, Special edition Mass Comunication Research Centre, Budapest, 1984, p. 183.

named the school, whilst only 6 per cent mentioned the family and 3 per cent their circle of friends. There were only two concepts which were frequently discussed amongst friends – money and God – it is hard to say that such concepts were directly political within Hungarian society, yet both have political undertones within any society. There were certain topics – capitalism, socialism, working class, party, revolution and king – which young people associated very clearly with their school curicula rather than with television. It would seem that the school's role is primarily to popularise the symbols of national and international identity, and the formal attributes of school festivities and voluntary work. Many young people complained bitterly about the very obvious connexion between the pioneer's scarf and school. The lack of choice about joining such groups was keenly felt by young people in schools.

NEW REALISTS?

In her discussions with young people in Budapest in 1991, Mita Castle-Kanerova described these men and women as 'a new generation of realists' (Castle-Kanerova, 1992, p. xv). Certainly one of the two brothers in discussion gives a graphic picture of how he believes change has occurred in Hungary:

> People don't want to hear about socialism anymore. They are so angry with the past that they want to throw the whole thing out. But even now they have been promised things and not much has come true. Most people don't vote (Castle-Kanerova, 1992, p. 140).

Other young people talked in similar vein about how their attitudes, particularly to Hungarian politics and culture, have become more sharply attuned – they no longer have high expectations of deeper, longer-term change within society. Anna Radnóti aged sixteen, from Budapest, stated that she felt that Hungary was 'going down' and that two major problems were the economy and the culture:

> There is still 5 per cent illiteracy. I can't see it getting any better for the next ten years. I have to change my thoughts. It would be good to see Hungary like other countries, say Austria.

> It is close to us. Their life is better. That's the maximum I would like to see here. It's not democracy here now (Castle-Kanerova, 1992, p. 142).

In speaking of the women in her family who have been involved in political activity, Eszter recognised the enormity of the task, for those who believed in communism, of having to reconsider their experiences:

> In our family, my grandmother belonged to the Communist Party. She was very active in it . . . The regime made it possible for her to become very socially mobile. She came from a low class and became an intellectual. So her relationship to the whole thing was very different. But one of her daughters is in the centre as an activist for the Free Democrats. Granny then had an insight into both parties and how they worked, and we had interesting discussions before the elections (Castle-Kanerova, 1992, p. 147).

Such opportunities were probably quite rare – to be able to discuss three generations of political involvement within such different sets of circumstances. For these young people, their only real involvement with the Communist Party was in the virtually compulsory attendance at 'ritual events' or within designated organisations. Olivia's remarks are not untypical of many young people with whom I have discussed this routinised participation:

> I was most irritated by the mass organisations – the pioneers, the Communist Party. Everyone had to join. Even if you wanted to express other sentiments like patriotism, you had to join. It should be choice (Castle-Kanerova, 1992, p. 153).

It remains the case that whilst these young people have had recent opportunities to challenge some of the received myths of their younger lives, they still to some extent have to bear the legacy of so-called 'socialist' education.

LEGACIES OF 'SOCIALIST' EDUCATION

The period after 1948 in Hungary was one in which educational institutions became centralised. This had several negative consequences including a lack of flexibility in both content of courses and student/teacher choice within the curricula. Structural considerations generally outweighed educational developments. If a pupil failed in physics, the whole year would need to be taken again. Gradings were on the Soviet 1–5 scale. Within this the difference between a low and high 4 could be up to 20 per cent but within this range students had very little idea of how they were progressing. Competition was high in schools, with much time spent on homework, yet student initiative and individuality was generally frowned upon.

At higher educational levels the sterilisation of ideas imposed by the ruling authorities was such that studying politics meant learning the 'line' on Marxism/Leninism without any relation to actual power relations within Hungarian political life. In philosophy often only 'acceptable' philosophers were studied and in sociology many aspects of life – such as poverty – were too 'sensitive' to be researched. One student described learning history in Hungary in the late 1980s as being like 'reading a telephone directory'. Students had to learn dates and 'facts' such as those concerning the 'counter-revolution' in 1956.[2]

In the current situation certain educational attitudes may prove hard to 'unlearn' both for students, who became attuned to a consumerist and uncritical notion of what education concerns, and for policy-makers who choose to manipulate curricula. It may be that the propaganda factor within education will again be used to serve the interests of the ruling powers. Spokespersons for the governing coalition are very much in favour of reintroducing religious education into schools throughout Hungary and of strengthening the 'moral' context of compulsory education.

In 'socialist' Hungary it was apparent that an avoidance of the political world was encouraged within families by the exclusion of politics from the relationship between parents and children. Children learnt that politics was independent from everyday life and from people's general experience and competence. In effect this gave an impression that 'politics' is 'out there' and does not concern 'us'. Within this is the implication that things which concern 'us' – within domestic situations – are organised along different lines and within a framework of different values from those of 'their' – external – political rules. What this means, in terms of 'reactivating' community actions and everyday participation within various political situations within 'civil society' is hard to gauge. In terms of people viewing the drive for women's equality as a 'political' issue, it is also debatable.

THE POLITICS OF WOMEN'S EQUALITY

One of the main sources of propaganda about women's emancipation was the official women's organisation known as the National Council of Hungarian Women (*Magyar Nök Országos Tanácsa*). This Council is now in its fourth and, some would say, last 'phase' of existence.

In many interviews with officials from the Council it was difficult to pin them down as to what the Council actually did in terms of organising for women. The women on the Council met three or four times a year and discussed basic social problems and brought the opinions of their workplaces with them. Of the thirty-five women in the praesidium in 1987 most were party-members, elected for four years. This speaks volumes about why most people, certainly all of the women with whom I spoke, saw this as an 'official' organisation, that is, like a sub-branch of the Party. Generally, there was a big women's conference every four years, the last one being in 1981. For many Hungarian women, for whom this organisation was supposed to exist, and of whom it was supposed to be composed, the Council was seen as nothing more than a 'paper organisation'. One young mother of two explained that:

> I don't think it does anything for women's liberation. It is only a paper organisation. I've never met anybody who has been in it, I don't even know where it is and I've no idea what sort of help I could ask from them nor do I know how they work . . . I think it may have some sort of negative role, because the initiatives might just be put aside saying that 'We have this *Nök Tanács* which takes care of such things' or 'You go there and ask them about it' (Edit: Corrin, 1986).

The one aspect of this organisation which was to an extent influential was its weekly paper *Nök Lapja* (*Women's Journal*) which was the only authorised women's paper in Hungary. It had a circulation of up to 1.2 million in 1988 and may have been read by as many as five million people each week. Whilst this paper did publish articles about women earning less than men in the same jobs, or about husbands who were not prepared to help their working wives in the home, it did not attempt to suggest any remedies or to propose any appropriate courses of action. There was very much an air of reading for the 'little woman' in it, in terms of reporting important women's gatherings by means of 'what the ladies were wearing' or the fact that recipes or patterns for clothing always outnumbered any articles on women's actual lives or problems.

This Women's Organisation has been described, not because of its positive significance for the lives of Hungarian women, but because of its essentially negative influence in terms of being the only authorised women's movement within 'socialist' Hungary. The fact that this organisation existed (on paper or otherwise) meant that any other group of women wishing to organise politically around issues affecting women became *de facto* illegal.

This was the case when some women attempted to organise a protest against the passing of the legislation restricting abortions in the Council of Ministers in 1973. At this time a group of young women (mainly students) wrote a letter to members of Parliament about the disastrous effects of this restriction. In a petition, the women argued against the outlawing of abortion for certain women pointing to the harmful psychological effects of this and suggesting that this was not a means which would encourage men and women to have children. Not only would unwanted births increase, but so too would illegal abortions. These women did not argue for abortion as a preferred method of birth control. Suggestions about how to create suitable conditions for encouraging births included resolving the housing shortage and building more crèches and kindergartens, in addition to implementing the equality legislation concerning women and making men legally responsible for sharing in child-care tasks.

Whilst the proposed bill was revoked from the agenda of Parliament, it was, in unchanged form, put into force by a decree of the Ministry of Health in September of that year. The alleged organisers of the campaign were excluded from Budapest university and were unable to finish their studies. In retrospect such an event highlights the difficulties women had, before 1989, in organising around women's demands and forming active movements. Yet, as we see in Chapter 8, these difficulties have not 'magically' disappeared in the changed political climate.

The issue of abortion is obviously one which affects all women in one way or another – older women would fear for their daughters or granddaughters. This issue of reproductive rights is but one in a number of women's issues around which women all over the world are organising themselves. Certainly in East–Central Europe at present this is a very 'live' issue to which attention is given in Chapter 8. Between 1973 and 1989 there were no more such women's activities in Hungary, but as Chapter 8 notes, women were active in the 1970s and 1980s in several movements including one of the largest protest movements, against the Danube dam.

The Women's Council became separated from the state forces for obvious reasons, during 1990, and has become the Alliance of Hungarian Women. Individual women within the new Alliance with whom I spoke during 1989 certainly wanted to try to change this old, official organisation into something dynamic and helpful for women, but organisationally and practically this would be an incredibly difficult task. For example, in 1988 the Women's Council as it still was, decided to initiate a campaign to combat poverty which had become a political issue through SZETA (foundation to assist poor people) and the new political movements such as the SzDSz (Alliance of Free Democrats). The Council wanted to set up links with other active groups but such groups did not want to be involved with this organisation which they saw as another branch of the Party and therefore something which would be better abolished than changed. The basis of the Alliance's funding was questioned within the new political climate, and rooms in the beautiful building in which they are accommodated were being let out to other groups for income. As in other areas of life in Hungary in these transitional times it remains unclear whether this Alliance can breathe new life into itself or whether it will fade away in due course. Yet women from this Council are still invited to speak 'on behalf of' Hungarian women,[3] and it might well be that they are viewed in governmental circles as the 'acceptable voice'.

INTERPRETATIONS OF WOMEN'S EQUALITY

As with all events, there can be different interpretations in terms of cause and effect, genesis and consequences. So far as the tensions in human relationships in Hungary are concerned there have been two main schools of thought. According to the first view these tensions stem from the fact that too few things have happened. For many, economic pressures and male interest crossed or stopped the real emancipation of women. Women's working capacity is still secondary: economic demands and not the needs of men either edged women out of their household, or they gave an impetus for women to return there; the system of social conditions and rules continued to be formed by the decisions of men, who still play an exceptional role in deciding even those decisions that most closely refer to women as in the question of reproductive rights. The real meaning of women's equality has never been clear and this subject always receives a question mark. All this can produce a women's 'identity crisis' with women becoming less self-confident about living amongst different kinds of forces, commands, expectations and ideals, and having to decide which direction they should take.

Such an 'identity crisis' may explain the results of experimental research concerning equality, in that among eleven kinds of social inequality, that between the sexes is noted as having the least significance. As women cannot realistically be good mothers, ideal mates, working women of value and influential persons in their everyday lives, they have to choose what to give up. Each choice would harm someone – either the children, or the marriage, or the husband, or the woman herself. In addition, the social judgement of their choices is not unequivocal and it changes quickly. This first view proposes the reanalysis of the so-called 'women's problem' by both collective and individual efforts.

In the second broad interpretation it is believed that too much has happened. Neither men, nor women, nor the whole of the society were prepared for the sudden changes. No one can adapt her- or himself to such fast change, but, according to some, in the case of women's liberation it meant a special problem in that these changes were 'unnatural'. Such an interpretation holds that going against the 'laws of nature' has brought Hungarian society to a state of disintegration and imbalance. Such changes as the decreasing number of births, and the increase in the mortality rate of middle-aged men, were counted as troubles arising out of the origins of women's liberation. On first consideration, this second view may seem insupportable – is it actually unnatural for women to wish to be accepted within society on equal terms with men? Few would argue this. Yet, so far as the speed of change within Hungarian society was concerned, this is certainly considered an important factor. Although the changes in terms of industrialisation and urbanisation and those changes brought about within the 'socialist' way of life (including those since the introduction of the New Economic Mechanism – NEM) have brought with them cultural and social improvements and gains for large sections of women, they also have their disadvantages. According to this viewpoint, then, the speed of change is one reason why people in Hungary have no anchors – in both the physical and the allegorical meanings of the word.

A secondary analysis which stems from this concerns the relative deprivation which men suffer from women's attainment of some measure of equality. According to this viewpoint, with the improvement of the women's situation, men did not actually lose too much. Their greatest loss may be that they are not so well personally supplied as previously. Their absolute gain can be seen in that they are no longer solely responsible for the survival of the family. They now carry much less of the economic (and psychological?) burdens for this. So what is discussed is relative deprivation.

One author does point out in this context that the situation of women is worse from various points of view than that of men even though: 'Men have lost their cultural and economic monopolies' (Szabo, 1984, p. 81). The respect towards the *paterfamilias* has been shattered as the guiding principle of family life. This can mean that some men cannot work off the pressure they get from the outside world as they previously did, within the home – by physically or psychologically abusing their wives. Economically independent women are less prepared to bear such ill-treatment. Therefore, according to elements within this view, women's liberation is causing the middle-aged male mortality to increase, so that these independent women are killing off men! This may be because such men are not able or prepared to organise their lives to include the increasingly changing environment, and therefore see themselves as relative losers. In addition, what is involved in society's expectations of men could be seen as much less clear than society's, albeit unrealistic, expectations of women. This male 'identity-consciousness' involves men thinking through their own situation and the means to coordinate the potentials of their role, their relationships with women and the possibilities for harmonising the situation.

It seems that this process in Hungary began in a somewhat surprising form. Its most striking appearance seems to have been that of men's rebellion both in Hungary and elsewhere. Katalin Hanak writes of this that:

> The Western neo-conservative trends, which started to strengthen from the mid-1970s and started their attack at the beginning of the 1980s – while generally questioning the values of the 1960s – considered the women's movement one of their targets. In the USA the so-called 'silent majority' condemned the legal possibility of abortion based on individual decision. It identified support for the equality of women with the 'exchangeability' of the sexes(?).
>
> According to other conservative trends, the preference given to minorities in a disadvantageous position and to women in the labour market was interpreted as a discrimination against whites and men (Hanak, 1984, p. 160).

As we know it was this so-called 'silent majority' which went on to become the very vocal 'moral majority' attacking the positive views on the changing social roles of women, defending the traditional views on the family and biblical Christian morals. The speeding up of legal, economic, cultural and family equality for women caused a form of anti-women campaign, both overt and covert, in the everyday political and academic thinking. This anti-women lobby was fundamentally concerned with the primary interests of men.

This debate in Hungary began around 1982 with the work of Dávid Biró and other 'dramatic' writings in similar vein.[4] Basically, what these authors were arguing is that the situation of men is worse than that of women, which can be proved by the increasing trends showing middle-aged men dying in a higher number than women and at a faster rate. The responsibility for this worsening situation is to a small extent placed within society (environmental damages and overworking) but the primary blame is attached to women. Women, it was claimed, over-use and abuse their emancipation and use it only for having chidren, then they leave the men. They know only rights, they do not know duties. A subdivision of the men's rebellion concerned maintenance payments – many men thought it contemptible to make contributions, whether voluntarily or enforced, to their ex-wives who were looking after the children.

The very nature of the latter group of writings gives cause for concern in terms of the validity of the statements made. Many of them show examples of wrongly understood statistics, shabby or misunderstood psychological 'reasons', or in some extreme cases sweeping generalisations are made. These works are based more on prejudice than on fact. Rather than trying to understand, they search for a scapegoat, making a basic problem of society into a problem of personal life – in terms of middle-aged men dying. It is possible that some of these works were written with a deliberate intention to shock.

One explanation as to why there was a swing towards biological explanations by the anti-equality group, has to do with the question of 'ancient values'. Given that there is, in many cases, a gap between ideals and reality for women's liberation, and that economic barriers have contributed to the slowing down of social change (in terms of attitudes changing very slowly) then the growing uncertainty about values and aims has become expressed in a search for 'natural' explanations.

So far as women's equality is concerned, forming a question in terms of 'natural' aims is an imbalanced formulation. It is interesting to see in which ways, if any, these ideas are present in the attitudes and activities of young people in Hungary today. Certainly in the later 1980s there has been a certain regeneration of positive and 'grassroots' types of youth activities.

POPULAR YOUTH CULTURE

In terms of popular culture there are distinct Western influences apparent in Hungary. For pop-music fans, the Hungarian equivalent of Kylie Minogue is Szándi – a fifteen-year-old schoolgirl who has sold thousands of records. Szándi believes young people need someone of their own age with whom to identify. Her debut album *Little Girl* went 'gold' after selling 100,000 copies. By mid-1991 her second album *Teenage L'Amour* was number one in the charts. The former state record company Hungaroton manages Szándi and another popular youth group Bonanza Bonsai. Two aspects, of Western and Eastern styles, are mingled in these performances and are treated differently by young people. Questions about 'your favourite singer' are often followed by 'your favourite Hungarian singer'.

Other popular groups include Rock Cafe, True Blue Box and Tilós As A. An interesting female duo called Padoo, sing rather outspoken songs about some new problems apparent in Hungary. A group called Bikini have a song – called *Nearby Places* – about ethnic Hungarians in Romania in which they encourage Hungarians there to try to fight for their rights. In the summer of 1991 Paul Simon, The Pet Shop Boys and AC/DC all played in Budapest. With tickets at around £20.00 each, which is nearly one week's wages, these are definitely seen as very special occasions. There are many open air concerts in Hungary during each summer and some concerts are now given in the growing number of clubs. These young people's experience and exposure to Western cultural activities is very different even from their parents' generation. Given that such 'subversive' activities as playing (or listening to) rock or jazz music was not only frowned upon, but actually banned, within certain 'ex-socialist' countries, particularly Czechoslovakia, the apparent 'thirst' for Western pop culture is understandable. That in Hungary these Western forms coalesce with 'Eastern' Hungarian forms, reinforces certain recognition of Hungarian youth culture, as being neither 'Eastern' nor 'Western' but Hungarian. In this area at least, young people in Hungary seem content and confident. As noted, their political and social futures in terms of their hopes and dreams are not at all certain, especially for young women, but in terms of their likes/dislikes in music, clothing, films and entertainment they are quite definitely enthusiastic and relaxed.

GENERATIONAL DIFFERENCES

It was an enlightening experience to gauge women's responses in August 1990 when collecting signatures for the petition calling for the Hungarian government not to change the abortion laws. Three of us – two women from the Feminist Network and myself – set up a table in a subway with posters calling on women and girls to sign the petition against changes to the abortion laws. Many women – mostly in the 30–45 years age bracket – were keen to come and sign. At one point a man came up and asked us to alter the sign which said 'Women and girls' to 'Women, girls and men' which we agreed to do. The most interesting aspect of our three-hour activity was that teenage girls and young women were not in the least interested in signing the petition. In discussion with these young women it became clear that not only were abortion rights not a problem for them in the foreseeable future, in part because they either took oral contraceptives or practised some other birth-control method, but primarily because they wanted to be able to live their lives differently from their mothers. There were a number of quite complex responses in terms of 'not wanting to have that sort of life' which they associated with their mothers.

By this they were principally alluding to childhood memories of their mothers always rushing – either to work, or home from work, preparing food in the evenings whilst trying to attend to the youngsters' homework – and primarily remembering their mothers as often tired, sometimes irritable and not really 'feminine' enough. Here Anna noted that:

> It isn't that we didn't care for our mother, it was because we cared that it was hard to accept that she was always tired and seemed pale. She worked hard yet never had any fun or time for herself. I don't want to live like that. I want to enjoy my children (Anna: Corrin, 1990).

It would have been wonderful to have been able to make an in-depth study of these young women's feelings about the ways in which they hoped that their futures would be different. From our brief discussions the main point which came through clearly was that these young women did not want the sort of 'emancipated' lives which their mothers had experienced, yet could not easily identify their own future aims. Some wanted to be more 'feminine' and to have the possibility of staying at home with their children, being 'cared for' by their husbands. In the context of their history this is understandable. Other young women just wanted something 'different' from their mothers and hoped that the more open social and political scene in Hungary would offer them alternatives which were not open to their parents. The context of their desires to have experiences different from those of their mothers may well lie within the greater 'openness' of the state authorities and power structures within Hungary since 1990. Rather than being viewed as 'objects of state policy' in worker/mother roles, these young women may well be able to achieve something of a bridge between the so-called public and private expectations placed upon them.

PUBLIC/PRIVATE DIMENSIONS

In much the same way as many black families in Britain might hesitate before calling in state forces, in the form of the police, to help in a violent dispute, so many people in Hungarian families strictly avoided any entry by state officials into their domestic lives. This was the case not just with police or state officials in cases of domestic violence, but also with any willingness to criticise or problematise conflicts within families and domestic life. This made it difficult for women to articulate and problematise the oppressive nature of their private, unpaid, domestic work. Why should the burden fall on women and what was to be done about it? These were questions that various groups of Hungarian women considered, but often answers such as Ilona's were given:

> We [women] are not prepared to make our family life even harder by causing strains between ourselves and our husbands. Things are difficult enough in Hungary in these times. It is natural that women take on the majority of the work in the home, after all men work so hard in the outside world. In Hungary, you know, our family life is important to us, especially to us women (Ilona: Corrin, 1986).

As other women talked a good deal on this theme, it became clear that two factors played equally decisive parts during the 1980s in confirming women's responsibility for home work and their desire for 'smooth' family lives. The state/society divide was probably the major factor in women's desire not to problematise their extra work in the home – the domestic division of labour. Many women, knowing that their partners also worked very hard often in second and third jobs within the second economy, felt that it was reasonable for them to carry out their second or third jobs in the home and caring for children. In addition, under 'socialist' conditions there was a solidarity of people against the state forces, so that a perceived common enemy in terms of the Party/state bureaucracies meant that problematising personal relations seemed almost treacherous. It is clear that 'equality for women' has many aspects to it when deconstructed from an equality on men's terms. A major aspect of 'equality for women' has to include those equal wishes and needs for sexual satisfaction and gratification. Within this comes the importance of recognition and expression of sexuality.

ATTITUDES TOWARDS SEXUALITY

A primary conception of equality in Hungary has been based largely on the maintenance and promotion of family units and to a great extent on women's roles as mothers and workers. Sexual relationships outside marriage and the family are not encouraged.

Given the housing shortage, relationships external to the family are, practically, quite difficult but certainly many extra-marital affairs continue – 'parallel' relationships are quite common. Couples cohabiting or openly being together outside marriage are not so common. Still, the high divorce rates in Hungary have shown that with many women suing for divorce on the grounds of alcoholism/cruelty, the situation within families is not always rosy. Whilst breakdowns of sexual relationships within marriage are not generally discussed, this does not necessarily mean that such reasons for couples parting do not exist. In schools, sexual education either does not happen, or is veiled in embarrassment on the part of both teachers and pupils. In magazines, such as the old Communist *Youth Paper*, where sexuality was discussed, it was generally written about in fairly crude terms and rarely in terms of emotional and physical satisfaction. Promiscuity of any sort was generally frowned upon, and even suggested as being bad for people's health.

As to why sexual relations and sexual freedom have been surrounded with differing degrees of silence and hostility in certain 'socialist' societies there does appear to have been a connexion between revolution and puritanism – certainly the Bolsheviks tended towards puritanism, despite writings of such revolutionary women Alexandra Kollantai. In her discussion of this subject Alena Heitlinger suggested that:

> The fact that all communist-ruled countries are today authoritarian rather than revolutionary may account for some of the obstruction of sexual revolution there. It can be argued that

> sexual freedom is incompatible with a strict authoritarian rule and child-socialization within an authoritarian family. While sexual freedom and permissiveness do not necessarily politicise people and make them revolt . . . they do represent independent thinking and deviation from accepted norms. People who experiment with their personal lives might not pose any real political threat, but they do not submit easily to rigid authority (Heitlinger, 1979, p. 22).

In the puritanical attitudes created in the late 1950s, questions of sex and related intimate issues were not addressed in public, unless 'scientifically'. The 1960s 'sexual revolution' that had such a formative impact on everyday life in Western societies, was absent from Hungarian society, so there was no progressive tradition to build upon. In the outlook of states needing soldiers and therefore requiring higher birth-rates, the political implications of homosexuality did not fit with the existing role-stereotypes of masculine warriors *versus* feminine mothers. In Hungary, even after the changes of the late 1980s, homosexuals do not fit the hard-worker/good-mother roles either. Homosexual acts were illegal as 'offences against the family and youth' until 1987. As with any other minority group in Hungary, there were no publicly known homosexual-rights groups. One of the few male homosexual bars in the 1980s was Egyetem in Budapest, but there seemed to be no such places for lesbians to meet. It was commonly understood that some homosexual men and lesbians married each other because of strong social and state pressure.[5] As marital status is considered crucial to some jobs this seems likely, and such marriages would help the people concerned to get some form of apartment – eventually. Few people discussed homosexuality in Hungary and even the most 'enlightened' members of the democratic opposition seemed to view homosexuality as 'unnatural'.

Section 199 of the Penal Code provides for a higher age of consent for gays and lesbians (18) than for heterosexuals (14) according to Section 201. The prison term for a violation of Section 199 is up to three years. A group called Homosexual Association for Leisure and Health Prevention (*Homeros Homoszexuálisok Szabadidős és Egészségvédő Egyesülete*) applied for recognition in October 1987. In January 1988 a speaker for the Ministry of Health and Social Affairs announced that the authorities would allow the founding of a gay and lesbian organisation. This organisation is now formed but has taken some time to get any real recognition.

Yet there were writers and artists who portrayed positive, or less negative, aspects of women's sexuality in Hungary. In 1980 Erzsébet Galgóczi's novel *Another Love* was published and two years later a film version was made. Essentially the semi-autobiographical novel parallels the life of a lesbian dissident, Eva Szalánczky, with the political 'life' of Hungary, following the 1956 revolution. Galgóczi looks at aspects of Hungarian history, culture and politics in coming to an understanding of post-war Hungary and particularly the devastation which the 1956 events caused. In expressing her intellectual and sexual identities the central character, Eva, is firmly situated in the historical and political realities of Hungary at that time. It is an exciting and yet a sad novel: exciting in that it realistically recreates the dangers of opposition during those years, yet sad in the impossibility of Eva being able to freely express her lesbian love or have it returned. Given that few women actually identified as 'leszbikus' in Hungary, even up to the 1980s, it is interesting that the film version, by Károly Makk, was instantly successful in Hungary. There is an irony that two Polish actresses, Jadwiga Jankowsk-Cieslak and Grazyna Szapolowska, were engaged to play the leading women parts. No Hungarian actress wanted to be associated with lesbian characters. Certainly, the combination of a leading woman who is daring enough to be a political dissident and a lesbian is a fiery one.

Another Hungarian artist whose work depicts women's strength and acknowleges lesbian identity is that of Ágnes Hay. Her cartoon series entitled *The Frog Saga* which was displayed in Budapest in 1987 was openly sexual and showed a small (female) frog experiencing various visions of sexuality. In one cartoon vaginas are being chased by large penises and the frog ends up in bed with a collar around its neck, next to a penis. Eventually the frog diminishes in size until it can slip the collar and run away. There are various 'endings' to *The Frog Saga*, including a lesbian-ending in which vaginas happily live together. When discussing her work in 1987 Ágnes claimed that she 'is not a feminist' but several of her sketches, including a series based on male and female symbols, with women's symbols hanging in butchers' shops or waiting on plates to be eaten, have been featured in Western feminist magazines. Ágnes was also involved in oppositional culture in Hungary in the 1980s around *samizdat* publishing with György Krassó. These women are examples of the different ways of thinking within Hungarian intellectual life which may now find more ways of expression.

Official attitudes to homosexuality seem to be largely similar everywhere in the industrialised world. Homosexuality is seen as a threat as it challenges the generally accepted monogamous, heterosexual family development. It is also seen as a threat by example to young people who are more open to question 'received wisdom' on all things. In most Western countries homosexuality is no longer illegal and although most lesbians and gay men experience discrimination to a greater or lesser extent, groups such as lesbian mothers do exist and will continue to develop support networks. Britain though is moving towards recriminalising men's homosexuality and making custody cases and adoptions for lesbians much more difficult. Lesbians and gay men in Hungary still live under the shadow of oppression, so it is unlikely that they would be tempted to 'come out' to their heterosexual friends or colleagues. The net result is that not only is homosexuality not discussed in the media, workplace, home or school, but perhaps because it is not discussed, it is regarded as 'sick', unnatural or at best immoral. Another so-called 'immoral' group within Hungarian society concerns those who are involved in prostitution.

PROSTITUTION

In 1949–50 all licenced brothels in Hungary were closed down. Prostitutes were trained for other professions, a large number became taxi-drivers. Many of them took up taxi stands outside the large hotels frequented by Western tourists and managed to work as prostitutes occasionally. There was no 'professional prostitution' in Hungary in the forty years before 1990, as it was illegal and punishable by up to one year's imprisonment, or up to three years for recurrent offenders. Inducing a person into professional prostitution received sentences from six months to five years and anyone managing a brothel, aiding a person to enter prostitution or living off the earnings of a professional prostitute could be punished by up to three years imprisonment, with increases of sixmonths to five years for recidivists.

Official statistics show very little on this subject, and the number of women arrested for prostitution is very small – only 127 in 1983. Cases of prostitution were reported in the Hungarian press and in 1985 there was a quite sensational case in which a 'prostitution ring' was discovered and punished. The 'Csuki gang' was a Hungarian prostitution ring that procured women for foreign truck drivers in return for hard currency. This gang operated out of the Csuki Espresso bar, which had been managed by Kálmán Racs (later nicknamed the gang's 'Godfather'). The bar's upswing in trade began in mid-1983 when prostitution was made available. It was in December 1984 that the gang was caught and they were tried in Szeged in May 1985. Racs was sentenced to three years and four months imprisonment on charges of procuring and currency offences. Whilst the shuttle service drivers received sentences of between twenty-two months and three years, the women all served between five and fourteen months. Instances such as this continued to be an embarrassment to the 'socialist' authorities in Hungary – as this 'immoral remnant of the bourgeois era' was supposedly eliminated.

In addition, a film was made (possibly based on these events) which centred on a young entrepreneur living on a large housing development on the outskirts of a city. This young man was a wall-driller, *falfuro*, which was the title of the film. The sexual connotations of his carrying his drill and drilling (the equivalent of 'screwing' in English) were abundant. In this film there was a prostitution circle of women (mainly younger women who were at home claiming the child-care allowance) who earned extra money by 'escorting' men at parties and having sex with them. There was no moral message in the film, other than that some of those involved were caught and punished, but the major impression which the film left was one of the bleakness of 'high rise life' in poverty and within this the obvious lure of money, drink and fun. One centre of prostitution in Budapest, Rákóczi tér, became a very well-known symbol. In the late 1980s a musical was written about it. There was also a very controversial documentary '*K*' (short for whore) made in 1988 about Hungarian prostitutes.

In 1990 only thirty-eight cases were recorded involving charges of prostitution, despite the fact that many more women are working in the streets. The Supreme Court heard the last prostitution charge some three years ago. Police in Hungary are currently linking prostitution with organised crime, which they claim is much harder to solve. This whole subject, of women earning money by selling sex is a difficult one for analysts – feminists and others. The whole subculture apparent in societies which do not have legalised brothels (and some of those which do), often appears as one of exploitation through sex, drugs and violence with male 'pimps' taking any money there is to be made. In the 'socialist' context, though, this was yet another area in which the expected changes in 'socialist morality' (with the socialisation of the means of production and the intervention of socialist policies in society) do not seem to have occurred, or have done so in an incomplete or unexpected way. In *The Origins of the Family*, Engels wrote that:

> Prostitution . . . demoralises men far more than women. Among women prostitution degrades only the unfortunate ones who become its victims . . . But it degrades the whole male world (Engels, 1976, p. 237).

Within Marxist analysis alienation in its starkest form was present in the condition of workers. For women, their general (alienated) relationship to men was one of prostitution, but this was only a specific expression of the workers' universal prostitution. Both these conditions could be changed only within a communist society. Yet, as Sheila Rowbothan points out, it is unclear how women are supposed to galvanise themselves to get out of their specific form of prostitution because there is no concept of an historical agency of women:

> Woman is still the other, part of the world outside as perceived, grasped, controlled by man . . . She appears as an indication of the state of society, not as a social group in movements, developing consciousness of history (Rowbotham, 1972, p. 63).

Such debates are now far away from the reality of street life in Budapest and other large towns in Hungary. Since 1990 many more women are 'working the streets', often very young women from the poorest groups and from rural areas with a high proportion being young Roma women. Prostitution is now important for survival for some women. It is hard to envisage how else some women can earn money. Perhaps one form of protection would be the establishment of a union, like the British Collective of Prostitutes, so that women working as prostitutes could protect their rights.

WORKING IN THE SEX INDUSTRY

Between 1990 and 1991 the sex industry in urban Hungary has expanded as a very definite growth area. In almost every district of Budapest bright neon signs light up lurid photo displays in attempts to attract customers. These 'erotic' nightclubs operate in a situation in which the laws are still unclear and unenforced. Presumably when the 'novelty wears off' and restrictions become clearer, many of these clubs might close. For the women working in them though they provide possibilities which were not present in 'socialist' times. Women working in the clubs appear to have a good deal of choice in the way they work and offer varying reasons as to why they choose this type of work. In her interviews with topless dancers Zsuzsa Ersek notes that one of the main attractions of certain clubs is that the women are encouraged to sit on the men's laps and invite foreplay in exchange for tips. One dancer explains her reason for taking the job:

> I didn't really plan to take this job. I had quit school because I didn't like it and moved back to my family. I was bored at home and I heard about this job. I decided to try it because strange things always attract me. I had no idea what to expect, really ('Ildikó', *Budapest Week*, 26 June 1991).

The answers mainly centre upon money, 'I can earn ten times more money here than people generally do. When I go over to the men, I get 500 to 1000 forints' ('Edit', ibid.). But not all women put the earning potential at the top of their list, and not all the women are from Hungary. Most clubs have at least one 'foreigner' be she from the former USSR or Romania and such women are often in very vulnerable situations, sending home food parcels and hoping they will be kept on when their visas expire. The present chaotic situation *vis-à-vis* the gaps in the laws will presumably be tightened in the coming years. Proposals have included that of some representatives from the Christian Democrats which suggested isolating part of Budapest for the sex trade

– a form of 'red-light area'. There is a cultural committee in Parliament which aims to enact some general legislation to avoid any extremist backlashes.

PORNOGRAPHY

Whilst there is a certain degree of male machismo within the Hungarian culture which allows for the treatment of women as sexual objects, this attitude was not heavily reinforced by strip clubs or brothels during 'socialist' times. Over the past ten years there has been a marked increase in the availability and acceptance of pornographic material in Hungary. Postcard-stands regularly displayed pictures of naked women or scantily clothed women dating from the mid-1980s. When all restrictions on pornography were lifted in 1990 there has been a virtual 'explosion' of pornography with strip clubs, sex taxis, pornographic magazines and videos freely available almost everywhere. With over forty pornographic magazines available, imported and domestically produced, the situation was becoming intolerable, with pornographic material on sale next to children's schoolbooks. The women's anti-pornography group made some stickers reading 'PORNO – why do you only adopt the bad things from democracy?' and stuck them over sexist advertising and pornographic pin-ups, magazines and books. These women realised that after the oppressive climate of the previous forty years for them to ask for the prohibition of pornography, which many argued was a 'liberal' aspect of 'the market', would not be acceptable. What they did demand was some legislation to stem the flood. In January 1991, the Mayor of Budapest, Gábor Demsky, banned newspaper kiosks near to schools from displaying pornography. Small victories such as this at least boosted women's confidence to continue their efforts.

VIOLENCE AGAINST WOMEN

There are various perspectives from which to analyse male violence against women. Rather than viewing male violence as individually motivated with few social consequences, feminist analyses argue that male violence has all the characteristics of a social structure and cannot be understood outside an analysis of patriarchal social structures (see Walby, 1990). Of three main theoretical approaches liberalism explains violence in terms of certain men's psychological derangement, class analysis looks at the frustrations of disadvantaged men whilst radical feminism considers male violence to women in terms of male power in a patriachal society. Feminist campaigns in many countries have led to the recognition of such violence as criminal and therefore not to be condoned by state forces. From the 1970s women's campaigns have led to the establishment of safe houses (refuges) for women suffering domestic violence and to specialised counselling, sometimes through 'rape crisis' lines, for women suffering violence.

In Hungary there is little or no information available on male violence against women. The very terms in which crimes are viewed, with indecent assault being considered an 'Offence against the Family and Youth', punishable by between six months' and five years' imprisonment – show that it is the 'ideal women' within families who deserve protection, not *all women* as their right. Rape is illegal (except within marriage). If 'force or threat' is used, or if a woman is unable to defend herself or to express her will, the penalty is two to eight years imprisonment. If the person attacked is under the care, supervision or medical treatment of the rapist, or if the attack is against a minor, or is gang rape, the penalty is five to twelve years imprisonment. There is evidence that if the accused rapist marries the victim before sentencing, then the punishment may be more lenient! Marital rape is not recognised by law. Official statistics for rape are not very high (in international comparison), ranging from 802 cases in 1973 (the highest) to 430 in 1977, 562 in 1981 and 654 in 1985. Reports of rape occasionally appear in the press as in the case of the boy of fifteen who killed his stepfather after he (the stepfather) had raped the boy's 13-year-old sister on several occasions when he was drunk.[7]

As with almost every country in the world, the number of reported rapes is probably so low because of prejudicial attitudes towards this crime and because raped women are, understandably, reluctant to go to the police. Obviously, the very nature of rape makes it an acute problem and the fact that no centres exist in Hungary where women can go for sympathetic support, means that women who have been raped suffer under the double burden of the attack and then, very often, having to deal with the consequent mixed emotions (of perhaps fear, guilt and shame) alone. Incidents of violence against women in domestic or public situations are seldom reported in the Hungarian press and official statistics on such crimes are hard to find. There is a good deal of everyday violence against women on the street in the form of verbal abuse and personal assaults which are hardly ever reported. Whilst there is no information available specifically on domestic violence, the general assault laws make battery illegal, and punishable by up to one year's imprisonment if the injured party recovers within eight days, or up to three years if the injured person suffers longer. Yet, whilst 'wife-beating' as it is commonly spoken of, is officially frowned upon, it is still considered by many to be a private affair between men and women. Certain reports show that the high rate of male alcoholism results in much battery and it is a fairly commonplace topic that 'so-and-so's husband hits her regularly'. 'Wife-beating' is not listed separately among crimes, but it is frequently cited as a cause for divorce, being politely called 'mental cruelty' by some women and 'rough handling' by others. There are no statistics available on battery, nor are there any special centres where women can go for help. Telephone lines equivalent to 'The Samaritans' exist in Budapest and certain of the big towns, but these are seen to be more generally available for potential suicide victims or young people with drug–drink problems, and there are far too few lines even to attempt to meet this demand. Most women who are battered feel there are few options open to them in terms of actually becoming separated (physically) from their violent husbands, primarily because of the lack of other places for the men to go. Even divorced couples often have to carry on sharing their marital home as there are no other possibilities available. Those women who are working towards developing SOS telephone lines and refuges for women have to cope not only with the persistent problems of funding and access to buildings and equipment, but also with the problems of being labelled 'feminist' and thereby not people to be taken seriously.

ATTITUDES TOWARDS FEMINISM

It would seem that feminism, often specifically 'Western feminism' is portrayed within the Hungarian media as something unnatural, and very bourgeois, certainly not something to which Hungarian women would wish to relate. When asked her opinion of feminist demands that men share all housework, one middle-aged mother of two replied:

> No. It isn't natural in Hungary. I could follow the lifestyles of couples where the woman is too manlike, too strong and who wants to divide all the work 50:50. These marriages after a time break down . . . It is too much for our culture that women are so strong and so equal because changes here in Hungary in all areas are very slow. Traditions are very deep (Mária: Corrin, 1986).

The word 'natural' is certainly much used/abused in debates about women's equality, and it is something which the media have had a hand in emphasising – that Hungarian women are 'naturally' kind, gentle, loving mothers and wives and not hard-hearted, selfish, grasping, 'feminist-type women', like certain feminists in the West. In terms of personal socialisation of Hungarian citizens then, it can be seen that whilst they may not agree with the official views of homosexuality being bad because fewer children might be born or whatever, the more (or in some cases less) subtle forms of socialisation through the media portrayal of what feminism is really about do affect the way that Hungarian women view feminism and feminist arguments. One young woman who was well-read and had an intellectual job which enabled her to travel to the West occasionally, when asked if she knew anything of the women's movements elsewhere, replied 'No, very little. Only from gossip – very funny or strange things. For example that they hate men, or they want men to bear children, etc. They make it all seem ridiculous here' (Judit: Corrin, 1986).

Several women when asked about women's movements in other countries replied that they knew very little, or that what they did know was probably distorted or one-sided. The whole question of women's liberation has become a 'loaded' one and some women go so far as to say they would not wish to become liberated women in the sense that they hear and see of liberation movements in the West. Such liberation, several women felt, goes too far, rather than wanting women to be equal they seemed to want women to be more equal than men. There is of course the counterpoint to this in that if 'socialism' was 'liberation' for women then many women in Hungary felt that they have had too much 'liberation' anyway! Most women stated that problems between men and women should be sorted out within families, and all stressed the need for more communication, more face-to-face talking between men and women. As time seems so precious, with people working long hours, sometimes there is even less discussion between women and men and less time to try to solve problems in peaceful ways.

REOPENING THE FEMINIST DEBATE

In the late 1980s there was an emergence of debates concerning feminism within the Hungarian press. An article called 'Where has Hungarian feminism gone?' was published in the weekly *Life and Literature* on 1 May 1987. The author, Pál Tamás, begins his work by reporting a discussion with his sociology students concerning attempts to define feminism. He notes that 'for the boys this is a rather dangerous and hardly conceivable women's aspiration for power (Tamás, 1987, p. 5), Whereas the young women in the group, whilst not classifying themselves as feminist – 'this would mean somethings unwomanly' –were of the opinion that feminism is not an aggressive phenomenon. In their opinion the successful woman and the feminist are contradictory poles. Tamás notes that 'according to nine out of ten recently interviewed professional women, the feminist has in some way become disappointed in the other sex. This disappointment is transferred into an ideology' (Tamás, 1987, p. 5).

This picture fits very much that given by most of the women who talked with the author – that is, feminism is seen by many women in Hungary as a negative, somewhat embittered movement, rather than as a positive force for change and development. Tamás points out that little of the feminist literature of the 1960s has been published in Hungary, and he notes that amongst the few 'educated' social scientists and journalists who are aware of the existence of ecological movements, alternative movements, and the New Left, they do not even know the names of the most disputed feminist ideologists. Despite the difficulties of 'getting things started' in terms of various movements in Hungary, Tamás asserts that of all the 'foreign intellectual movements' only feminism has been missed by Hungarians. There are some standard 'reasons' given for this which include the fact that feminism has never existed in Hungary, even the suffragettes at the turn of the century were isolated in Hungary, and as soon as the Hungarian bourgeois radicalism slipped out of intellectual life, so Hungarian feminism also disappeared.

The second version proposed is that no 'isms' of any kind exist within Hungarian society so that an autonomous women's movement is bound to have problems, given women's inexperience in public affairs. Yet another 'answer' is that the basic aims of the Western feminist movements have been fulfilled, so that feminist movements would only serve to increase women's problems in Hungary, and as people in the West do not seem to have realised that Hungary is over such problems this is one of the reasons why feminism is laughable, or occasionally annoying, for Hungarians.

In the final version – probably the most common – the argument goes, 'Have we not troubles enough with problematising the female/male relationship?'. In this view other things are more important, so that if feminism is concentrated upon, 'real conflicts' are avoided. This argument is not uncommon within the Western left. According to this version, women and men must work together to fight social injustice. Tamás goes on to point out that whilst there was a Hungarian feminist movement at the turn of the century, the Association of Feminists, which published a journal called *Women and Society*, it did not become a real political force.

Discrimination still exists for Hungarian women workers in terms of the devaluation of 'feminised' profession:

> At the same time a group of highly educated, self-respecting, well-to-do women with a lot of leisure time, is missing in Hungary, which is the basis of the Scandinavian and American upper middle class feminism (Tamás, 1987, p. 6).

The lack of a women's movement in Hungary has meant, in Tamás' view, that state regulations which worsen women's situation, such as the restrictions on abortion and the new divorce act, are not being 'adequately resisted'.

Given that at least some of the conservative beliefs associated with public participation in politics have now been challenged and that a Parliament of the multiparty, more democratic variety is now in place, it remains to be considered in Chapter 8 how the reforms in the political world will be reflected in women's everyday worlds.

CONCLUSION

It is perhaps in the personal/political realm that Hungarian people's attitudes could be seen to differ from those in other advanced industrialised countries. It is evident that Hungarian citizens became used to a strong, protective state framework, yet were not prepared for the state forces to intervene too directly into their very 'private' lives. So far as attitudes towards women's equality are concerned, one point is forcefully made by Mária Márkus in terms of women not even being viewed as equals within the workforce, the entry to which in the 'socialist' period had 'liberated' them:

> Firstly, because the dominant 'instrumentalist' attitude towards women makes use of the very strong, conservative, patriarchal practices and values of the majority of the population. And – as everywhere – where no real movement challenges them, these values are, to a degree interiorised by women themselves; they constitute a part of the socialisation model. Secondly, this is so, because the incorporation of women into the 'public economy' almost completely realised in Hungary, was accomplished without the creation of the corresponding conditions necessary to ensure an equal participation of women in professional life (Márkus, 1979, p. 25).

Differences between the ways that women are viewed as workers and as mothers feed into differing notions of 'roles'. In terms of attitudes towards women's political participation, generally in Hungary there appears to have been a conservative attitude that as 'politics is a dirty business' it should be left to the men. In this context the distancing which parents cultivate, consciously or otherwise in their children from 'external' politics is one which seriously changes the terms of debate when considering 'political activity', in terms of, say, women's liberation. This subject, of the possibilities for and barriers to, the development of Hungarian women's movements, is considered again in the final chapter.

So far as sexuality is concerned, it was expected that under 'communism', free from their economic dependence upon men, women would share in the new human relationships thus made possible. This belief was based on the attainment of a situation of both material and moral advancement from capitalism. That is, women would have to be able to support themselves adequately, together with any children, women or men they chose to care for, in addition to being part of the community with equal sexual rights and expectations. Yet, as has been shown, the void created by 'official' negligence on sexual matters and the lack of everyday openness was so easily filled by pornography after the rapid liberalisation in the late 1980s. In Hungary, as in many other areas, certain present-day attitudes towards homosexuality are often legacies of a rigid official mentality which had an 'instrumental' attitude towards human sexuality. Putting this crudely, this attitude equates sex with procreation and sexuality as an area in which 'control', both personal and social, is necessary. It is within this area that the illogical, biological arguments again come to the fore in terms of 'natural' and 'unnatural' sexuality. This also has major implications for women's 'choice' in terms of controlling their own bodies and their fertility. The Christian–nationalist (largely Catholic) attitudes of the current ruling coalition are unlikely to welcome any 'opening-up' of debates on sexuality and freedom of individual choice.

So far as social attitudes towards male violence against women are concerned, the situation in Hungary seems to be such that so long as violence against women is considered as an 'issue for women' it will not become problematised, and therefore dealt with, as a social problem. The feminist perspective by which violence is analysed within patriarchal social relations allows the 'private' violence to be recognised as an illegitimate abuse of power by men over women. Certainly there are the beginnings of work being done in this area in Hungary, by Hungarian feminists, as is seen in the final chapter. Yet, for the most part at present, women are often 'privately' having to bear the brunt of increasing competitiveness and violence within Hungarian society.

From the two sides of the 'equality/anti-equality' debate issues concerning the liberation of women have engendered some partial debates in Hungary. These have been largely intellectual debates and have not had any wider social significance. Such a lack of debate often signifies a lack of interest in a particular situation, which could mean that women and their needs and wants are not considered 'important' within Hungarian society. It is some aspects of this question which are now to be assessed in terms of how far the changes since the demise of Kádár and the Party have opened up the Hungarian political scene since 1988–9 and whether more civic spaces are being created for women's social and political participation at various levels in Hungarian society.

8 Politics in Transition

INTRODUCTION

With the democratic developments and the formation of new political cultures in Hungary the questions for many women within the current political context include:

- Have these political openings brought with them spaces for women's activities?
- If so, how can such activities be considered and compared in terms of 'formal' participation, community activities and/or feminist politics?
- What are women's relationships to formal and informal politics in Hungary today?
- How are women's activities being defined in the 'new' Hungary?
- What are the possibilities for women's cooperation and networking into the 1990s?

Within this discussion the overall meaning of equality is central. Equality on whose terms and towards what visions of future society? By considering something of women's activities within Hungary over recent years some potential answers to these questions emerge. The speed of events in 1989 caught almost everyone, especially the political leaderships, by surprise. It could not have been foreseen how quickly changes would occur following the June 1989 elections in Poland. As noted in Chapter 2, the rapid loosening of the power of the Hungarian Communists during their efforts at 'controlled reform' pushed the opposition social movements into an electoral situation more quickly than was envisaged.

With events in the former GDR, Czechoslovakia and Romania following in quick succession, the Hungarian case could appear rather unexciting. Of course the pace and history of change in each of these countries was very different, with Poland and Hungary having a much richer recent history of oppositional activities, so that communist power was becoming undermined from the early 1980s. Developments in Hungary and Poland placed the leaders in Prague and East Berlin in difficult situations. Events in Czechoslovakia, former GDR and Romania became telescoped and seemed more 'revolutionary' than 'refolutionary' (a mixture of reform from above and revolution from below) as Garton Ash might have it (Ash, 1990, p. 14). In 1989 these regimes were showing the weaknesses that had been 'papered over' in preceding years. That they had supposedly provided security of life in terms of employment, housing and basic material necessities now had to be assessed against the reality of economic decline temporarily bolstered by Western borrowing. The disastrous policies followed by the Communist leaderships up to the late 1980s did have one rationale – the maintenance of the Party's hold on power.

POLITICAL CHANGES FROM 1989

There are now many accounts of the election processes in Hungary (Vasary, 1991; Racz, 1991). Consideration here is given to several important features concerning the nature of post-communist politics in Hungary. First, the methods of selecting political legislators was such that the cores of each political group emerged from the tight political networks of the former opposition. Whilst these individuals were well-known within their own circles, generally in Budapest, they were not widely known throughout Hungary. A second group were professionals who had been coopted into the new élite as experts in the three-sided (triangular) talks, the Hungarian version of the Polish 'round-table' talks. The third group entered Parliament because the parties needed candidates at local levels. As it was important that these local candidates did not have communist connexions, many came forward from professions, such as doctors, priests or teachers.

Various factors, such as candidates being little-known, the barely distinguishable 'party programmes', an election campaign fought as battles between groups/indidividuals rather than on issues, and a complex and confusing electoral process, meant that turnout at elections decreased. At the first poll in March 1990 average turnout was 63 per cent nationally and in the second round in April it dropped to 45.5. per cent. That parties had no roots within the population and were not representing people's interests, meant that none of the foregoing negative factors were cushioned by party identification and allegiances. Pleased as Hungarian citizens initially were with the new, democratic opportunities opening up, there was also a sense of muddle and chaos about the elections, not least because of the complex voting system. Several older people with whom I spoke in polling booths on the first-round election were clearly having difficulty finding the Party/candidate for whom they wished to vote. Considering the declining number of people voting, the staggeringly high vote in smaller communities for those 'independents' was a shock to the parties in parliament. This has since led to a measure of confusion as to where power lies and how relations are mediated from centre to region, and from region to locality. The turnout of 18 per cent at a local election in September 1991 highlighted a further element of people's disillusionment. Basically, the 1990 election produced a parliament of male, well-educated and politically inexperienced representatives. Despite the fact that women in Hungary had certainly been very active within different party offices and in the polling booths on election days in March and April 1990 they were clearly not represented within the parliament.

REPRESENTATION OF WOMEN

One noticeable feature of the new government was a distinct absence of women. Table 8.1 the representation across the parties of women Members of Parliament.

As can be seen, Table 8.1 includes the MPs' 'family situation', which would not be included for male MPs. It is perhaps notable that individuals such as Solt Ottilia and Szelényi Zsuzsa have not had their family situations included. There is only one female minister-without-portfolio in the Cabinet, and of the thirty-three under-secretaries only two are women. Although 17 per cent of mayors are women, this figure falls to 3 per cent in the cities (of over 10 000 inhabitants). Just 5 per cent of presidents of big companies, 14 per cent of bank directors and 7 per cent of rectors of universities are women. There are few women in leading positions in political parties or trade unions (see Katalin Koncz, *Women's International Network News*, WN, vol. 18, no. 2, Spring

Table 8.1 Women Members of Parliament in Hungary, 1991

Name	*Party*	*Family situation*
Béke Kata	MDF	
Béke Gabriella	SzDSz	divorced, 2 children
Bossányi Katalin	MSzP	married, 1 child
Dotos Katalin	MDF	married, 2 children
Büky Dorottya Sára	SzDSz	married, 1 child
Dr Csehák Judit	MSzP	divorced, 2 children
Dr Dávid Ibolya	MDF	married, 2 children
G. Nagyné Dr Baczó Agnes	MDF	married, 3 children
Dr Hajdu Istvánné	FKgP	married, 2 children
Hága Antónia	SzDSz	married, 2 children
Hodosán Róza	SzDSz	married
Jakab Róbertné	MSzP	
Király B. Izabella	MDF	married, 1 child
Kónyáné Dr Kutrucz Katalin	MDF	married, 2 children
Dr Kóródi Mária	SzDSz	married, 1 child
Kósányé Dr Kovács Magda	MSzP	married, 2 children
Lakatos Józsefné	FKgP	divorced, 1 child
Dr Pusztai Erzsébet	MDF	married, 1 child
Dr Remport Katalin	MDF	
Rózsa Edit	SzDSz	divorced, 1 child
Solt Ottilia	SzDSz	
Dr Szabó Erika	SzDSz	
Szelény Zsuzsa	FIDESZ	
Dr Tarján Lászlóné	FKgP	married, 2 children
Dr Ugrin Emese	KDNP	single
Ungár Klára	FIDESZ	divorced, 1 child
Vargáné Piros Ildikó	Peasant assocn.	married, 1 child

Source: Personal communication to the author, adapted from parliamentary printouts.

1992). Two women have since left Parliament so that in 1992 there were twenty-six women out of a total of 386 members.

Of these twenty-six only Solt Ottilia has written anything recently concerning women's situation in Hungary. Her article in Beszélö early in 1991 stressed the need for women to organise themselves to gain proper representation of their interests to compensate for the absence of women in politics. Several MPs with whom I spoke stressed that they do not think that women have particular needs or interests which need representation. In the SzDSz, and to a lesser extent, the Hungarian Democratic

Forum (MDF), women politicians often echo their male colleagues in stating that the most urgent task facing Hungary today is to 'sort out the economy' and everything else must follow that. Given the previous discussion of poverty and those vulnerable groups for whom there is inadequate or no social provision, this single-minded attitude is hard to comprehend.

What are the consequences of this virtual absence of women within the political élites?

Given that the quota systems under the former regimes had largely meant 'women in seats', rather than politically active women voicing demands in the decision-making arenas, was it to be expected that there would be a sudden increase in women politicians? It seems more plausible that the legacies of communist politics would affect women's representation most critically for two major reasons. First, the idea that politics is a 'dirty business' which some men are prepared to undertake, yet few women are willing to become power-holders. Within this is also the legacy of the public/private divide in Hungary, in which women are perceived to be more concerned with the domestic side of the new politics, in terms of assisting active men, and working in the offices and on policy documents – 'behind the scenes'.

The second argument is that 'people would not vote for women'. Although this argument was voiced in general terms many times during the Hungarian elections, the prejudice behind it became most clear in the case of the 'Socialist' (ex-Communist) Party leader, Anna Petresovits. Whilst Ms Petresovits was widely criticised, mainly because of her politics, she was also quite blatantly criticised for the way in which she dressed, and was generally given the 'gossip' treatment by several national newspapers. No other candidates were criticised for their dress sense, despite an apparent lack on the part of some male candidates. This second aspect seems to be part of an overall prejudice within Hungary against the notion of women as powerful, capable and able to assume leadership qualities. Some of this prejudice has been internalised by women themselves so that some of Petresovits' worst critics were indeed women. Yet former British Premier, Margaret Thatcher had a good press within Hungary as strong leader. 'The Iron Lady' was also very much admired, within certain circles, for her strong views on the need for privatisation and to cut back on 'welfare scroungers'. The double-edged nature of debates on 'widening' within the EC during 1990 also brought her much praise in Hungary, despite the questioning within domestic circles as to whether this issue concerned inclusion of Hungary in the European Community or Britain's loss of 'sovereignty'.

Given the inequalities in terms of the time and effort women put into work within the home in comparison with men, and the increased responsibility that women take for child-care, women generally have much less 'free' time for politics which often involves evening and weekend meetings. Whatever the underlying reasons for women's reluctance to participate at the higher levels of decision-making and citizens' reluctance to support women who chose to stand for such office, the concern of this chapter lies with those women who do want to challenge their lack of representation in decision-making positions and trade unions. Such women are calling for radical changes in the overall approach to women's issues and are dissatisfied with many aspects of their situation. These women's groups and organisations are trying to translate their dissatisfaction into political action. Since their first beginnings, these groups have been fighting very much 'against the odds' but do have a women's 'herstory' upon which to build.

ACTIVE WOMEN

It seems to have been assumed in some Western writings that there were no 'real' women's activities within central and eastern Europe prior to 1989. Perhaps this misconception stems from those viewing women's activities through the lens of Western feminism, but clearly women have been active in political movements throughout central and eastern Europe for a long time. A fundamental point to remember is that as women in a 'socialist' context were recognised publicly as workers, then this tended to be the political context within which they were seen to be active. Given the devastating legacy of 1956 and the changing situation in terms of the NEM and the second economy, there were different levels of struggle taking place, in which women were active, again, within the so-called 'private' sphere of fighting state encroachment into family lives and of engaging in alternative work – bypassing state interventions. The strains for

Hungarian women and men in taking these opportunities to work harder in order to be able to survive are all too clear in the early 1990s. Even though women were viewed primarily as workers (and mothers) in the same way as their counterparts in Poland and elsewhere, oppositional activity in Hungary could be seen to be 'privatised' in a curious way. Both the results of the NEM and the parallel growth of the second economy within Hungary, meant that rather than resisting state forces by direct confrontation, Hungarian citizens were resisting in alternative forms of by-passing state activities through privately-generated work and spending.

A whole 'second society' of another sort was developing within Hungary, in both rural and urban areas, and the state forces as they were then structured could not easily directly intervene in these processes. Rural people stepped up their work on domestic plots so that they were not only producing enough for their own consumption but more for sale on open markets. In towns, the semi-legalised work on factory machines for other suppliers in the evenings was much better-paid than machinists' day jobs.

One of the consequences of this form of resistance through extra work, was that many people in Hungarian society were working up to fourteen hours daily, often at weekends and through their 'holidays'. This activity was challenging the existing state structures in a number of ways, primarily by opposing the Party/State monopoly of power relations *vis-à-vis* employment, house-building and activities around control of markets in labour, goods and scarce resources. There was a form of *embourgeoisement* emerging which set up differing expectations throughout Hungarian society, part of which concerned political expression and representation. Within this divisions between 'rich and poor' became sharper and more apparent as state support for vulnerable groups was not keeping pace with other changes. So far as political representation of various groups within Hungarian society was concerned most of the main six parties went for a broad-based appeal with the possible exception of two. The Socialist Party restated its claim to represent particular groups within society, basically working people whose livelihoods would become threatened by privatisiation and marketisation processes. Included within their brief were working women, for whom they claimed to uphold arguments of 'women's equality' *vis-à-vis* the workplace at least. The second party which seemed to have a particular constituency (which was later to prove very widely appealing) was the Association of Young Democrats (FIDESZ). Their brand of youthful enthusiasm and political astuteness has certainly been a unique feature in Hungarian politics.

YOUTH POLITICAL CULTURE IN HUNGARY

Given the earlier consideration of attitude formation in Hungarian society it has been stunning to recognise the speed and style with which young Hungarians took charge of their political affairs and generated an entirely new political group within the Hungarian political scene. According to opinion polls in Hungary in early 1991, FIDESZ was one of the most popular parties. FIDESZ was started secretly in 1988 by thirty-seven students. Often their rallies were broken up by police and although many supporters were arrested there were no trials. In 1989 one member, Tamás Deutsch, was arrested in Prague for demonstrating, then he returned to Hungary to campaign and became elected as an MP. FIDESZ politicians argue that they represent a new political culture, as their policies are independent and free of forty years of past experience. No one over thirty-five years old was able to be a member, but FIDESZ speakers argue that they are not a youth party as they represent all interests. They do have a wide spectrum of support. It was noteworthy that the oldest person to vote in Budapest, a woman of 101 years of age, voted for FIDESZ. The youngest MP in Hungary is twenty-three years old and overall there are twenty-two of the youngest MPs in the world in the Hungarian Parliament.

Oranges are the FIDESZ symbols, representing for them freedom and independence. FIDESZ chose the symbol of the orange also as a reference to a famous film by Béla Bacso, *The Witness*, where a small, acid and pale Hungarian orange appears – but it is ours! In terms of their public profile, one of their election posters was very much discussed and commented on. It showed two couples kissing – the first were two old communist officials, Honecker and Brezhnev, kissing each other in formal communist greeting, the second were a young couple, kissing on a park bench. The request was simply stated – please choose us! Connotations of old formal communist politicians with young, enthusiastic, modern ones were very obvious. Their direct style gives them a good rapport with people. Their foreign office spokesperson, Zsuzsanna Szelényi, supports arguments for a new campaign on human rights, which is an important issue within Hungary today. Their magazine, *Magyar Narancs* (*Hungarian Orange*) has given space for feminists to contribute and writers reported favourably on the establishment of the National Gay Council in Hungary. Yet legacies of former ideas and attitudes do linger on in Hungary.

CHAUVINISM AND PATERNALISM

Despite the outlook of some of the new political groups it remains the case that in Hungary there has been a legacy of chauvinism, much of it pre-dating the 'socialist' regime, but certainly not discouraged within such a rigid and formalistic system. In the work of several scholars (Siklova, Dölling and Adamik) the weight of the past upon women's lives today is emphasised. Nowhere does this seem more apparent than in women's consciousness of their everyday situations. Being 'emancipated' as workers and living under the dual burdens of paid and unpaid work, women throughout Hungary have had no opportunity to consider actively, make choices and give priority to different aspects of their own lives.

As various scholars have pointed out (see Miroiu, 1992) the varying authoritarian regimes in power within East-Central Europe worked hard to create abstract 'socialist' images by actively destroying the individual outlooks of people. In terms of the 'new socialist man' Mihaela Miroiu notes:

> This term 'the new man' was the thematic obsession of all communist training. I believe that this term was an obstacle to the creation of both masculine and feminine genders, which obstinately tried to deprive the individual of his or her individuality and to obtain the gradual dissolution of the person and the melting of the individual into anonymity (Miroiu, 1992, p. 6).

In this context, the Romanian experience was certainly an extreme one, but on a continuum, as women in Hungary do speak of similar situations with regard to a 'vacuum of values' and their own low self-esteem. One woman in here early thirties described to me her thoughts on this:

> I do know that I am a capable and a caring person. But sometimes it is very hard. Much of my energy goes into creating a good home environment for my family, although my [paid] work is also important to me. I suppose the difficulty is to gain confidence, to rely on myself or to remember my strengths. It sound strange, I know, but sometimes I feel 'useless' somehow (Katalin: Corrin, 1990).

In many of my conversations with women in Hungary it did seem clear that women undervalued their strengths and achievements. To my mind various aspects of chauvinism/paternalism combined to reinforce the view that women are generally regarded merely as someone's wife, mother or daughter and so have no personal identities, nor indeed worth, as individual women. Many women's low self-esteem and lack of confidence becomes a barrier for them in terms of recognising their own power to change concrete situations. When coupled with economic hardships, in terms of day-to-day survival it could certainly become the case that many women will not be able to participate in any civil initiatives for change, in the immediate future.

As has been pointed out by different researchers (Sas in Hungary, Siklova in Czechoslovakia) cultural change has been very slow, despite, or perhaps as a consequence of, immense political upheaval. Old myths do live on, particularly that of women's 'natural roles'. In this context the political outlook of the major party in the governing coalition in Hungary, the MDF, in its distinctly conservative mode, is having practical consequences for women throughout Hungarian society. On the issue of women's reproductive rights and abortion it is clear that throughout 1990 when members of the Catholic Church were encouraging people to sign petitions about restricting or outlawing abortions the Hungarian government 'sat on the fence'. No official statements were issued about whether or not the laws on abortion would be changed, yet rumours were rife. If there had been a groundswell of opinion in favour of changing the law, undoubtedly the government would have moved to do so. Given that the Feminist Network and other 'concerned citizens' worked to get signatures for petitions against restricting women's rights to abortion, government officials appeared to be biding their time.

Many statements by members of the ruling coalition, notably the Christian Democrats, emphasised the strong forces in favour of outlawing abortion altogether. As cheap and safe contraception is not available to every woman who needs it in Hungary, the fall-back position of having the right to abortion is essential. In a public opinion poll on abortion which the Szonda-Ipsos Media Opinion and Market Research Institute conducted on a 1000-strong representative sample in November 1991 an overwhelming majority (86 per cent) agreed that it is one of the human rights of a woman to decide to give birth or not and that the state may not interfere in this decision. Table 8.2 shows the percentage of responses agreeing to abortion.

Many issues are raised by this poll, not least regarding the way in which questions were framed, but essentially the 86 per cent agreeing that it was a basic human right for women to determine their own fertility is certainly a positive outlook. When the abortion issue became 'newsworthy' in November 1991 various arguments concerning the paternalism of the old regime came into focus. As many Hungarians still associate the issues surrounding women's equality and abortion with the old communist administration, then it is relatively easy to dismiss the abortion issue as a communist issue. Yet in response Hungarian feminists claim that:

> We regard any regulation drastically interfering in the life of the citizen impermissible. The era during which individiuals' private lives were shaped via centralised issues, prohibitions and demands is now a thing of the past (Béres in *Budapest Week*, 20 December 1991).

Table 8.2 Percentage of responses agreeing to abortion

Condition	*Percentage*
If the birth jeopardises the mother's life	96
If the pregnancy is the result of rape	93
If the child is expected to be born handicapped	93
If the mother already has three children	75
If the couple do not have a flat	61
In any case, if requested	56
If the mother is not married	50

Source: *Daily News*, vol. 25, no. 65, 6 December 1991, p. 4.

In terms of legality, the arguments of those from the group Peace in the Womb: Lawyers and Physicians Against Abortion claim that abortions were never specifically approved in the constitution, but were allowed under a ministerial regulation passed in the communist era. A decision regarding this regulation was taken in December 1992. The tenor of debate reached quite extreme proportions so that there was some relief at the choice of the so-called 'liberal' option. However, women in Hungary can now only have an abortion in a 'crisis' situation – not clearly defined. They need two different people – a doctor and one other – to sign their permission. With the compulsory three days' 'thinking time' on top of the agony of having to make this decision, it could all be too much for some women. Some observers suggest that the well-off, well-educated and assertive women will be the ones who will get access to abortions.

PARTY PATERNALISM?

Irene Dölling makes the point that the behaviour patterns created and spread by a patriarchal State 'socialism', have had the effect of making women susceptible to parties which are ready to relieve them of their responsibility once again. This expectation that women and their children or families will be taken care of can, by all means, be used to support strategies for social adjustments to unemployment, devaluation of qualifications and degrees, cutting social supports and so on. In this context the underlying motives of certain government policies concerning 'women and the family' in Hungary are appealing to some groups of women who wish to be 'looked after'. It is ironic that the MDF version of state paternalism is enthusiastic about women 'returning' to the home and having more children, when little is offered in the way of social welfare legislation. As many women in Poland have discovered it is not a progressive step to be at home trying to raise a family on less money in a situation of rising costs. Having to spend time going from shop to shop to see what can be afforded cannot be seen as a positive development. In Hungary, crèches are still being closed down, with arguments centring on the choice between making more workers redundant or closing the crèche, therefore the crèches are being closed in piecemeal fashion, and within arguments about unemployment, such closures are harder to resist. Given that women's rights to return to work after child-care leave were withdrawn in July 1991, many women are in a difficult economic situation. In terms of the provisions for child-care leave and caring for sick children, many women in Hungary are now viewed as 'expensive' to employ. Some women have been questioned at job interviews concerning their domestic arrangments for child-care or their expectations regarding having children. Young married women are vulnerable in such an environment. The double-edged contradiction is again apparent here in that whilst young women are expected to have children, and of course often look forward to having children, the economic climate has become such that they are often penalised *in advance* for this potential.

There is an atmosphere in which women's employment is once again seen as secondary, yet economically it is still primary. Most families in Hungary still need two wages on which to survive. That women are no longer guaranteed their jobs when they finish child-care leave could mean that many working mothers will join the ranks of the long-term unemployed. Despite the rhetoric within the MDF in terms of women becoming important once again within the household, strengthening family ties (and responsibilities) and replacing the moral vacuum of 'socialism' with Christian values, the reality for hundreds of thousands of women may well be very difficult indeed.

SOCIAL WELFARE

Within this context it is clear that there is confusion within not only the ruling coalition in government at the present time, but also within the opposition groups in Hungary, regarding the social welfare aspects of the changing environment at present. Given that poverty is increasing amongst young families with children, and the rate of growth is very high amongst single-parent families, the threat of the feminisation of poverty is significant and publicly unproblematised at present. Social security does not tackle these problems directly – there is no indexation of family and child benefits, there are major inequalities of incomes, and the taxation systems remain inadequate.

It remains the case that the general proposals in the context of social welfare measures outlined by spokespersons within the governing coalition, tend towards market-based schemes, such as encouraging a voluntary sector involvement in health-care. Whilst in the short-term this may ease, in part, the massive burdens on the health service in Hungary such measures are not applicable to issues of poverty and unemployment. The 'active unemployment' proposals from the Ministry of Labour are not part of a coherent strategy and can be seen as stop-gap measures. It seems that the government in Hungary is currently able to conceive of only short-term measures, certain of which seem to favour those who are better-off within society.

In this context one public opinion survey showed that many people in Hungary think that the government looks after the better-off (see Figure 8.1).

Figure 8.1 Whom does the government represent?

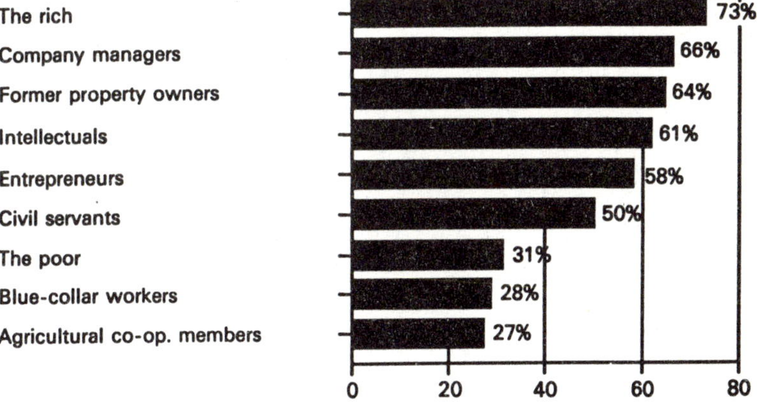

Source: Budapest Week, 26 June 1991, p.3.

This poll, as can be seen, showed that people took exception to the government's economic policy moves, and the main charge was that it supported the interests of those who were better off, to the detriment of the lower classes. The paper noted a comment from one of the pollsters, Guy Lázár of the Medián Kft, in *Magyar Hírlap*:

> This approach indicates that the social (and not the *political*) bias of the majority of people is not manifest in the power relations that exist in the Parliament . . . While the majority of

> the respondents said they would vote liberal [i.e. opposition] their approach still seems to be dominated by the egalitarian and authoritarian motives of the past.

This legacy from the 'socialist' past will not disappear overnight.

In this context the recent work of Iván and Szonja Szelényi centres on this aspect of the social-democratic constituency in Hungary. Given that, by their very nature, the power relations within the Hungarian Parliament cannot encompass the social tendencies of the majority of people, then it would take not only a change of Parliamentary forces but a change in the priorities of certain groups of politicians, to allow the social-democratic constituency to be mobilised. Given that the Free Democrats, the SzDSz, had broad appeal across varying political fields, some observers expected it to remain ineffectual unless it was able to transform itself, to move to a centre-left position and to construct a social welfare programme which emphasised welfare-state priorities. There were some indications that this was being discussed in early 1991 within SzDSz circles when new proposals on social welfare were drawn up. The resignation of János Kis from the post of president of the SzDSz in early October 1991 was indicative of the realisation that the opposition in Hungary is facing enormous difficulties. Kis told the economic weekly, *Heti Világgazdaság,* that, never having considering himself a 'profession politician', 'I do not see myself as the SzDSz's candidate for the post of prime minister. Clearly, the long-term leaders of the party must be people who have a vocation for politics.' This highlights not only a certain crisis of opposition, but something of the difficulties of making a transition from opposition to a 'socialist' regime where battle-lines were clearly drawn, and opposition to a centre-right Christian–Nationlist coalition in which all distinctions are blurred and the way forward looks distinctly uncertain. That all parties hold to largely radical 'liberal' economic views yet none have a consistent emphasis on social welfare measures, may well mean that citizens' organisations will need to play a larger role in the coming years.

DEMOCRATIC DEBATE

There was heated political debate after the 'leaking' of a secret governmental party document in August 1991. Critics were quick to attack the apparently authoritarian style of the 'tougher action plan' proposed by the Hungarian Democratic Forum (MDF). Writers György Konrád and Mihaly Korniss led a response by initiating the *Democratic Charter 1991*. Some excerpts from Konrád's description of the aims of the Charter give insight as to its intentions:

> A 'Made in Hungary' civil initiative, but not tied to our borders. It could impel similar attempts in our region and further afield, not only in Central Europe, but in Latin America, Southeast Asia; indeed, perhaps in the European Community there is also value in democratic charters. This plurality means that nobody has a monopoly on the democratic charter, which suggests more a type of work than a one-time text (*East European Reporter*, January–February 1992, p. 36).

Within its context the Charter is very much concerned about civil initiatives and the activities of 'civil society':

> Civil society is constantly changing its expectations with respect to the system of government and the public life to which it is tied. The Democratic Charter can exist only when thinking people in individual cases agree with it. Civil society continually searches for and experiments with appropriate forms for expressing itself.
>
> It does not want to replace representative democracy, only to place the political class and, more narrowly, the governing administration in the environment of a democratic society. It wants to act as a third side in bilateral conflicts, as in national–ethnic confrontation, for example (ibid.).

At the time of writing it is difficult to gauge the impact of the work of those involved with the Charter. So far as women in Hungary are concerned, though, one can hazard a guess that they will have to work very hard to gain their rightful place within this new vision of 'civil society' as they will not be automatically included on any agendas.

WOMEN IN OPPOSITION

Women have been active in oppositional movements in Hungary for many years, but, it would seem, not in large numbers nor in influential positions. The dissociation of most Hungarian women from political activity has many underlying roots, including distancing from 'socialist' politics, as politics was seen as dangerous (underground activities), the double burden taking up all 'spare' time, but key factors of male arrogance and sexism must not be forgotten. Many Hungarian men remain narrow-minded and chauvinistic about their beliefs concerning 'women' generally, and Hungarian women in particular. These historical, gendered notions follow the lines that 'real' Hungarian women do not want to become active participants in politics nor to argue against men as this would not be 'womanly'.

Hearing such comments as they grow up is bound to affect women's attitudes to political activity and their desire to take part, as well as confidence in their abilities to do so. In addition, if women believe that not only will they *not* be welcomed, but will be actively discouraged or discriminated against, if they become politically active then the whole situation becomes much more complex. Sadly, as women internalise such prejudices, they in turn can put off other women who do want to be active in opposing certain outdated and sexist prejudices and practices. As has been seen, though, official media images and interpretations of feminist activities have been very negative in Hungary. One unusual figure has been Ottilia Solt, who has long been active within oppositional circles, and her activities in the Foundation for the Poor (SZETA), initially drew criticism within the Hungarian opposition for being too much of a 'welfare' organisation. From her work within SZETA Solt was able to write some devastating critiques of the stark levels of poverty within Hungary, and about the police harassment of poor people which was very much a 'taboo' subject.

Perhaps the major engagement of women within oppositional politics developed initially within peace groups and then with the environmental movements such as those against the Danube dam. In the early 1980s women were active within the Dialogue groups – independent peace movement groups – in Budapest, Szeged, Debrecen and Pécs. These groups were consistently oppressed and suppressed by state forces. In July 1983 officials prevented the Dialogue group from holding an international peace seminar in Hungary by refusing visas, expelling Western peace activists and detaining Dialogue members (Gáthy, 1989, p. 104). Women were also active within the *klub* movement in Hungary which played a significant role in unversity colleges such as the István Bibó College of Law, where subjects such as environmental issues, minority problems (the Roma and Jewish questions and the Hungarian minority in Romania) and peace and human rights questions, were discussed. Certain issues of dissent were not open to women: these included conscientious objection which was punishable by five years' imprisonment for all but certain small sects in Hungary. The Catholic Church in Hungary condemned conscientious objection, whereas the Polish Catholic Church openly supported it.

Whilst some women were involved in the intellectual opposition and *samizdat* publications, more women began to participate in environmental protests in the mid- to late 1980s culminating in actions against the Gabcikovo–Nagymaros Danube dam. Hungarian women did participate in large numbers within the environmental movement from the mid-1980s onwards. The Danube Dam was an important focal point. Although a contract was signed between Hungary and Czechoslovakia in 1977 to build the Gabcikovo–Nagymaros system of barrages and a power station on the Danube, serious construction only began in 1984. Criticisms and protests against the project began in 1988 and in September of that year 50 000 Hungarian citizens stood outside the Parliament building for the largest peaceful protest against the 'socialist' regime – the cause was ecology, specifically the Danube dam. By May 1989 when 164 000 citizens signed a petition, a few MPs spoke against the dam and work was suspended. The impact of this large demonstration in central Budapest and the 'success' of the protests and petitions in actually changing government policy certainly spurred the confidence of democratic forces in Hungary. There are still some ecological debates within Hungary – not least whether or not nuclear power will be cut back. The Ministry of the Environment opposed nuclear power in Hungary, but the debate within the government on this subject is due to come up for a final decision in early 1993.

Women from different age groups and levels of society have shown concern about the dangers of pollution within Hungary. A group of young women were very important activists in the environmental movement which organised large demonstrations against the Danube Dam. These activities were widely supported by women, but as yet much of this history is unrecorded.

Hungarian women certainly have not been absent from politics of this kind. Yet, no 'women-oriented' activities were apparent before 1990.

WOMEN'S ACTIVITIES IN THE 1990S

Since 1990 various women's groups have emerged in Hungarian society representing a variety of different interests. Of the two main 'types' of group, the Women Entrepreneurs and the Feminist Network offer very different analyses and options for changing women's situations. In some sense two models of change – assimilation and liberation – could be utilised here. In the assimilation model, women's 'equality' is to be gained by entering the male world. Even though women entering this world do so on men's terms within an already-given framework, the assimilationists believe that this is the aim of women's 'equality'. To some extent the Women Entrepreneurs 'fit' this model in that they want women in business to have equal access to all that men in business have. They are not attempting to change the 'rules of the game'. Women in the Feminist Network, on the other hand, are trying to change the terms of debate, and can be seen to work within the liberation model, when women, men and children work together to change the terms of reference, including what human equality entails.

Founded in 1991, the Women Entrepreneurs chose to break away from the main Entrepreneurs Association because their voices were not being heard. Whenever women professionals within the Association spoke at a large gathering, many men paid no attention to what was being said. Yet often women knew that their ideas were innovative and useful if representing other women's interests. They recognised two different types of women interested in their work:

1. Those who have been working for many years as top managers but are not fulfilled in their jobs. These women have personal aims to do better for themselves; and
2. Rural women forced to do some new work as they have lost their jobs. Such women are from various social strata including some with just the basic compulsory education –

> one woman opened a petrol station; others with *gymnazium* education who try to improve tourism in their rural area.

The primary aim of the Women Entrepreneurs is to help and encourage those women who wish to start their own enterprises but do not have the necessary bookkeeping or other skills and cannot pay for such help.

Certainly in the new economic climate in Hungary, women and men who set up in business are more 'alone' than they were in previous situations. Often they cannot 'afford' to be ill as there are no supports for them. The Women Entrepreneurs are hoping to learn a good deal from their international connexions –from the American Association of Entrepreneurs and Italian Cooperative Associations. In particular, they are utilising information on marketing and on gaining credits. Their plan is to create a Foundation which could provide guarantees for the banks from which women could gain credit. Eventually fees could be paid to women working for the Association, plus some holiday and social funds.

The group which eventually became the Feminist Network began with just three women meeting together to discuss issues such as the media representation (or misrepresentation) of women. Their Tuesday meetings in an old building of the trade unions became channelled into university lectures from 1990 on the basic theme of 'Women in Society'. Women attending these talks were not all 'academics' and several wished to be involved in 'doing something' when the course ended. As noted in its Declaration of Intent (see Appendix III), the Feminist Network was established to provide a forum in which women and men could formulate their own ideas, interests, questions about certain social 'norms' and received attitudes, thereby developing a woman-centred interest group which could represent women's interests. Such a group could also give women a voice in Hungarian society, and political and cultural life.

In this sense the Feminist Network falls very much into the 'liberation' model in that it aims to help women, men and children to renegotiate the terms of debate regarding women's situation and women's aims. The Network expects to remain small for some time to come, perhaps for quite a long time. Given the practical constraints for women organisers, of time, money (for leaflets, fares) resources (places to meet, phone lines) energy (women are tired from everyday activities) and lack of support in terms of wider community attitudes, creating women's groups and campaigns is not an straightforward task. An added problem which several women involved in various women's activities have pointed out is the lack of solidarity amongst women. One women summed this up by stating that:

> If a woman sleeps with someone else's husband she is not betraying any sort of solidarity amongst women because there is no real trust amongst women in Hungary. We have had to compete for so long in almost everything that somehow we don't really 'talk' to each other (Eszter, 1990).

This is an aspect of Hungarian women's lives that will take a lot of time, energy and trust to overcome. If there had been the opportunities for the consciousness-raising activities that many feminists from elsewhere had experienced, some of these issues could be raised. As things turned out for the Feminist Network in Hungary, no sooner had they got together than they were out collecting signatures against the proposed changes in abortion legislation. In such a climate it is hard to find the opportunity for the women themselves to discuss, assess and generally discover their own ideas about women's possibilities and activities.

Some of the activites within an active 'civil society' context such as those associated with the Feminist Network have suffered from the more general malaise following the 1990 elections. Expectations were high, perhaps inflated, of the possibilities that a complete change of government heralded. Basically change in many areas was very slow. People in Hungary complained that the government 'was all talk and no action'. Much time was spent in Parliament discussing the need for religious education in schools, whilst important budgetary decisions were made in the last hour of any given session. People did become disillusioned. This did not mean that the change of governmental structures was not considered in a positive light, but that a readjustment of expectations of change had to take place. The first feminist groups were started among intellectuals at the same time as trade unions and political movements were emerging in the late-1980s. One was set up within the TDDSz, the Democratic Union of Scientific and Research Workers and another embryonic women's group was established within the SzDSz, but was short-lived.

The timing of the 'Women in Society' course is interesting in this context – the latter part of the academic year 1990. This was a time of great social and political change and there were some feelings of optimism in the opportunities that could be taken. However, by mid-1991, one year later, the group had not attracted many new members and when a women's course was offered at another university in Budapest it was cancelled, primarily because of lack of student interest. This may well be a reflection of the disappointment many Hungarians were feeling about the extent of the new possibilities opened to them by the political changes. This highlights the peaks-and-troughs element of this transitionary period, in that the course which was available in 1992 on *Gender in Culture and Society* was again a success. This lecture series *Gender in Culture and Society* was developed on Thursdays at ELTE (the English Language Department of Eötvös Lóránd, Budapest) by Antonia Burrows and Scott Long. It looked at issues such as pornography, sexual identity, violence against women and other issues related to women's interests. These lectures were in English, but Hungarian interpreters were provided and certainly the wide range of topics covered meant that debates could be wide-ranging and challenging.

Another group working towards creating a gender-balanced outlook on society and culture is that of the Ariadne Gaia Foundation (AGA). Two of the main aims of the Foundation are:

> to provide the necessary means to meet these urgent needs by acknowledging the fact that effective change can only come from within, by developing personal, interpersonal and spiritual capacities to attain the wholeness of our human divinity;
>
> seeing the world of today 'out of joint' asserts the need to enhance the 'feminine' so as to counterbalance the one-sided dominance of the 'masculine'.

In various discussions with one of the founders of AGA, Ágota Ruzsa, it became clear that she has a very far-sighted vision of how to achieve a more balanced outlook, not only within Hungarian society, but globally. Elements of this outlook are obviously shared by other Hungarians who regularly apply to take part in various training courses provided by AGA in education and health areas in order to raise awareness on different issues.

Having visited courses in the entirely self-funded premises of this Foundation, I have consistently been struck by the way that the shared aims of the participants – gaining greater communication with others and recognition of some of the global issues concerning the environment, spirituality, communication, peace – concern us all.

In the women-only sphere, both founders Ágota and Magda, are committed to providing courses on assertiveness for women and on various health and welfare areas such as those dealing with violence against women or child sexual abuse. Such an atmosphere as has been created via AGA is essential for those willing to share in such deeply emotional experiences as are required to come to terms with such fundamental issues.

FEMINIST GOALS

In the discussion about the goals of the only openly feminist group – the Feminist Network – ideas centred on various aspects: training for women in consciousness-raising, forming sheltered homes for women experiencing violence, and other longer-term plans. The choice of the term 'feminist' was hotly debated and many felt that this would put women off joining the network. Eventually 'feminist' was chosen in part because other equally suitable terms such as 'women's association/council' had been devalued by their use in official Party women's organisations. Terms such as 'autonomous' and 'independent' did not fit the particular Hungarian context. On the positive side women argued that very few people in Hungary actually knew what feminism was and as there is a good deal of prejudice against it, then the women in the network wanted to work towards giving the term 'feminist' meaning within the Hungarian context. Their choice of the term 'network' was perhaps too optimistic, implying as it does a number of groups linked together. Although this was the aim of the Budapest group, the only other group with direct connections is one in Szeged, although others may well be forming. Their founding statement (see Appendix III) outlined their goals and showed how the network expected to work.

WOMEN NETWORKING

A signficant barrier to extending the Network's contacts has been the resistance of many of those within the new political parties to supporting the Network's initiatives. At a meeting on the abortion issue in the summer of 1990 there were representatives from many of the major parties. Unfortunately many of the women in parties felt that they could do little within their parties as it was not a 'party issue'. This party identification is worrying for those women who want to be able to attract 'across- the-board support', as groups such as the National Abortion Campaign in Britain attempt to do.

One fundamental aspect of the Network, though, is its actual existence, in that groups from other countries can now invite members of the Network to attend international women's conferences such as that of the Women's CSCE (Conference on Security and Cooperation in Europe) in Berlin in November 1990. It was at that conference that the Central and Eastern European Women's Network was set up, in part to give those women trying to create and support women's activities in the 'ex-socialist' countries the opportunities to work first with each other in order to compare experiences, setbacks and potential ways forward. The text of this network is printed in Appendix IV.

Other major conferences have included three conferences of the European Forum of Socialist Feminists (EFSF). At the EFSF conference in Gothenburg, Sweden, in November 1989, women from various 'ex-socialist' countries including the Soviet Union were present. For many Western feminists it was their first chance to exchange ideas with women active within the 'ex-socialist' countries – that is, women who were active outside the communist-controlled women's organisations. There were many fertile discussions and much 'networking'. It was agreed that the women from Jugoslavia would host the next conference but this proved impossible for various reasons. At this point some members of the Feminist Network agreed to host the conference in Budapest but again things proved difficult. The Hungarian women had little experience of budgeting a conference for more than a hundred women and their task was not made easier when there was galloping inflation during the first months of 1991. In addition the solidarity angle became important in that some women did not feel they were getting support from others and yet other women felt that it was the wrong time for the Feminist Network to be attempting to organise such a conference. Communications were a problem. The conference did not take place that year.

Discussion of whether or not to change the name of the Forum from 'socialist-feminists' at the EFSF conference in Britain in 1991 produced a fascinating array of arguments. Principally the voices in favour of moving away from socialist-feminist came from participants from the former Soviet Union and Czechoslovakia, their reason being that such labels were not useful to them in their own environments. However, arguments in favour of keeping the term 'socialist-feminist' also came from one woman from Leningrad and another from Budapest, who argued that the traditions and histories behind socialist-feminism in the Western context should not be 'thrown out' because of the 'Eastern experience'. The decision was to keep the name and reopen the debate at the next conference in Brussels in October 1992. At this conference the decision was made to change the name of the Forum to 'European Forum of Left Feminists'.

Such discussions provide rich grounds for real meeting-points for women from different historical, cultural and political situations. Several of the women from Hungary and the former Soviet Union afterwards discussed their interest in the points made by the speaker from a London-based women's group Southall Black Sisters, in that there were obvious common themes – violence against women, ethnic conflict and patriarchal domestic and statist attitudes – yet there were enormous differences – principally in how the Southall women chose to resist actively and gain support for their work. The negative side of such networking is that relatively few women can participate in such conferences, and circumstances could lead to the formation of a 'feminist élite' unless more meetings take place within Hungary, Poland and elsewhere, which is beginning to happen.

One such was a gathering of women from 'east' and 'west' which took place in Dubrovnik in June 1991 and this meeting included women from the USA who had organised the funding for women from East-Central Europe to travel to Dubrovnik. The Network of East–West Women was set up following this conference and this network has continued to work as a support group (of women from the USA) for women's initiatives in East-Central Europe.

Networks such as the Women's Commission within the Helsinki Citizen's Assembly (hCa) are active in bringing together various groups on particular, practical issues. In December 1991 forty women from all over central and eastern Europe and some from western Europe met in Prague to discuss women's health and reproductive rights. This was organised by the hCa Women's Commission as a foundation from which to build a reproductive rights network within central and eastern Europe, not only to provide information resources for women, but also as a practical step in sharing cross-country information so that women can learn more of the situation in neighbouring countries, where hitherto such networking has been restricted by lack of resources and opportunity. The booklet from this meeting, *Reproductive Rights in East and Central Europe* is available from the hCa Secretariat (June 1992).

At the second Assembly in Bratislava in March 1992 more than forty women attended a follow-up session on Women's Reproductive Health. Various groups reported on their progress in translating leaflets, and outlined their plans for further activities. The Feminist Network in Hungary reported on their grant received from the Global Fund for Women to enable them to carry out a media campaign in support of women's reproductive rights in Hungary. A very useful networking session was held in Bratislava in which women from the SOS telephone lines in Belgrade and Zagreb exchanged information and ideas with members of the Feminist Network from Budapest. In publishing the resource booklet the Women's Commission of the hCa was keen to ensure its translation into as many languages as possible so that the information could be made widely available.

Some of these meetings were amongst the issues discussed in the first feminist magazine to appear in Hungary, in September 1991, *Nöszemély*. This name in translation means 'female person', which is itself a statement. The terms 'people' and 'person' are generally masculine in Hungarian, which does not have linguistic gender distinctions. This fifteen-page magazine was produced jointly by women's groups, including the Women's section of the LIGA (League of Independent Trade Unions), Green Women's Group (environmentalists), Society of Women Entrepreneurs, Feminist Network, Women's Council and others. This joint intiative represents a turning-point for women's activities within Hungary in that such a representative collection of groups has not before worked *together* on a joint project aimed at women from all walks of life. As with any social development, getting information to people is one of the most important steps in gaining wider support. A magazine for women which is written by women, some feminist others not, which aims to put forward a variety of viewpoints, is an essential part of this ongoing process of widening people's ideas about women's strengths and possibilities. Given that the only major women's magazine in former times was the *Women's Journal* issued by the offical Women's Council which did not try to represent any different views, this new magazine is a radical departure.

CONCLUSION

As with any political developments the changes set in motion from 1989 onwards in Hungary have worked through peaks and troughs and remain very variable in terms of openings for women. Women's formal political participation remains low, yet, as has been shown, citizens' participation generally within the formal political sphere in Hungary has remained quite low. Certainly at the electoral level people have not been motivated to vote, let alone campaign on behalf of the various political groups. Such a situation could have negative consequences in demoralising people so that they no longer believe in the legitimacy of the parliamentary groups. Yet, conversely, a measure of disillusionment in politicians could lead certain groups to try to organise some things for themselves. Certainly the Democratic Charter initiative is something along these lines.

The developments in women's political organisation show that, at least in a very embryonic way, women are organising for themselves. A refuge for women suffering domestic violence was set up in August 1991, just outside Budapest. As noted, there is now a 'coalition' of women's groups who are members of the Social Council, set up in August 1991. Whilst such women cannot be said to be 'representative' of Hungarian women, they do at least represent those groups of Hungarian women who have chosen to organise themselves, at this point in time. The publication of their joint women's magazine was a first step in enabling the voice of women to reach more people and in trying to broaden some of the outlooks towards women and their places in Hungarian society.

As has been noted, the political and economic future of Hungarian society is by no means settled or optimistic in terms of its smooth development towards a more market-oriented society. Within the continuing processes away from 'socialist' organisation women in Hungary will be suffering a great deal. Some women are setting themselves up in various enterprises, perhaps with help from Women Entrepreneurs. Others, especially pensioners, are living in incredibly bad conditions as members of a very vulnerable group. Yet other women are going to evening meetings, be they of trade union groups, feminist groups, spiritual sessions or school/parent meetings. Basically Hungarian women are becoming active on behalf of themselves and others, and are working in a variety of ways to effect change within their society.

In many senses some women are at least able to challenge certain of the received 'myths' about what women in Hungary are supposed to be like, and what they are supposed to expect in terms of future possibilities. In such a situation the opportunity to change and challenge unwanted processes, remains open. Until the historical, gendered notions held by many Hungarian men and women are at least explored, in terms of masculinity and femininity, women's 'roles' and the over-expectations placed upon modern women in Hungary, then the debate remains too narrow and does not easily allow women's full engagement in it.

9 Conclusion

In concluding this study, it is clear that relations between women and state forces, between ideologies and their consequences for women's situation, changes in family structures and state transformations, and between women's domestic and public work are fundamental. Included within the ideological framework have been the psychological elements of strain, stress and illness which women suffer as a result of conlficting ideas and ideals concerning what women *should* be, as ideal mother, worker, wife, daughter and the varying and conflicting aspects of social policy provision. In terms of transition, given the slow pace of cultural change, it is the case that there will be legacies from the former ways of thinking. For women such legacies can include not only assumptions about 'natural women's roles' but also internalized beliefs about what women can or perhaps more importantly, what women cannot achieve. That some women are not confident in their own abilities nor in those of other women is understandable in this context.

So far as male violence against women is concerned, the growth of pornography and the sex industry generally highlights something of the hypocrisy attached to images of women in terms of 'good' and 'bad' women. Again, by viewing the sex industry within a framework of patriarchal social relations it is possible to locate distinct elements of this particular abuse of power by some men in Hungarian society. Work in all of its forms is central to many areas of consideration. Definitions of, recompense for, state policy on, attitudes towards, value and status of, work are but some of the ways in which this concept affects everyday lives and imbues our consciousness.

WORK

There are particular ways in which work became significiant within 'socialist' policies towards women's 'liberation'. From its theoretical significance, in terms of women gaining equal access to public particpation in the workforce, to the practical application of the mass entry of women into paid employment, there has emerged much far-reaching social change which has affected the perceived value and status of work – 'feminised industries', child care. Consideration will be in the four broad areas – relations between women and state forces, ideologies about women and consequences for women's situations, democratisation of the political structures, and family situations within state transformations – before concluding on women's self-images and activities.

RELATIONS BETWEEN WOMEN AND STATE FORCES

It was within the rigid, planned framework of the early post-liberation period that economic 'solutions' were taken up to solve social and political problems which resulted in alienating much of the Hungarian population and setting up strong state/society tensions. It was in the post-1956 atmosphere that Kádárist policies of compromise were offered to 'appease' the Hungarian people, yet within this the policies for women were not given any priority in terms of easing the dual role women had been carrying out since the war years. Not only problems which disadvantaged women but significant welfare areas such as housing, were not prioritised in the first years of the 'normalisation'. Indeed, it was not until the discussions in the early 1960s surrounding the introduction of the economic changes (NEM) that we see the 'woman problem' in various guises being openly discussed by planners. When areas such as the falling birthrate and rising divorces were discussed there was a good deal of input concerning what would be best for 'women'. Yet the fact that there was much discussion concerning the needs of women does not mean that such perceived 'needs' on the part of researchers and analysts were regarded as important needs by planners, nor that certain perceived 'needs' be prioritised over others.

When were women consulted in any of these proceses? What attempts were made to encourage women in political education. Unlike in the early years in Soviet Union where active attempts were made by the authorities to politically mobilise women, albeit for Party mobilisation, at least there was recognition of women's energies and strengths and the need to harness these for social progress. In this context, in Hungary, 'women' as an official category were treated in a more economically instrumental way by the authorities, basically Hungarian women were, and are, viewed as an unstable and unreliable workforce because of their role as child-bearers and child-rearers. Throughout the policy debates of the 1960s and 1970s it was clear that there were apparent tensions in state requirements for women workers and mothers. Again in the 1990s it is the mother/worker tensions which are making certain groups of women be viewed as too 'expensive' to employ.

THE DREAM OF EMANCIPATION?

In reviewing a balance sheet of gains/losses over the last fifty years for women in Hungary, it is evident that on the surface the gains can appear impressive. With political emancipation, roughly equivalent opportunities to education, protected maternity rights within the labour market, provision of creches and kindergartens, and fathers' ability to claim child care benefit and to spend time with sick children. Such 'gains' were unimaginable fifty years ago. Yet from closer inspection it has been shown that many other problems have become actual, practical losses for many women. The average number of men in better qualified and higher-paying jobs is much higher than that of women, the sexual segregation in employment is strong and men get more money for their work. For various reasons, very few men take the child care allowance and choose to remain in the home caring for their children. There were not enough creche places available so many women had little choice as to whether they remained in their homes with children or continued to work outside the home. There are many evident stresses and strains involved in becoming the homemaker – which is sometimes forced upon couples who would prefer a more active role for the father – as economic necessity limits the time and energies available.

So far as the worlds of paid work and family life are concerned these remain separated from each other. Tensions between home life and 'productive' life have also become apparent in terms of the shortage of houses in Hungary. Due to the lack of apartments, the building of homes by individuals has been encouraged and as such work generally falls to men, this has meant that women are being further forced into domestic and child-caring work by external circumstances. This tension between economic production and social reproduction continues to cause strains within relationships on both the individual and societal levels.

WORKING MOTHERS OR SUPERWOMEN?

Whilst women's entry into the labour force in Hungary has been massive, the socialisation of the tasks associated with the household and childcare has not been achieved. What has this meant for the expectations placed upon women? It would seem that many women have been expected to carry out successful careers, or at least substantially contribute by paid employment to the household budget, in addition to carrying out the majority of household work and childcare. If children were in child-care institutions, the duties of the parents, often carried out by women, included having to drop children off at centres and collect them each day.

The average length of time women have to enjoy as leisure time is substantially lower than that of men and working mothers have the least free time. In her work on this situation Mária Márkus points to the central problem that:

> All this leads to a situation where there no longer exists any 'natural' behaviour for women and everything has to be 'explained'. When she is staying home, she has to explain why she is not working and contributing to the welfare of her family; when she is working, but has no family, it is this latter that has to be 'explained'. In the case where she is trying to fulfil both functions, she may have a sense of bad conscience about not being a good mother (when she is at work) and not being a good worker (when she is at home – e.g with an ill child). The existence of this 'bad conscience' can be verified in almost all sociological investigations dealing with the problem of motivation to work, and life satisfaction (Márkus, 1979, p. 35).

These conflicting demands do not seem to be broadened into a general group consciousness, but remain at a personal level. There seems to be a tendency for women to internalise some form of 'ideal' attainment and for them to attempt to achieve this by trying to juggle each of their different spheres together, with a great deal of effort being put into each. Given the impossibility of achieving this, the strain is bound to show. Starting from a point which holds some faith in such an ideal, in terms of seeing it as a practical possibility, the situation often results in an unconscious competition being engendered amongst women, and when the strains appear, individual women then begin to feel that they have failed in some way. In her book about women drinking Szalai notes a hangover of patriarchal attitudes as barriers to women's self-development:

> Even though most women work, so that they also finance the formation of the family, the archaic, traditional, patriarchal conception of the role of women and men is continuing to live in practice. The conservation of these traditional sexual roles makes it difficult for women to develop in their jobs or in their social life . . . So the patriarchal relations are the real dams of women's emancipation (Valkai, 1986, p. 70).

It is evident that the idea of women gaining some emancipation through work is much more complex than it at first appears. Unlike in many Western societies where women are not generally forced to justify their choice of lifestyle, the very existence of such 'choice' has been denied to Hungarian women. This is not to say that all Western women can choose to remain at home, given unemployment this can be an enforced decision. Nor is it to imply that those women who work choose so to do, as many women work in appalling conditions out of economic necessity. The difference in the two situations for women has been that in Hungary women are expected both to work and to be 'full-time' mothers. Even single parents were expected to work. Although welfare provision has improved for single mothers, in that they can claim the child care benefit for longer and receive more welfare benefits, these women were still expected to work outside the home. In this context the right to work becomes fused with the social obligation to work.

For women in Hungary the fusion of 'rights' and 'duties' by the statist powers meant that women always lost out. Conceptions of citizenship were pivotally tied to duties, and women's duties were so all-encompassing that they were oppressed under the weight. For many men in this situation their so-called rights and duties were not only compatible but complementary. For many women the 'right' to work conflicted with their 'duties' as mothers and given that women's duties are generally more emotive and stressful than those of men, women are often made to feel failures if the domestic world is not perfect. Women are in the Catch-22 situation that their domestic repsonsibilities are not so important as men's 'wordly' ones, yet men can generally countenance failures without being personally devalued.

So far as the 'beautiful dream' of emancipation in 'socialist' times was concerned, Szalai writes about how women wanted to believe it, and that teachers, schoolbooks and television programmes kept encouraging women to believe that it was happening, even though most women could not see changes in their everyday lives. It is in this discussion that Valkai pinpoints another confusing aspect for women's self-realisation and images of themselves – that of the duality in terms of learning from the example of home life, and from the ideas taught to young people at that time. Belonging to the post-war generation herself, she tells how she and many of her contemporaries 'woke up to the drastic reality . . . a lot of us did wake up with divorces or disappointment' (Valkai, 1986, p. 70).

Within the broad consideration of social relations in Hungary, major factors which stand out have been the changing relations engendered through the economic reforms of the NEM and those of the second economy. In comparing oppositional activities in Poland and Hungary since the early 1980s it became clear that rather than direct confrontation with state forces in the form of strike actions, the Hungarian people either chose, or felt constrained, to work against the 'socialist' regime in other ways – primarily through bypassing state mechanisms in their 'extra' work. Some of the consequences of this extra working rebounded particulary onto women. In large measure this way of working meant that gendered indentities were confirmed, so that although many women were still in paid work their primary responsibility remained within the home. Those women at home on child care leave felt the loss of their external world by domestic constraints all the more keenly. These stresses faced by women were not broadened out into any group consciousness at the public level.

In certain ways then the opportunities for people to earn more in Hungary by various means led to a situation in which people could and did take more initiative and responsibility for generating part of their income, but in some ways this made social relations even more atomized, especially where women were concerned. Given that in the pre-1990 period state authorities were the primary employers for everyone, it was those with second economy work who were for the first time experiencing the responsibility and control that accompanied 'private' work, that is, work from which they could affect the outcomes. For many women who were still working in state enterprises and within the home, no new horizons were opened on the employment front. It was from some of these expectations, generated from the possibilities within the second economy that ideas arose concerning other demands which challenged statist monopolies in other areas, notably the political arena. As always, these changing social relations were not operating within a vacuum and the ideological dimension was an important one.

IDEOLOGIES CONCERNING 'WOMEN' AND THEIR CONSEQUENCES

There are distinct aspects to ideological considerations concerning women in Hungarian society. The 'socialist' ideology of women collectively becoming liberated through paid work was destructive of women's images of themselves. There was a constant confusion of expectations and pressures. Many women were feeling guilty about not being at the same time good workers/mothers and had little choice about how they presented themselves in any of these assigned roles. Collective authoritarian actions carried out on women's 'behalves' was generally patronising and meant that women became apathetic to such initiatives. Examples of women being presented with bars of soap from the communist-led trades unions on International Women's Day (March 8th) each year, were laughable. That such a day could be the cause of genuine celebration for, and of, women strengths as it is in other parts of the world, seemed incredible to Hungarian women. Such examples of the mandatory 'socialist' gloss on women's activities meant that Hungarian women came to believe that there was no point in solidarity amongst women, as everything was channelled through official organisations such as the communist-led Women's Council.

Another negative spin-off from the 'collectivist ideal' of the former regime was the 'anonymity' factor through which women and men experienced a distinct lack of personal identity. The collective 'we' always outweighed an individualist 'I'. There is some evidence, especially in terms of increases in male violence against women, that whilst men are now reclaiming some form of 'masculinity', this can often be at direct cost to women. One young women recalled the experience of her cousin in early 1991:

> She became employed by her husband, which is a situation which could not have arisen before. Soon she was working for him in his small 'butik'. But when they argued he fired her – he was testing his power. When she had no work she had to ask him for every forint to buy food, clothes, etc. Sometimes he said no. She was in a very bad situation (Edit: Corrin, 1991).

Such 'transitional' attitudes do not bode well for the development of new expressions of masculinity and femininity. That work within the home was not problematized, in terms of the gendered division of labour, was a major drawback for women. Given that the introduction of women in large numbers into paid employment had not been accompanied by any marked socialization of housework and adequate child care, women in Hungary remained disadvantaged by their double burden/shift. Social relations between the authoritarian 'socialist' structures and people's everyday lives were such that the domestic sphere remained a safe haven from the interventionist state forces, so women could only 'problematize' domestic relations at their own costs. That so-called women's issues were actually social issues and as such needed discussion on public agendas, was not tackled during these times.

In terms of women's images of themselves it was apparent that during the 'socialist' period whilst some women felt 'de-sexualised' by having to work all day and evenings too, other women felt that the domestic sphere was the only area in which they had some personal control so they worked hard to please their husbands in what they considered an appropriately feminine way. Sometimes women were unwilling to share their domestic 'power' by encouraging men to cook, clean or 'help' in any way. As the work by Szalai on women drinking illustrated, many women in Hungarian society viewed themselves in relation to men, and those women without male partners for whatever reasons, felt that in some ways they had 'failed'.

Another area of ideological views on women's possibilities, is in the democratising political arena, post 1989, which shows marked changes, but not necessarily in favour of extending women's possibilities towards 'liberation'. On the one hand the general liberalising atmosphere in Hungary since 1990 has meant a growth in new industries such as the sex industry. Pornography, prostitution and sex shows are all readily available in Budapest and some other large towns in Hungary. That this is a 'right' for a liberal society is almost taken for granted, yet no public debate has taken place concerning the possible impact of pornography on crimes of violence against women. Nor has any discussion been generated about why women, particularly young women, are prepared to work as prostitutes. Linkages between poverty, need and availability of other types of work for women have not yet been made. Nor is there any public discussion about power relations in society in terms of patriarchal social structures. How certain images of women have been socially constructed and maintained – the 'mother' image is idealised, yet the 'whore' image is used for servicing certain groups of men and maintaining certain power relations. The governing coalition proposes outlooks for Hungarian women which revolve pivotally around family relations. The two views of women – good and bad, Madonna and Whore – are starkly apparent within Hungarian society at present. Some women will remain classified as 'bad' and as such not worthy of detailed attention, while those 'good' Hungarian women who wish to be married, have children and abide by Christian (and nationalist?) values will be 'cared for' by the government.

As has been noted, that the present government cannot live up to its promises for these 'good' Hungarian women, is currently being faced within Hungarian society. Even 'good' women are, and will become, poor in Hungary. That all women, as women, have rights needs to be recognized. Domestic work not only has not been problematised in the current era, but in fact the gendered division of labour seems to be applauded by the present administration. Given the lack of choice about whether or not to be in paid work, many women in Hungary do want choice to care for their families full-time. Equally though, many women still wish to work in paid work, either full- or part-time. Current economic changes and consequent policy decisions may well mean that many Hungarian women will experience the worst of both worlds – in reality the state forces cannot provide the cushion of paternalism – so that the increasing income differentials without social welfare supports will mean that women lose out on all fronts. Many women may 'be returned' to their homes to suffer poverty.

FAMILY STRUCTURES AND STATE TRANSFORMATIONS

An enduring feature of Hungarian family development now includes that period in which the mother stays at home caring for the children. Within this it is apparent that many traditional household arrangements are strengthened in terms of the sexual division of labour. It is in this context that the consideration of the debates concerning family structures in Hungarian society centre upon: (a) the strengthening of the nuclear family; and (b) the support given to 'modern' policy prescriptions. In terms of the first, it is apparent that the policy-makers in Hungary distinctly favour policies which serve to support and strengthen the monogamous, heterosexual family model of two adults and 2 or more children – both in the 'socialist' and in the current period. Yet, despite the fact that within policy making circles this model is the dominant one, so far as policies are concerned there is a duality in terms of the 'ideal' and reality. The 'ideal' is held to be the nuclear family of two plus two/three, developing towards the modern, progressive type of family, in which household tasks (and child care to some extent) are shared between spouses, with democratic decision-making and equal opportunities for both partners. Underlying this is the reality in which the two-parent, two-children model is not the major mode of life for most Hungarian people. Even when there are periods when two adults and two children share households, the power relations within these situations are generally unbalanced, in that women still tend to have to take major responsibility for the domestic sphere. The current policies of the governing coalition aim to create a male 'breadwinner' or family wage situation, in which women will become wholly dependent upon men financially. Given this contradictory nature of strengthening the unrealistic 'ideal', the question arises as to what this means for the position of women?

From the consideration in Chapter 3 it is apparent that far from Hungarian families becoming more homogeneously modern, democratic and so on, there is a definite separation between families in towns and villages, and between worker-peasant, and worker families on the one hand, and families in the upper strata on the other. Whilst these divisions are by no means rigid or clear-cut as there are various layers of overlap, it can be proposed that many familial groupings within Hungarian society are fairly backward-looking, certainly in terms of equality of decision-making and leisure time for women and the sharing of household tasks. This is in direct contrast to the optimistic picture painted by some contemporary sociologists and it is a far cry from the radical thinking of such writers as Heller and Vajda concerning social movements developing a revolutionary consciousness to dissolve monogamous marriage in favour of communal life.

Although the importance of this gap between the ideal type and reality cannot be underestimated, the ideal is still upheld within many policy measures. Much of the legislation concerning families in Hungary has actively promoted a particular form of family. The apparent fragility of modern 'family life' has been of concern to policy-makers, in their attempts to ensure not only its stability but its durability. The changes in divorce laws have been evidence of this desire to keep families 'together', despite the costs.

There appears to be no evidence in Hungary of attempts to plan for, or to build communal housing, like that of Sweden.[1] This was not because of economic constraints – there is no evidence that communal housing costs more than individual units either to build or to run, probably the reverse is the case – it was due to ideological constraints. Revolutionising familial relations was not, in fact, part of the Soviet model of development, nor did the Hungarian authorities wish to experiment in this area. Nevertheless, as the reality of social life is that people live together in an almost infinite variety of ways, it is reasonable to ask how social policy measures can become more attuned with this variety of familial groupings? In her work on social policy, Gillian Pascall makes the link between state support for the family and responsibility for social welfare:

> The real meaning of supporting the family is supporting family responsibility for dependants young and old. State support is primarily a series of policies for a particular family type, that in which there is a male 'breadwinner' and a female 'carer', who fortunately does not have to be paid. These policies underlie social security practice, as well as provisions for dependents of all ages (Pascall, 1986, p. 43).

It is important in this context to remember that in Hungary there was basically only a financial association between state authorities and 'the breadwinner'. In the case of family allowance sums were paid directly into men's wages via the enterprises, and for women caring for children on GYED the amounts were collected by them. There were no networks of people employed within social work offices to mediate between state structures and differing social groups or individuals. If people had problems claiming their benefits or working out which bureaucracy they had to go to there were few ways to sort them out. In such a situation people's dependence on state authorities was virtually complete in that no external citizens' advice bodies were available nor was there any voluntary sector. People in vulnerable groups, with learning difficulties or with little access to larger settlements or towns often suffered in very poor circumstances.

As noted, within the rigid structures of the former 'socialist' era there were two societies. These could be described as the 'external' world and the 'internal world'. The external world consisted of relations between Hungarian citizens and state forces, and almost everyone was engaged in this world, as almost all adults worked or were in education, and as most work was for state authorities these linkages were reinforced daily. In the internal world the situation was very different in that this sphere was 'non-political', except that it was here that children learnt the 'true' histories of their people, and it was a world which resisted the interfering arm of 'the power'. That this internal sphere was both a site of women's oppression and a 'haven' for the external world meant a that women experienced differing sets of pressures associated with these divisions, which men did not.

POLITICAL PERCEPTIONS OF 'CHOICES'

One legacy of this period was that politics was viewed by most women as a dirty business, so that when opportunities to oust communist rule and create more democratic forms arose, women were not encouraged to put themselves forward. In the current climate, the legacy of past chauvinism arising in part from the rigid social relations of the 'socialist' past has meant that the new state structures which have been created are no more accessible to women that those of former regimes. The governing Parliamentary coalition of Christian-Nationalists openly state their wish to transform family relations towards what appears to be an historical (rural?) ideal of extended family networks, with a primary role for women as carers, whilst women would supposedly be 'cared for' by men and the state authorities. On a surface level this appears to be not such a different outlook for women than in the 'socialist' times except that women would have less opportunities to participate in paid work. Yet this represents a tremendous change for women who have become used to working outside the home, having the right so do to and the independence of their income. Current government proposals of restructuring which include women's 'return to the home' would make many Hungarian women economically dependent on men and limit their social relations to the domestic sphere. Given the high incidence of divorce in Hungary at present, divorced women bringing up children would be placed in very vulnerable economic situations if they could not find employment. Instances of having to take ex-husbands to court in claims for maintenance would probably increase but how this would affect women's images of their situations is hard to calculate.

It remains the case that many women in Hungary are tired of their dual existences. They are tired of working in boring jobs for state enterprises that were never particularly efficient, nor did they engender any loyalty or initiatives from their workforces. It is perfectly understandable that arguments concerning a 'family wage' such as those generally (if incorrectly) believed to have been the norm in many western countries, strike a positive chord with Hungarian women and men at the present time. Many men would prefer to have their wives at home caring for the family and home and not having to go off to the factory each day. As the survey material in chapter two showed, in terms of their own images many men would feel more fulfilled if they could support their families by their own work. However, Hungarian reality at the present time is such that for more than one person to live on an 'average' wage will not be possible in the coming years. Many women are still going to need to earn money to help with domestic budgets. If child care benefits are not raised, with rising prices, many women may not be able to 'afford' to take child care leave, certainly as their jobs will not be guaranteed. In such a situation the closure of creches and kindergartens will form part of an irreversible process through which many women will be barred from taking up employment because of lack of child care services. Such state-funded institutions will be extremely difficult to replace.

PUBLIC/PRIVATE DIMENSIONS

In terms of the much-considered public/private divide with regard to women's work there are various schools of thought as to how to achieve change. Primary amongst these are the 'wages for housework' arguments which broadly speaking want to raise the value of domestic work to that of paid work. In the process of so doing, recognition of the importance of domestic work within the overall economic structure of a society would be gained. At the present time in Hungary, apart from the 'socialist' policies concerned with paying women to care for children in the home, the present Hungarian government appears to be moving in a direction opposite to that of any 'wages for housework' argument in that even if home care benefits remain, they will definitely remain gendered. Men will not be encouraged to care for children in the home. The Christian-nationalist ideology of the present government has distinctly prescribed 'roles' for women, and men, and within that women have few rights. Rights to decide whether, and when, to have children may be be denied to women if there are further constraints on the current abortion legislation.

The ideological complexities engendered within the abortion debate in Hungary have been touched upon in Chapter 6 in terms of the anti-abortionists being able to argue that the current laws concerning abortion were legacies of the old communist mentality and have no place in a new 'Christian' Hungary. For the feminists and others who are opposing changes in abortion legislation arguments centre upon precisely those rights which were denied women in the communist past – rights over their own bodies, choice regarding when and whether they have children, and rights to better health care in terms of availablity of safe, reliable, and cheap contraception.

The alternative arguments around the domestic/public working contradictions also centre on issues of reducing the barriers of paid and unpaid work with more emphasis on timing. Arguments for a three-day paid working week or encouragement of job-sharing so that public and domestic work can also be shared by adults have much validity in the modern world in which there is not enough paid employment to engage people. Yet this set of arguments work in direct contradiction to a market-led economy. The demands of markets are such that they are by their very nature differentiated, necessitating a specialised workforce and particular sets of equipment and utilities. Within market situations central intervention is seen as preventing the 'free' operation of different forces. Essentially employment in market systems is not open to all – vulnerable groups, especially older women and single parents with young children (usually women) and those with less skills generally, cannot benefit from employment in market conditions.

SOCIAL POLICY PROVISION

It is strikingly apparent that strong social policy provisions within government policies are needed if women in vulnerable groups are not to suffer even more over the coming years. Yet, it is equally apparent that the ideological framework of liberal economic thinking which is shared both by the ruling coalition and the opposition parties in Hungary, does not make adequate allowances for the needs of those who are disadvantaged within the present situation. It is unfortunate that some positive social welfare policies can be attacked as interventionist and reminiscent of the old 'socialist' policies. At some point there will be a more general recognition that egalitarian policies are basically about ensuring that vulnerable groups are not further disadvantaged and that these are not to be confused with the 'classless society' propaganda which became oppressive in former times. However, the general economic situation in Hungary at present is not rosy and the 'economistic excuses' concerning social welfare issues find quite wide general support at present. Structural reforms were quite far advanced in Hungary at the beginning of 1992. Privatisation processes through redefining property rights are complex and the Hungarian privatization policies have been based on the principle of selling assets – not giving them away. Privatisation via distribution of assets to the population via vouchers was not considered and privatisation via restitution for former owners was also rejected, though partial compension is being given. A significant amount of state assets have been sold and foreign investment played a significant role here, yet property rights remain uncertain in several respects.

In addition, the pre-privatisation programme had not been very active because of various conflicts between local governments and the central government over the ownership of real estate. Cooperative members have not been encouraged to restructure their agricultural and industrial entities in a market-oriented manner. As in other 'ex-socialist' countries, Hungary faces many difficulties in terms of past legacies. External debt is a particularly heavy burden and the loss of markets in the former Soviet Union added to these difficulties. Cuts in subsidies coupled with rising unemployment will mean falling living standards for many millions of Hungarians in 1993 and beyond. In such a situation, if social welfare measures are not radically re-thought, the arguments concerning the government representing the rich and better-off may well become every louder.

Sometimes, needs/desires are contradictory. Not all groups (in age, gender, class, ethnicity) can have complementary needs at all stages of development. Yet in general terms – of women's needs in the workplace and in terms of child care – it is clear that even on the broadest level these do not fit in with the modernising desires of the current administration. That 'socialist' goals for women tended to centre on 'emancipation through employment' caused multiple problems for many Hungarian women. Yet the Christian-nationalist goals of the current administration within the framework of increasing differentiated and unequal social relations, will also have negative implications for many women's lives in Hungary in the 1990s. Whilst economic constraints are certainly the major concerns given by policy-makers in terms of styling policies geared towards the various familial groupings, the other major constraint, which is ideological, must not be underestimated. In her discussion of family ideology, Gittins notes that family ideology, although it does not represent the way people interact, does come near enough to the reality of people's lives to make it possible for those who are divorced, unmarried, childless, to at least identify with a childhood image or whatever, and then such people feel that their own 'failure' to achieve the ideal has been an individual failing rather than something based on an unrealistic ideal. Gittins points out that:

> The distribution of guilt, however, in unequal. Because it is predominantly women who are identified with the family, who are allocated primary responsibility for its well-being, unity and happiness, failure to achieve such goals is overwhelmingly seen as a woman's problem and failure – her guilt. Men's responsibility for the family now, as in the past, is seen as solely a financial one. In this sense, socialism has been a crucial factor in 'lifting' guilt from men. But because of the close identity between the family and women, a perceived crisis in the family tends also to be seen as women's fault both as indidivuals and collectively (Gittins, 1985, p.165).

This certainly seems to have been the case with many of the women spoken with concerning this study, who felt that the responsibility for creating a nice home environment fell squarely on women's shoulders.

WOMEN'S HEALTH

It is from such pressures to create a 'nice home environment' in isolated and often very strained economic circumstances, whilst working many hours each day, that many women experience health problems. Problems connected with stress, neuroses and alcoholism are often experienced by women in Hungary. Here Márkus notes that it is certainly not only the problem of time, which does remain a problem, but it is also connected with the impossibility of harmonising the various contradictory values and requirements which cause women to live in a state of tension, feeling that they are unable to fill all their 'roles' adequately.[2] The 'superwomen' complex referred to in this connection, with women juggling impossible tasks, is definitely no joke when the cracks start to appear and women's health suffers as a result.

It was in this area that many analysts looked to the psychological elements in the 'socialist' perspective of how women were expected to achieve, or in some cases were believed to have achieved, equality. That gendered, historical family structures, authority relations, and educational patterns had not been radically altered within Hungarian society meant a reinforcement of sex-role stereotyping, yet with significant particularities. That younger women in Hungary want something different for themselves than that which their mothers experienced may mean that they wish to be cared for by their husbands' family wage and be able to remain home with children. It could also mean that these young women choose not to marry young but to take up some of the opportunities available under various different educational programmes, such as TEMPUS (Trans-European Mobility Programme for University Staff and Students) in order to travel and gain more knowledge of the world. Young women in urban areas may also choose to work in types of employment which women are now gaining high-level recognition, such as banking. For young women in rural areas, however, it would appear that there will be less opportunities for employment than before, and the choice concerning early marriage or migration may well take on a great sense of urgency.

YOUNG PEOPLE'S PERCEPTIONS

It is apparent in the Hungarian context that family structures and authority relations are not seen as a prime area in need of change by policy makers. This strengthening of the nuclear family models does not bode well for any major changes in sex-role differentiation. Changes in aspects of everyday lifestyles towards a more progressive model of life which includes women as equal participants in every sphere and has notions of men being primary to child care and home life, are at best *very slow* and at worst contradictory. The conflicting trends of traditional and progressive thinking underlay much of the 'socialist' education which children received from their televison programmes and the views taught in schools. So far as family patterns learnt at home are concerned, these too were often contradictory in terms of the various 'roles' mother performed. Here it was evident that whilst girls saw it as their 'right/duty' to work in paid employment the (realistic) expectation was that they would also be primarily responsible within their future families for child and home care, whilst their husband was 'out earning the majority of the family income'. In the current climate attitudes towards these issues are by no means obvious or clear cut.

So far as political education is concerned the distancing process which went on within many Hungarian families resulted in the creation of a duality of outlooks – of 'our' private, family life and 'their' external, political life with little meeting of the two. In this context, that women's liberation and the so-called 'women's movement' in Hungary were seen to be connected with the external political world, had negative consequences for the development of an autonomous women's movement. This was certainly the case before the 1989 political changes. On the question of women's organisation the need to recognize that there were no forceful, autonomous political movements within Hungary is important. As Pál Tamás noted:

> it is true that a strong women's movement does not exist [in Hungary] but anyway, what kind of movement can be found? In our region, movements have to face difficulties, their crystallization is slow and usually stopped (Tamás, 1987, p.5).

This sums up the major political obstacles to the formation of an autonomous women's movement within Hungarian society before 1989. The existence of an 'offical' women's movement formed a secondary strand to this problem.

That the Hungarian Women's Council was an official Party organisation meant a good deal to the average Hungarian woman. Firstly, such an organisation was regarded with suspicion – if for no other reason than because was 'official'. Secondly, the very fact of its existence precluded the opportunities for women to form any sort of grouping (social or political) which could include a 'self-help' group on a large housing estate or a form of toy-library in a certain area, as well as a rehabilitation group (for say, alcoholics) or any number of such groups which exist other industrialised countries. The main reason that these were impossibilities in Hungary was not just that of restrictions on forming organisations (as these could sometimes be circumvented by the informal nature of the gatherings) it was the fact that such groups need some access to resources – be it in the form of buildings to meet in, some means of distributing information or even to the possibility to engage part-time workers. All access to such resources in Hungary remained closed to any but official organizations. Ironically, some of these problems remain today for the groups which are starting up. This is the case not because 'access' is restricted officially, but that access is restricted by the market mechanisms, in that people have to pay to hire rooms in which to meet and this is perennial problem for voluntary groups in terms of how to raise funding.

WOMEN'S ACTIVITIES

In terms of the potential for the development of autonomous women's movements in Hungary, the institutional and psychological pressures still weigh heavily against such activities. It is evident that before 1989, no autonomous outlets of any kind existed in Hungary within which women could mobilise to confront inequalities within the workplace and home, work against sexism in the society or to stand up for women's rights and oppose any encroachments on the gains women had won. Now that some women's groups are emerging, be they Women Entrepreneurs, Feminist Network, women in independent trades unions or political parties, they will face a good deal of resistance.

This resistance concerns not only the lack of priority given to matters concerning women's equality but also the fact that few women are present within the important decision-making circles so that there are very few opportunities for women in Hungary to influence planning decisions or prioritise matters relating to discrimination of women at work, or matters concerning the sexual division of labour. This remains the case in Hungarian political circles today – as noted the number of women members of Parliament elected in 1989 was very low with 28 out of 386. Hungarian women are still discriminated against in the area of work, which is a primary area in our everyday lives in many contexts, as people work for money, for status, for self-respect, for duty, for love and for many other reasons. Such work that is for money, some types of status and self-respect often seems to go to men, whereas those who carry out many of the socially undervalued 'caring' jobs in society are often women, who do a great many things for their children out of love. This is not to say that men do not care for their children (nor elderly relatives) it is to point out this basic division apparent in Hungary and many other societies, between the 'important, external, political and economic' world mainly populated by men that is the world which sets the agenda for the 'less important, domestic, social and caring' world of women and children, who suffer as a result.

How far governments are prepared to change this begs the question: 'How far will any bureaucracy change its power-base and undermine its own authority?' If women were to become an 'active force' in either an evolutionary sense, by becoming office-holders and decision-makers pressing for women's demands or in a revolutionary sense by challenging the sexism within the monogamous nuclear family 'ideal' – the majority of Hungarian men would feel not only threatened but angry because their 'little women' had turned against them. In such a situation, if men chose to counter women's demands, the power imbalance (in favour of men) would become even more of an obstacle for women. This would not be an ideal situation.

As evidenced by the 'anti-equality' groups, if men feel threatened they can very often use attack as the best form of defence. With this in mind, any major moves towards women's equal opportunities and development in Hungary would need to have not only the support of large sections of Hungarian women but also at least some sections of Hungarian men. In this connexion, the development of a women's 'coalition' within the Social Council, from September 1991, is very positive for future developments. The Social Council is a recognised government-supported body and as such could facilitiate a nationwide developmnet of citizens' initiatives through which social issues could be debated. There are problems with this fledgling 'Second Chamber' in terms of the democratic input being limited via officially-recognised groups, and so it is not as inclusive as it first appears. In addition, problems of representativity remain in that groups of 20 and 200 000 obviously need to have differential impact. Yet for women's groups this opportunity to work together with a recognised, supported context is of paramount importance. Also access to decision-making, even if 'only' within the social sphere could well give women access to other areas of decision-making. Even though it is only a small number of women included in this Council and in the groups within it at present, this joint working on such projects as the women's magazine, are important for spreading positive images of women and the belief in women's strengths and future possibilities. In addition, it may well allow various ideas from women's activities in other parts of the world to be discussed within the Hungarian context and give women outside Hungary an opportunity to realise more of what life is like for Hungarian women.

Yet it remains the case that there is a long way to go before women in Hungary, and almost everywhere else on the globe, are regarded as fully equal on their terms within society. In the meantime, discrimination is bound to exist. Women in Hungary are still living with the double burdens of the unrealistic expectations placed upon them, whilst their 'problems' are being judged and 'solved' by men in a male-dominated, market-oriented society. Until women can at least have some significant input into the male-oriented perspective of decision making and thereby influence work priorities, re-evaluating the 'important' areas and including some of the hitherto undervalued areas, then those attitudes which endgender sexism will continue to thrive in Hungary. It remains to be seen what differences will come from women's voices within the present government coalition and opposition parties, and how effective the new women's groups within Hungary can be in gaining a political voice and intervening in social and political areas.

Viewing politics within its broadest, feminist context as being concerned with differential power relations in society at varying levels from governmental structures to familial settings, the various women's groups acting at different levels within Hungarian society will be able, if they choose, to develop positive progressive images of Hungarian women and to challenge many of the stereotypical myths still hampering many women's development.

WOMEN'S STUDIES

As has been noted, several courses have taken place at universities in Budapest which have paved the way for the development of active women's groups. The first in 1990 along the lines of 'Women in Society' was a starting point for the establishment of the Feminist Network in Budapest. Despite some false starts in 1991, another course was presented in 1992 which was concerned with 'Gender in Culture and Society' and explored important issues of sexuality, violence against women and images of women. Despite the tiny group of people involved in such courses, relative to the Hungarian population, the spin-off effects of the developments in Women's Studies courses within a changing higher educational framework in Hungary could be quite impressive. Given that the radical movements of the 1960s and 1970s apparent in north America, western Europe and elsewhere had no chance to develop within the rigid authoritarian climate in Hungary, there were no women's movements emerging either. Unlike in other countries at this time when women's achievements were being recorded through the history of their campaigns and struggles, women in Hungary were being granted statist 'guarantees' of 'equality'. Unlike their counterparts elsewhere, women in Hungary and other Soviet-type societies were not involved in developing their own histories of women's activism and could, in Dölling's words, be seen as receiving 'paternal statist' care.

In this context a whole new arena could be opening up within Women's Studies in East-Central Europe so that the particular feminisms apparent in Hungary and say, Bulgaria will emerge. Attitudes towards the balances between masculinity and feminity could vary widely within newly-emerging feminisms. Given that the political regeneration towards multi-party democracy in Hungary did not bring with it any new civil space for women, different groups of women will have to work hard to create such spaces. Unlike those involved in education in countries with established women's movements, active women in Hungary will not have autonomous women's 'movements' as such to support them in the next few years. Yet, the power of education is such that if women who are active within different fields can come together and discuss and analyse their experience and write it down for a broader audience, then more and more women can become actively involved in different arenas of interest to them. Certainly the women's magazine *Nöszemély* is an important step in this direction. It is hoped that this book will make a positive contribution to the on-going discussions about Hungarian women's situation, their activities and expectations over the coming years.

Further developments may well include courses in Women's Studies either at universities or colleges, and evening groups which would discuss women's history, women's literature, violence against women, and so on. Coming together on many related themes is what women do very well, when they can overcome any legacies of isolation, lack of confidence and disbelief in their own power to change things. Issues such as the changes in abortion legislation are of such importance to women that they will become active on them, yet overcoming four decades of 'paternal statist care' is something which takes time to achieve. Times will be hard in various ways for many groups of women within Hungarian society as the 1990s continue to unfold, yet it will often be the power of women's initiatives and examples that will direct social change in the coming years.

Appendix I
Election Results

Seats in the National Party Assembly, March–April 1990

	Individual	*Regional*	*National*	*Total*
Magyar Democratic Forum (MDF)	114	40	10	164
Alliance of Free Democrats (SzDSz)	35	34	23	92
Smallholders (FKgP)	11	16	17	44
Hungarian Socialist Party (MSzP)	1	14	18	33
Alliance of Young Democrats (FIDESZ)	1	8	12	21
Christian Democratic Peoples Party (KDNP)	3	8	10	21
Agrarian Alliance	1	0	0	1
Independents	6	0	0	6
Joint Deputy	4	0	0	4
Total				386

Source: National election results, April 1990.

Appendix II Conditions for Granting Permission for Abortion

The committees give permission for abortion in the following six cases:

- If the application is motivated by considerations involving the health of the parents or the probability that the child will be physically or mentally abnormal.
- If the woman is not living in the married state or has been living alone for at least six months.
- If the pregnancy is the consequence of a criminal act.
- If neither the woman nor her husband owns an apartment that can be occupied immediately or if it is impossible for them to rent one.
- If the woman has three or more children, or has given birth to three or more children; or if she has two children and in addition has suffered at least one 'obstetric mishap' (spontaneous abortion, stillbirth, extra-uterine pregnancy).
- If the woman has reached the age of forty.

There are also four instances in which the committee exercises discretion, and may give permission for an abortion:

- If the woman has two children and the health of the baby to be born, or its development, is expected to be endangered.
- If the woman's husband is doing regular military service or is detained for special service in the armed forces or a similar organisation, and if at the time the application is filed he still has at least six months to serve.
- If the woman or her husband is serving a prison term of at least six months.
- If the application is motivated by other weighty social considerations.

Appendix III Declaration of Intent

During the past forty years, just as before the Second World War, women have not been able to play an active role in social and political life. In the countries behind the iron Curtain women could not join in the positive and progressive actions taken by women's movements around the world. Despite the recent political changes that have taken place in Hungary, women must still face their virtual non-recognition as full citizens.

The founding of the Feminist Network demonstrates the persistence of needs long declared non-existent. The Feminist Network aims to achieve the recognition of specific female interests and points of view, the participation of women in public life and decision-making, the realisation of women's and men's real emancipation, and the abolition of all kinds of discrimination. We intend to change the political, economic and employment practices that have been perpetuating women's current disadvantageous situation both in the society and in the family. Through dialogue and public debates we wish to reshape the structure of interests so as to make possible a real, rather than a forced and false harmonisation of interests.

We will fight for the improvement of our life conditions, our right to work, our autonomy, our health and for our basic and broadly defined existential security.

We hope to join in a united Europe, and we are convinced that these specific women's interests are also the values of a civilised society, serving women, men and children.

The 1949 constitution recognised women's emancipation. In practice, this was reduced to the right to work, and under the given economic conditions this right became a necessity. This 'emancipation' grass-roots organisation in a basically conservative society with a double standard of morality has only succeeded in producing deeply uncertain and self-doubting women prone to accept the scapegoat role they are often given.

In order for this situation to change:

- The impact of the past forty years on women's roles, status, and self-conceptions on male–female relations, and on family must be analysed and these analyses must be widely disseminated.
- The current efforts of the renewed and strengthened conservative religious groups, aided by the mass media, to secure the dominance of their moral views in society must be opposed.
- The parliament, with its overwhelming majority of men as members, must be prevented from making decisions in haste and without social debate, especially such decisions that can have particularly far-reaching consequences for women.

If these tasks are not accomplished, the great majority of women – surrendering the few positive developments of the past forty years – will have to 'choose' resignation and submission in order to survive.

The former omnipotence of state power, disabling or deforming all members of society, destroyed support communities and exploited the natural forces of human life, including human relationships. Women, men and children have been forced to bear their burdens alone.

Women have become a 'bad' but cheap workforce; State social policies have made them responsible for the size of the population; with the degradation of human relationships they have become sexual objects; the lack of decent educational institutions and service infrastructure has ensured both that they remain unpaid household servants, and that they do not have an equal chance with men in the world of paid work.

Those few women who have been in sufficiently favourable situations to become independent modern women, have seldom found similarly modern men to be their companions. Authoritarianism and paternalism, in addition to their everyday burdens, have also made men vulnerable (rising mortality rates) and distorted their personalities. The consequences of their inability to renounce their privileges and dominance shapes private and public life in Hungary even today.

The Feminist Network commits itself to the goal of extending to children, women and men equally, opportunities for self-realisation without regard to gender, religion, nationality, racial origin or social class. From this it follows that our understanding of emancipation is universal and is directed toward the whole of society.

To this end, the Feminist Network demands that effective steps be taken against unemployment, that the employment structure which is so disadvantageous to women be changed; that the formation and operation of strong trade unions with proportionate numbers of women in leadership positions be facilitated within all ownership sectors of economy; and that the introduction of new technologies be not permitted to force women into jobs with low prestige and obsolete technology. Legal opportunities should be created for flexible working hours and part-time work for both men and women.

The concept of work must be redefined so that the work required to care for family and children and the tasks needed to sustain everyday life should be included within the sphere of important activities deserving social and material recognition. Men and women must be assured equal rights and obligations to participating these activities. A high-quality system of child-care institutions and family services must be created out of public funds. A free and high-quality health system, including a more enlightened women's health network, is essential for the entire population. The availability of abortion must be legally guaranteed and contraception must become a responsibility of men as well as women.

Social and moral constraints which penalise forms of cohabitation outside the traditional marriage and family must be struggled against and must not characterise state policy. The possibility for participation in Social insurance must be created for and extended to every man and woman regardless of family status. Strong efforts must be made to increase society's tolerance of all 'otherness' – whether cultural, sexual, racial or religious – and its acceptance of mentally and physically disabled people, and of pensioners. The books and activities of nurseries and schools must be examined critically in order to prevent the continued propagation of obsolete and destructive prejudices regarding gender roles.

We protest against violence within families against women and children, which is widely known about but not discussed. Now is the time for it to be given the public attention it deserves, for only with public education can this tragic situation be ameliorated. We urge stricter and stronger judicial handling of such cases, as well as the creation of refuges, telephone and taxi crisis services for those suffering from such violence.

The feminist movement is an organic part of Western democracy. The political activity of feminists is aimed at overcoming those aspects of male–female relations which are based on a relation of unequal power. We are also working for the real – not simply formal or legal – equality between the sexes in every area of social life. We hope finally to free the word 'feminist' from the misunderstanding and uniformed prejudices under which it currently labours.

FEMINIST NETWORK

Appendix IV Declaration of Women from East-Central and Eastern Europe

Women from East-Central and East European countries present at the first Women's CSCE came to the conclusion that it is of vital importance to create a network of East-Central and East European women in order to coordinate activities of women's organisations in their countries and share information about the actual situation of women on the broad international level. Such a network is necessary especially as the newly emerging democracies have proved to be conservative and authoritarian regarding women. They perpetuate and promote male dominance in these societies. The best examples to prove this statement can be found in the tendencies to raise the percentage of unemployed women beyond that of men and to curb or even ban the right of abortion.

It is necessary to develop close relations with women from all other parties of Europe and the world because we share the same problems, even if the manifestations are different – in East Europe increasing nationalism and ethnic conflicts, and in the West racism and xenophobia have similar roots in the patriarchy and have the same disastrous impact on all women.

East-Central and East European participants of the Women's CSCE are convinced that the worsening situation of women in their countries, which is due to the transition period could be stopped, and the most difficult problems overcome only if women organise themselves and struggle against the still-very-dominant patriarchal culture and structures in their societies.

With the spreading of the women's movement from below, women from East-Central and Eastern Europe have a general chance to change the societies they are living in and influence all levels of power structures.

Appendix V List of Women's Groups and Organisations in Hungary

Ariadne Gaia Foundation
Szép utca 3
1053 Budapest

Budapesti Közagdaságtudományi Egyetem
Budapest University of Economics
Fövám tér 8
1093 Budapest
Contact: Katalin Kancz

Eötvös Lóránd Tudomány Egyetem
Szociálpolitikai Tanszék
Lóránd Eötvös Science University
Faculty of Social Policy
Kun Béla tér 2
1083 Budapest
Contact: Mária Adamik

Homeros Lambda
(Lesbian and Gay Rights)
c/o Peter Ambrus
Menesi ut 17b/I/7
118 Budapest XI

Hungarian Feminist Network
Forach u. 18
1139 Budapest

Hungarian Women's Alliance
Népkoztarsaság utja 124
1062 Budapest

Központi Statisztikai Hivatal
Central Statistical Office
Keleti Károly u.5–7
1024 Budapest
Contact: Rózsa Kulcsár

Magyar Nök Szövetsége
Association of Hungarian Women
Andrássy u. 124
1062 Budapest
Contact: Ibolya Ujváry

MTA Szociológiai Kutató Intézet
Hungarian Science Academy
Research Institute of Sociology
Uri u.49
1014 Budapest
Contact: Olga Tóth

Munkaügyi Kutató Intézet
Research Institute of Labour
Mozsár u. 14
1066 Budapest
Contact: Zsuzsa Orolin

Népességtudományi Kutató Intézet
Demographic Research Institut
Semmelweis u.9
1052 Budapest
Contact: Marietta Pongrácz

Oktatáskutató Intézet
Hungarian Institute for Educational Research
PO Box 427
1395 Budapest
Contact: Katalin R. Forray

Országos Müszaki Múzeum
Museum for Science and Technology
Kaposvár u. 13–15
1117 Budapest
Contact: Éva Vámos

Phralipe
Independent Organization of Gypsies
Felsöerdösor 16–18, 1/13
1068 Budapest

Pro Familia Hungarian Scientific Society
(family planning service)
Buday László u 1–3
1024 Budapest

Semmelweis Orvostudományi Egyetem
Semmelweis University of Medicine
Nagyvárad tér 1
196 Budapest
Contact: László Molnór

Society for Equal Chances
Hazafias Népfront Országos Tanacsa
Népkoztarsaság utja 94
1062 Budapest

Szegedi Feminist Group
József Attila University
Egyetem utca 2
Szeged
6722 Hungary

TIN-TA Teenage Advice Service
Közösségi Ház
Lévai utca 34
2040 Budaörs

Women's Information and Research Network
Felhévizi utca 26
1025 Budapest

Women's Section
Democratic League of Free Trade Unions
Város fasor 45
1071 Budapest

Women's Steering Committee of Trade Unions
Dózsa György ut 84/b
1415 Budapest

Appendix VI Statistics on Hungary

Area: 93 030 km^2

Population: 10 375 000 including 5 388 000 women (1991).

Capital: Budapest.

Languages: Hungarian (Magyar) official, Romani, German, Slavic.

Races and Ethnic groups: Magyar 98 per cent of which up to 1 million are of Romani (Gypsy) origin and are counted as Hungarian. German 0.5 per cent, Slovak, Croation, Romanian – many more Romanians have settled in Hungary since the purges in 1989 and many refugees from the violence in the former Yugoslavia are now residing in Hungary.

Religion: Roman Catholicism approximately 60 per cent, Protestant (Calvinist), Jewish.

Education: Free and compulsory from 6 to 16 years. At 14 choices are made between gymnaziums and technical and vocational schools. Girls make up about two-thirds of students in gymnaziums, which provide education in many fields, including preparation for university entry. Because girls prefer to study in these secondary grammar schools (which provides a general education only), this does not guarantee strong chances for work. Boys and men tend to attend mainly vocational schools and obtain up-to-date skills.

Percentage of women in national parliament: 7.1 per cent 1992.

Birth rate: In 1990 – 11.7 per 1 000 population.

Death rate: In 1990 – 13.8 per 1 000 population.

Maternal mortality: In 1990 – 15.41 per 100 000 live births.

Infant mortality: In 1990 – 15.8 per 1 000 live births.

Ratio of abortions: In 1990 – 734.00 per 1 000 live births.

Life expectancy: female 73.8, male 65.4 (1989).

ECONOMY

Currency: Forint (July 1991 exchange £1 = 150 fts). Now almost convertible, no major difference in legal/illegal exchanges.

Women's wages as percentage of men's: Women still earn between 70 and 80 percent of men's wages, but this varies across sectors. Most women remain in the lower levels of the income brackets. Whilst the earnings of 75 per cent of women were below the national average in the 1980s, this was the case with only 33 per cent of men.

Equal pay policy: Guaranteed in law in Article 70/B of the Hungarian Constitution (amended 1972).

Agreed minimum wage: On 1 April 1991 official minimum monthly wage in Hungary was set at 7 000 forints (US $100).

Average personal incomes: In 1990 – 13 205 fts (gross), 9 960 fts (nett).

PRODUCTION

Agricultural: corn, wheat, sunflower oil, potatoes, sugar beets, vegetables, wine grapes, fruit, dairy produce.

Industrial: transport equipment (mainly buses), textiles, pharmaceuticals, measuring equipment.

Women as percentage of labour force: Total active earners 4 467 000, of which women make up 1 992 500 (1990); included in this figure are over 200 000 women on child-care leave. Proportion of women out of the total workforce in 1991, 48.5 per cent.

Employed women's occupational indicators: In the 1980s the majority of women still entered the job market without professional skills, despite rising educational levels. The sectoral distribution of women wage-earners in 1988 was 29.4 per cent in Services (non-material sector), 29.1 per cent in industry, 16.4 percent in Agriculture and Forestry, 15.3 per cent in commerce, 5.1 per cent in Transport, Post and Telecommunications, 3.0 per cent in Construction and Industry, 0.9 per cent in Water Works and Supply, with 0.8 per cent in 'others'.

Unemployment: Little reliable gender-specific data available. In January 1989 an unemployment benefit scheme was launched. Of those receiving unemployment benefit in 1990 it appeared that women were less affected by unemployment than men. This had significantly changed by 1992.

Rate of unemployment (total population): In January 1992, 10 per cent.

Percentage of women in total unemployed: In January 1992, 42 per cent.

Notes

1 Introduction

1. 'Eastern Europe' has never been a particularly useful label for countries in this region. See the explanation later in this chapter under the heading 'Terminology and Sources'.
2. I use marks around the term 'socialist' to let the reader know that this term is used as a short form rather than descriptively.
3. The term 'the power' is fairly widely used throughout Hungary and other neighbouring countries to denote not just the government but the whole apparatus that went with the old-style authoritarian regimes which were in place from the later 1940s.
4. It is not possible to speak of 'the state' or 'the family' in terms of state forces and family structures. The concern here is with precisely those ill-defined yet very powerful idealised forms of state paternalist intervention and the notions of 'ideal' families.
5. See, initially, Heitlinger (1979), Lapidus (1978) and Scott (1974).
6. See, especially, Wolchik Sharon, 'Ideology and Equality: The Status of Women in Eastern and Western Europe', *Comparative Political Studies*, vol. 13, no. 4, June 1981, pp. 448–56.
7. See Heitlinger (1979), Scott (1974), Lapidus (1978) and Molyneux (1981).
8. See particularly Mária Márkus (1979).
9. Friedrich Engels, 'The Origin of the Family, Private Property and the State', in *Marx–Engels: Selected Works* (Moscow: Lawrence & Wishart) pp. 461–566.
10. Other, 'capitalist' methods of computing women's labour for such needs as insurance policies tend to assess women's work at well above the average (male) income.
11. There was much discussion at the Conference in June 1991 in Norwich (UK) regarding whether or not the European Forum of Socialist Feminists should change its name. After discussion from those in favour of change, several women from the former Soviet Union and central and eastern Europe discussed the fact that they could not make use of such a 'label', the name was left unchanged as there was recognition from those within central and eastern European countries that the term had a long history and that there were positive reasons for those women who favoured retaining it.
12. See, initially, Ann Oakley's consideration in her work on the sociology of housework and the arguments of Liz Stanley and Sue Wise in *Breaking Out*.
13. Under the Ceausescu regime, with compulsory monthly pregnancy testing for women, the ideal family was a *minimum* of five children.

2 Transformations

1. Both words, 'liberation' and 'socialist', deserve consideration. The so-called 'liberation' period according to official history in Hungary was that in which the Red Army liberated Hungary from the Nazis and began the development towards 'socialism'. 'Socialist' in turn refers to the authoritarian, hierarchical, top-down developmental approach taken by the Soviet-inspired Hungarian authorities.
2. After the mid-1950s there was a recognition in Hungary that the first sense of 'liberation' by the Red Army was not liberation in a true sense at all. For women, on the other hand, the official delusion carried on for forty years in terms of their so-called liberation through work.
3. See, initially, Elemér Hankiss, *East European Alternatives* (Oxford: Clarendon Press, 1990)
4. See Hankiss (1990) and Heinrich (1986) as general introductions to Hungarian history.
5. Agricultural production remained 10–20 per cent below the level of the years 1934–8.
6. It became clear during the later 1940s that research into 'sensitive' areas which contradicted official propaganda would not be tolerated. For sociologists wishing to look at living standards, the subject of poverty has always been a 'thorny' area. No money was made available for research into this subject, but much useful ethnographic work was carried out.
7. W. Brus, 'Concept of the Hungarian Economic Reform', talk delivered at the Social Studies Faculty Centre, Oxford, 5 March 1983.
8. In Hungary, people have spoken of 'the power' since the communist takeover in 1948. This term covers not only the statist apparatus including the army and police but also all the outgrowths of bureaucracy that were built up during the dominance of the hierarchical power structures of authoritarianism.
9. Iván Szelényi, 'Eastern Europe in an Epoch of Transition: Toward a Socialist Mixed Economy?', in Nee and Stark (eds), *Remaking the Economic Institutions of Socialism: China and Eastern Europe* (Stanford University Press, 1979) p. 220.
10. Exceptions were the Entrepreneurs Party organised to mediate the interests of people involved in private ventures, and the Party of Generations supporting old-age pensions. FIDESZ, although youth party, aimed to represent all interests.

3 Women's Paid Work

1. See István Kemény, 'A magyar munkásosztály fejlödése' (The development of the Hungarian working class), *Szociológia*, no. 2, 1972; and György Konrád, Iván Szelényi, 'A késleltetett város fejlödés társadalmi konfliktusai' (The social conflicts of delayed urbanisation), *Valóság*, no. 12, 1971.
2. See, for example, Aliz Mátyus, '*Holnapon Innen, Tegnapon Tul*' (This Side of Tomorrow, the Other Side of Yesterday) (Budapest: Szépirodalmi Könyvkiadó, 1980).

3. This case was not successful at the industrial tribunal but was won through independent arbitration.
4. Social policy analysts claim that these people are just 'the tip of the iceberg'.

4 Domestic Work and Family Considerations

1. *Magyar Nemzet*, 27 July 1980, noted in Radio Free Europe Situation Report,18, 6 October 1980, p. 16.

5 Social Policy Developments

1. See István Huszár, 'People at a distadvantage in Hungary', *Társadalmi Szemle*, no. 6, 1981; and Antal Böhm, 'Debate on groups of people suffering multiple disadvantage', ibid.
2. Social policy analysts claim that these people are just 'the tip of the iceberg'.
3. In the mid-1980s discussion centred upon allowing women to retire at fifty with full entitlements so that they could care for elderly or sick relatives. By the early 1990s, though, debates focused on increasing retirement ages for men and women by five years in order to ease the economic pressure of pensions/benefits.
4. See Judit Somnor, 'Those who have been written off', *Uj Tukor*, 6 June 1982
5. See Katalin Peto, 'A modern Taygetus or the end of the road', in *Mozgó Világ*, May 1982. Mount Taygetus was a mountain from which, according to Spartan traditions, crippled and unfit children were thrown to their death.

6 Hungarian Health Care: Women's Health

1. Statute II, 29 April 1972, para. 25(1).
2. The Patriotic People's Front was one of a number of mass organisations in Hungary which according to the 1972 Constitution was expected to 'galvanise the social forces in the interest of the complete construction of socialism, the solution of political, economic and cultural problems and to participate in the elections and the work of elected organs of popular representations' (para. 4(2)). Essentially, the PPF had its most important activities centring on the organisation of elections. Its programme and activities attempted to symbolise national unity and areas such as women's concerns, and youth activities were often high on the agenda.
3. For literature on this concerning British women see, initially, Ann Oakley, *Housewife* (Harmondsworth: Penguin, 1974).

7 Attitudes in Transition

1. The term 'state' is used here as a shorthand description of the structures and powers of those involved in the various bureaucracies, governmental organisations and decision-making circles.

2. In the years before 1990 the official version of the 1956 revolution was that it had been a 'counter-revolution'. When this version of history was corrected there was much celebration in Hungary
3. In this context note *Women of Europe*, no. 68, February/May 1991, p. 33.
4. Dávid Biró, 'A "teremtés koronái" és a "gyengébb nem"' (The 'master-piece of creation' and the 'weaker sex') *Valóság*, no. 9, 1982.
5. Robin Morgan, *Sisterhood is Global* (Harmondsworth: Penguin, 1984) p. 291.
6. Radio Free Europe, HSR/9, 7 August 1985.
7. *Magyar Hirlap*, 26 February 1983.

9 Conclusion

1. See Hilda Scott, *Sweden's Right to be Human* (London: 1982, Allison & Busby) ch. 8.
2. See Mária Márkus, 'The Position of Working Women' (n.d.).

Bibliography

UNPUBLISHED PAPERS

CSEH-SZOMBATHY, László, 'Családpolitika – családgondozás' (Family policy – Family welfare), not dated.

FERGE, Zsuzsa, 'The varying rhythm of change in women's situation in Hungary', not dated.

KULCSÁR, K. and GERGE, Z. (project co-ordinators) 'Social policy research in Hungary', (Institute of the Hungarian Academy of Sciences, 1979).

KULCSÁR, Rózsa, 'The development of the socio-economic conditions of women in Hungary', Conference paper for 'Changes in the Status of Women in Eastern Europe', George Washington University, December 4–6 1981.

SZALAI, Julia (with the contribution of Ágota Horváth), 'Alternative policies for caring for children under the age of 3: the Hungarian case', (Institute of Sociology, Hungarian Academy of Sciences, 1978).

PRINTED SOURCES

Official documents

HCSO (Hungarian Central Statistical Office), *Population Census Data* (from 1949), (Budapest, 1964).

HCSO, *Statistical Social Surveys in Hungary: Stratification and Time-Budget Studies* (1966).

HCSO, *Longitudinal Marriage Surveys in Hungary 1966–1980* (Budapest, 1984).

HCSO, *Public Opinions Research on Demographic Issues* (Budapest, 1985/2).

A Népességtudományi, A Gyermekvállalasrol és a Népesedes-politikárol alkatott Vélemények több gyermek gondozó anyák körében, Kutató Intézet Kozleményei, 1980–1.

Hungarian News Service, *Women's Position in Socialist Hungary* (National Council of Hungarian Women, 1985).

A MSzMP határozatai és dokumentumai, *Decisions and Documents of the Hungarian Socialist Worker's Party* (1978).

Press material

The primary Hungarian newspapers used for this study are:

Magyarország	(Hungary)	
Magyar Hirlap	(Hungarian News)	
Magyar Nemzet	(Hungarian Nation)	Daily of the PPF
Népszabadság	(People's Freedom)	Party newspaper since 1956

Népszava	(People's Voice)	Hungarian trade union newspaper
Szabad Ifjúság	(Free Youth)	Newspaper of the Hungarian Young Communist League

Radio Free Europe Background and Situation Reports (1970–86) have provided useful information.

Hungarian articles, books and pamphlets (includes translated materials)

Journals

Demográfia	(Demography) Quarterly of the HCSO
Élet és Irodalom	(Life and Literature) Literary paper
Ifjuság Szemle	(Youth Review) Monthly
Kortárs	(Contemporary) Literary journal
Közgazdasági Szemle	(Economic Review) Monthly economic journal
Mozgö Világ	(Moving World) Critical monthly magazine
New Hungarian Quarterly	Literary, current affairs, arts journal
Nök Lapja	(Women's Journal) weekly magazine
Statisztikai Szemle	(Statistical Review)
Szociológia	(Sociology)
Társadalmi Szemle	(Social Review)
Valóság	(Reality) Sociological journal

Articles

CSÁSZI, Lajos, 'As egészégügy szekularizációja Magyarországon' (The secularization of health care in Hungary), *Valóság*, no. 5, 1982, pp. 77–87.

FERGE, Zsuzsa, 'Kell-e Magyarországon feminizmus?' (Does Hungary need feminism?), *Ifjúság Szemle*, May 1987, pp. 3–7.

HANKISS, Elemér, 'Második társadalom? Kisérlet egy fohgalom meghatározása és egy valóságtartómány leirása' (The second society? Attempt to define a concept and to describe a province of reality), *Valóság*, vol. 5, 1984, pp. 25–44.

HUSZÁR, István, 'A bátrányoshelyzetüek Magyarországon' (The deprived in Hungary), *Társadalmi Szemle*, no. 6, 1981, pp. 89–100.

JUHÁSZ, Pál, 'A neurózis és alkoholizmus néhány szolciológia vonatkozása' (Some sociological aspects of alcholism and neurosis), *Szociológia*, no. 1, 1980, pp. 69–80.

KÁDÁR, Béla, 'Preparing to meet the challenge: the Hungarian economy in the Eighties', *New Hungarian Quarterly*, no. 88, Winter 1982, pp. 88–100.

KOLOSI, Tamás, 'Egyenlötleséy – Életkörulmények' (Equality – inequality – living conditions), *Társadalomtudományi Közlemények* (Papers in the Social Sciences) 1978/4.

KULCSÁR, Rózsa, 'Marriage and Social Mobility', *New Hungarian Quarterly*, Winter 1978, no. 72, pp. 141–6.

LEVENDEL, László, 'A Népegeszégügyi Reformról' (The reform of public health in Hungary) *Valósag* no. 5, 1982, pp. 65–76.

PATAKI, Judit and MOLNÁR, Edit S. *Public Opinion Research on Demographic Issues*, (Central Statistical Office Demographic Research Institute, 1985/2).

SZALAI, Julia, 'Mire Kell az óvoda és kinek?' (Who needs a kindergarten and for what purposes?), *Nök és Férfiak*, (Budapest, 1985) pp. 196–212.
SZALAI, Sándor, 'Women in the light of time budget research' *New Hungarian Quarterly*, no. 64, 1973, pp. 74–92.
POLGÁR, Zsuzsa *et al.* 'A sex questionnaire for the young', *New Hungarian Quarterly*, no. 43, 1970, pp. 71–80.
TAMÁS, Pál, 'Hova Lett a Magyar Feminizmus?' (Where has Hungarian feminism gone?) *Élet és Irodalom* (Life and Literature), 1 May 1987, p. 5.

Books

CSEH-SZOMBATHY, László, *A Mai Magyar Család* (The contemporary Hungarian family), Bydapest: Magyar Nök Országos Tanácsa, 1983).
FERGE, Zsuzsa, *Fejezetek a Magyar Szegénypolitika Történetérböl* (Budapest: Magvetö Kiadó, 1986).
GERGELY, Anikó (ed.) *Nök Magazinja Évkönyv* (Budapest: Kossuth Könyvkiadó, 1986).
HANKISS, Elemér, *Társadalmi Csapdák Diagnózisok* (Budapest: Magvetö Kiadó, 1983).
HAVAS, E. Szuhay, *The Situation of Women in Hungary* (National Council of Hungarian Women, 1975).
HIRSCHLER, Dr Imre, *Nemcsak Nökröl – Nemcsak Nöknek (Not just about women – not just for women)* Magyar Nök Országos Tanácsa (Budapest: Kossuth Könyvkiadó, 1984).
KABOS, E. and ZSILÁK, A. *Studies on the History of the Hungarian Trade Union Movement* (Budapest: Akadémiai Kiadó, 1977).
KAMARÁS, Ferenc, OROSZI, Zsuzsanna and BÁRÁNY, Lajos, *Longitudinal Marriage Survey* (Budapest: Population Statistics Department, Hungarian Central Statistical Office, 1984).
MASS COMMUNICATIONS RESEARCH CENTRE, *Jel-Kép* (Symbol) Telévizió Rádió Sajtó (special edition) 1984.
NAGY, Katalin (ed.), *A Viselkedés – Kultúráról* (Budapest: Kossuth Könyvkiadó, 1984).
SÁNDORNÉ, Dr Erika HORVÁTH, *A Gyestöl a Gyedig* (From the child care allowance to the child care benefit) A Magyar Nök Országos Tanácsa (Budapest: Kossuth Könyvkiadó, 1986).
SZABODY, E. (ed.) *Nök – Gazdaság – Társadalom: Tanulymanyok A Nök Helyzeterol* (Women – economy – society: essays on the situation of women) (Budapest: Kossuth Könyvkiadó, 1976).
SZÁNTÓ, Miklós (ed.) *Ways of Life: Hungarian Sociological Studies* (Budapest: Corvina Press, 1977).
VALKAI, Zsuzsa, *Miért Isznak a Nök?* (Why do women drink?) (Budapest: Magvetö Kiadó, 1986).

Articles

The major journals used are:

Acta Oeconomica
Capital and Class

Critique
Comparative Politics
Daedelus
European Sociological Review
Feminist Review
Labour and Society
Labour Focus on Eastern Europe
Soviet Studies
Telos

ANON., 'Hungary – the new mechanism: a balance sheet', *Labour Focus on Eastern Europe*, Spring 1981, pp. 18–19.

ALEXANDER, Leslie L. 'Hungarian public health', *Journal of the National Medical Association*, vol. 67, pt. 5, 1973, pp. 389–91.

ANDORKA, Rudolf, 'Comparative demographic analysis of socio-cultural determinants of fertility in European socialist countries where fertility is around the replacement level', *International Population Conference*, Manila, 1981, pp. 139–158 (Union Internationale pour l'Etude Scientifique de la Population).

BÉRES, Zsuzsa, 'Women's liberation: words of ill repute', *Budapest Week*, vol.1, no. 2, March 1991.

BEVÉRIA, Lourdes, 'Reproduction the sexual division of labour', *Cambridge Journal of Economics*, no. 3, 1973, pp. 203–25.

BRUS, W. 'The East European reforms: what happened to them?', *Soviet Studies*, no. 2, 1972.

CARTWRIGHT, C. 'The myth of the economic reforms in Hungary', *Critique* no. 5, 1975.

COCKS, Joan, 'Wordless emotions: some critical reflections on radical feminism', *Politics and Society*, vol. 13, no. 1, 1984.

DAVIDOFF, L. 'The separation of home and work? Landladies and lodgers in nineteenth and twentieth centure England', in S. Burman (ed.) *Fit Work for Women* (London: Croom Helm, 1979).

EDHOLM, Felicity, 'The Unnatural Family' in E. Whitelegg (ed.) *The Changing Experience of Women* (Oxford: Open University Press, 1982) pp. 166–78.

FERGE, Zsuzsa, The relations between paid and unpaid work of women, a source of inequality – with special reference to Hungary', *Labour and Society*, vol. 1, no. 2, April 1976, pp. 37–52.

FERGE, Zsuzsa, 'Cooperation and conflict between researchers and planners in social policy', *Acta Oeconomica*, vol. 30, no. 3–4, 1983, pp. 425–32.

FOSTER, Bridget, 'Suffering from equality', *Trouble and Strife*, no. 6, Summer 1985, pp. 17–23.

GRONMO, Sigmund and LINGSOM, Susan, 'Increasing equality in household work: patterns of time-use change in Norway', *European Sociological Review*, vol. 2, no. 3, December 1986 (Oxford).

HALAY, Tibor, 'The Development of Health Care and Social Development in Hungary', *Szociológia*, no. 1, pp. 47–52.

HANKISS, Elemér, 'The "Second Society": Is There An Alternative Social Model Emerging in Contemporary Hungary?', *Social Research*, New York, 55 nos 1–2, Spring/summer 1988.

HESS, Bess B. and SUSSMAN, Marvin (eds) 'Women and the Family', *Marriage and Family Review*, vol 7, nos 3/4, Fall/Winter 1984.

HUBER, Joan (ed.) 'Changing women in a changing world', *American Journal of Sociology* (special issue) vol. 78, no. 4, January 1973.

JANCAR, Barbara, 'Women's lot in Communist societies', *Problems of Communism*, vol. 25, no. 6, November–December 1976.

KISS, Judit, 'The Second 'No': Women in Hungary', *Feminist Review*, vol. 39, 1991.

KULCSÁR, R., 'Results of the first nationwide prestige survey in Hungary', (Review), *Acta Oeconomica*, vol. 36, no. 1–2, 1986, pp. 155–67.

LADÓ, Mária, 'Women in the Transition to a Market Economy: The Case of Hungary', United Nations Conference paper on the Impact of Economic Reform on the Status of Women in Eastern Europe and the USSR, Vienna, April 1991.

LAND, Hilary, 'The family wage', *Feminist Review*, no. 6, 1980, pp. 55–77.

LASLETT, P. and RAPPORT, ?, 'Collaborative interviewing and interactive research', *Journal of Marriage and the Family*, November 1975.

LÖCSEI, Pál, 'Women's employment and the traditional Hungarian family', *Kortárs*, October 1985, pp. 78–90.

MÁRKUS, Mária, 'Factors influencing the fertility of women: the case of Hungary', *International Journal of Sociology of the Family*, no. 2, 1973.

MÁRKUS, Mária, 'Change in the function of socialization and models of the family', *International Review of Sociology*, no. 3, 1975.

McAULEY, Alastair, 'The woman question in the USSR', *Slavic Review*, vol. 38, no. 2, June 1979.

MICKLEWRIGHT, John, *Income Support for the Unemployed in Hungary*, Suntory–Toyota International Centre for Economics and Related Disciplines, London School of Economics discussion paper, February 1992.

MIROIU, Mihaela, 'The Vicious Circle of Anonymity, or Pseudo-Feminism and Totalitarianism', mimeo, 1992.

MOLYNEUX, Maxine, 'Women's emancipation under Socialism: a model for the Third World?', Discussion paper, Institute of Development Studies (Brighton: University of Sussex, 1981).

MOLYNEUX, Maxine, 'Mobilisation without emancipation? Women's interests, state and revolution in Nicaragua', *Critical Social Policy*, September 1984, pp. 59–76.

RÁCZ, Barnabas, 'Political pluralisation in Hungary: the 1990 election', *Soviet Studies*, vol. 43, no. 1, 1991, pp. 107–36.

RAKOVSKI, Marc, 'Marxism and Soviet societies', *Capital and Class*, no. 7, 1977.

ROGERS, S. C. 'Women's place: a critical review of anthropological theory', *Comparative Studies in Society and History*, vol. 20, no. 1, 1978, pp. 123–62.

ROSSI, Alice, 'Equality between the sexes: an immodest proposal', *Daedalus*, vol. 93, no. 2, Spring 1964, pp. 607–52.

ROSSI, Alice, 'A biosocial perspective on parenting', *Daedalus*, vol. 106, no. 2, Spring 1977, pp. 1–32.

STACEY, Judith and THORNE, Barnie, 'The missing revolution in sociology', *Sociological Problems*, vol. 32, no. 4, April 1985.

STIEHM, Judith H. 'Socialism and women's equality: looking backward and forward', *Studies in Comparative Communism*, vol. XIV, nos 2 and 3, Summer/Autumn 1981, pp. 208–18.

SZELÉNYI, Iván, 'Notes on the Budapest School', *Critique*, no. 8, 1977.
SZELÉNYI, Iván and Szonja, 'The Vacuum in Hungarian Politics: Classes and Parties' *New Left Review*, no. 187, May/June 1991, pp.121–39.
TIMÁR, János, 'Income distribution and social equality in Hungary', *Labour and Society*, vol. 2, no. 1, January 1977, pp. 75–88.
TÓTH, András, *The Social Impact of the Restructuring in Rural Areas*, paper given at 'New Directions in Hungary in the 1990s', Glasgow, June 1992.
VASARY, Ildikó, 'Comrades its over! The election campaign in Hungary 1990', *Anthropology Today*, vol. 7, no. 4, August 1991, pp. 3–6.
WHITE, Stephen, 'Political socialization in the USSR: a study in failure?', Paper presented to the Annual Conference of the Political Studies Association, Liverpool, 1977.
WOLCHIK, Sharon L., 'Ideology and equality: the status of women in Eastern and Western Europe', *Comparative Political Studies*, vol. 13, no. 4, January 1981, pp. 445–76.
WOLCHIK, S. L. 'The status of women in a Socialist order: Czechoslovakia 1948–78', *Slavic Review*, vol. 38, no. 4, December 1979, pp. 593–4.
WOLCHIK, Sharon L. and MEYER, Alfred G., 'Women in Communist System', *Studies in Comparative Communism*, vol. XIV, nos 2 and 3, Summer/Autumn 1981.
WOMEN'S COLLECTIVE, 'Labour Focus on Eastern Europe Special issue on women' (London: Community Press, 1978).

Books

ASH, Timothy Garton, *We the People* (London: 1990).
ANDORKA, Rudolf and KOLOSI Tamás, (eds), *Stratification and Inequality* (Budapest: Institute of Social Sciences, 1984).
ANDORS, Phyllis, *The Unfinished Liberation of Chinese Women* (Brighton: Wheatsheaf, 1983).
ARTHUR, C.J. (ed.) *Marx & Engels: The German Ideology* (London: Lawrence & Wishart, 1970).
ATKINSON, D. A., DALLING, S. A. and LAPIDUS, G. W. (eds) *Women in Russia* (Brighton: Harvester press, 1978).
BAHRO, Rudolf, *The Alternative in Eastern Europe* (London: Verso, 1978).
BARKER, Diana L. and ALLEN, Sheila, *Sexual Divisions and Society: Process and Change* (London: Tavistock, 1976).
BARRETT, Michéle and McINTOSH, Mary, *The Anti-Social Family* (London: Verso, 1982).
BARTA, Barnabás, KLINGER, András, MILTÉNYI, Károly and VUKOVICH, György, *Fertility, Female Employment and Policy Measures in Hungary* (Geneva: International Labour Office, 1984).
BEAUVOIR, Simone de, *The Second Sex* (New York: Bantam, 1964).
BEBEL, August, *Society of the Future* (Moscow: Progress Publishers, ch. VIII, 1971).
BEVÉRIA, L., *Women and Development* (New York: Praeger, 1982).
BEREND, I.T. and RANKI, G. *Hungary – A Century of Economic Development* (Newton Abbot: David and Charles, 1974).

BEREND, I. T. and RANKI, G., *Underdevelopment and Economic Growth: Studies in Hungarian Social and Economic History* (Budapest: Akadémiai Kiadó, 1979).
BERNARD, Jessie, *Women, Wives, Mothers* (Chicago: Aldine, 1975).
BIERMAN, A. K. and GOULD, James A., *Philosophy for a New Generation* (New York: Macmillan, 1973).
BLUMEN, J. L. and BERNARD, J., *Sex Roles and Social Policy* (California: Sage, 1979).
BÖHM, Antal and KOLOSI, Tamás (eds) *Structure and Stratification in Hungary* (Budapest: Institute for Social Sciences, 1982).
BOZOKY, Eva, *The Hungarian Woman Today* (Budapest: National Council of Hungarian Women, 1985).
BROWN, Archie and GRAY, Jack, *Political Culture and Political Change in Communist States* (London: Macmillan, 1979).
BROYELLE, Claudie, *Women's Liberation in China* (Brighton: Harvester Press, 1977).
BRUNT, Rosalind and ROWAN, Caroline (eds) *Feminism Culture and Politics* (London: Lawrence & Wishart, 1982).
BRUS, W., *Socialist Ownership and Political Systems* (London: Routlege & Kegan Paul, 1975).
CASTLE-KANEROVA, Mita (ed.) *High Hopes: Young Voices of Eastern Europe* (London: Virago Press, 1992).
CORRIN, Chris, 'Gendered Identities: Women's Experience in Hungary', in Rai, Pilkington and Phizaklea (eds), *Women in the Face of Change* (London: Routledge, 1992).
CORRIN, Chris, *Superwomen and the Double Burden: Women's Experience of Change in Central and Eastern Europe and the Former Soviet Union* (London: Scarlet Press, 1992).
CLIFF, Tony, *Class Struggle and Women's Liberation* (London: Bookmarks, 1984).
CLÉBERT, Jean-Paul, *The Gypsies* (Harmondsworth: Penguin, 1967).
CSEH-SZOMBATHY, Lászlo, *Hungarian Sociology Today* (Budapest: Institute for Social Sciences, 1982).
DAHRENDORF, Ralf, *Class and Class Conflict in an Industrial Society* (London: Routledge & Kegan Paul, 1959).
DALY, M., Gyn, *Ecology: The Metaethics of Radical Feminism* (London: Women's Press, 1975).
DEACON, Bob, *Social Policy and Socialism: The Struggle for Socialist Relations of Welfare* (London: Pluto Press, 1983).
DEACON, Bob and SZALAI, Julia, *Social Policy in the New Eastern Europe* (Avebury: 1990)
DEACON, Bob *et al.*, *The New Eastern Europe: Social Policy in the Past, Present and Future* (London: Sage 1992).
DRAKULIC, Slavenka, *How We Survived Communism and Even Laughed* (London: Hutchinson, 1992).
EBERHARDT, Eva, *Women of Hungary* supplement to *Women of Europe*, (European Communities, January 1991).
EVANS, Mary (ed.) *The Woman Question: Readings on the Subordination of Women* (London: Fontana, 1982).
FEHÉR, Ferenc and HELLER, Ágnes, *Eastern Left, Western Left: Totalitarianism, Freedom and Democracy* (Cambridge: Polity Press, 1987).

FEHÉR, Ferenc and HELLER, Ágnes and GYÖRGY, Márkus, *Dictatorship Over Needs: An Analysis of Soviet Societies* (Oxford: Basil Blackwell, 1983).

FEHÉR, Ferenc and ARATO, Andrew (eds), *Crisis and Reform in Eastern Europe* (New Brunswick, New Jersey: Transaction Publishers, 1991).

FERGE, Zsuzsa, *A Society in the Making: Hungarian Social and Societal Policy 1945–1975* (Harmondsworth: Penguin, 1979).

FIRESTONE, S., *The Dialectic of Sex* (London: Jonathan Cape, 1971).

FOURTH INTERNATIONAL, *Women's Liberation and the Socialist Revolution* (London: Pathfinder, 1979).

FOREMAN, Ann, *Femininity as Alienation: Women and the Family in Marxism and Psychoanalysis* (London: Pluto Press, 1977).

GALGÓCZI, Erzsébet, *Another Love* (Pennsyvania and California, Cleis Press, 1991).

GELLNER, Ernest (ed.), *Soviet and Western Anthropology* (London: Gerald Duckworth, 1980).

GITTINS, Diana, *The Family in Question: Changing Households and Familiar Ideologies* (London: Gerald Duckworth, 1980).

GOUGH, I., The Political Economy of the Welfare State (London: Macmillan, 1979).

HANKISS, Elemér, *East European Alternatives* (Oxford: Clarendon Press, 1990).

HANN, C. M., *Changing Cultures – Tázlár: A Village in Hungary* (Cambridge University Press, 1980).

HANSSON, Carola and LIDEN, Karin *Moscow Women* (London: Allison & Busby, 1984).

HARASZTI, Miklós, *A Workers in a Worker's State* (Harmondsworth: Penguin, 1977).

HARDING, Neil, *Lenin's Political Thought: Theory and Practice in the Democratic and Socialist Revolutions* (London: Macmillan, 1983).

HARE, P. G., RADICE, H. K. and SWAIN, N. (eds), *Hungary: A Decade of Economic Reform* (Winchester Mass: George Allen & Unwin, 1981).

HARTSOCK, Nancy C. M., *Money, Sex and Power: Towards a Feminist Historical Materialism* (New York and London: Longman, 1983).

HEGEDÜS, András, HELLER, Ágnes, MÁRKUS, Mária and VAJDA, Mihaly *The Humanisation of Socialism: Writings of the Budapest School* (London: Allison & Busby, 1976).

HEGEDÜS, András, *The Structure of Socialist Society* (New York: St Martin's Press, 1976).

HEINRICH, Hans-Georg, *Hungary: Politics, Economics and Society* (London: Frances Pinter, 1986).

HEITLINGER, Alena, *Women and State Socialism: Sex Inequality in the Soviet Union and Czechoslovakia* (London: Macmillan, 1979).

HIBBIN, Sally (ed.), *Politics, Ideology and the State* (London: Lawrence & Wishart, 1978).

HOGWOOD, Brian W. and Guy B. PETERS, *The Pathology of Public Policy* (Oxford: Clarendon Press, 1985).

hOOKS, bell, *Ain't I a Woman: Black Women and Feminism* (Boston: South End Press, 1984).

HOLLAND, Barbara (ed.), *Soviet Sisterhood* (London: Fourth Estate, 1985).

HUFF, Darrell, *How to Lie with Statistics* (Harmondsworth: Penguin, 1973).

HUSZÁR, Tibor, KULCSÁR, Kálman and SZALAI, Sándor (eds), *Hungarian Society and Marxist Sociology in the Nineteen Seventies* (Budapest: Corvina Press, 1978).
INKELES, Alex, *Social Change in Soviet Russia* (Cambridge, Mass: 1968).
INTERNATIONAL LABOUR OFFICE *Women at Work* (Geneva: International Labour Office 1979).
JAGGAR, Alison M., *Feminist Politics and Human Nature* (Brighton: Harvester Press, 1983).
JARDINE, Alice and SMITH, Paul *Men in Feminism* (London: Methuen, 1987).
JAQUETTE, Jane S. (ed.), *Women in Politics* (Chs by Jancar and Lapidus) (New York: John Wiley, 1974).
JANCAR, B. W., *Women under Communism* (Baltimore and London: Johns Hopkins University Press, 1978).
KÁDÁR, János, *Selected Speeches and Interviews*, with an introductory biography by L. Gyurkó (Budapest: Akadémiai Kiadó, 1985).
KAMERMAN, S. and KAHN, A. G. *Child Care, Family Benefits and Working Parents* (New York: Columbia University Press, 1982).
KASER, Michael, *Health Care in the Soviet Union and Eastern Europe* (London: Croom Helm, 1976).
KEANE, John, *Democracy and Civil Society* (London: Verso, 1988).
KOLLONTAI, Alersandra, *The Autobigography of Sexually Emancipated Woman* (New York: Herder and Herder, 1971).
KOLLONTAI, Alexandra, *Selected Articles and Speeches* (Moscow: Progress, 1984).
KONRAD, György, *Anti Politics* (London: Quartet, 1984).
KONRAD, György and Iván SZELÉNYI, *The Intellectuals on the Road to Class Power* (New York: Harcourt, Brace, Jovanovich, 1979).
KOVRIG, Bennet, *Communism in Hungary: From Kun to Kádár* (Stanford: University Press, 1979).
KUHN, A. and WOLPE, A. (eds), *Feminism and Materialism: Women and Modes of Production* (London: Routledge & Kegan Paul, 1978).
LANE, David, *The End of Social Inequality? Class, Status and Power Under State Socialism* (London: George Allen & Unwin, 1982).
LAPIDUS, Gail Worshofsky, *Women in Soviet Society: Equality, Development and Social Change* (London: University of California Press, 1978).
LAPIDUS, Gail Worshofsky, *Women, Work and the Family in the Soviet Union* (New York: M. E. Sharp, 1982).
LENIN, V. I., *The Emancipation of Women* (Moscow: International Publishers, 1966).
LENIN, V. I., *On Women's Role in Society and the Solution of the Question of Women's Emancipation in Socialist Countries* (Moscow: Soviet Women's Committee, 1973).
LIVERMORE, G. and F. SCHULZE, (eds), *The USSR Today: Perspectives from the Soviet Press* (The Current Digest of the Soviet Press, Ohio, 1981).
LUKÁCS, G., *The Meaning of Contemporary Realism* (London: Merlin, 1963).
LUKÁCS, G., *Studies in European Realism* (London: Merlin, 1972).
McAULEY, Alastair, *Women's Work and Wages in the Soviet Union* (London: George Allen & Unwin, 1981).

McNEIL, Maureen, *Gender and Expertise* (especially chapter on work) (London: Free Association Books, 1981).

MACKIE, Lindsay and PATTULLO, Polly, *Women at Work* (London: Tavistock, 1977).

MALOS, Ellen (ed.), *The Politics of Housework* (London: Allison & Busby, 1980).

MARX, K., ENGELS, F. and LENIN, V.I. *Marx and Engels: Selected Works* (London: Lawrence & Wishart, 1968).

MASSELL, Gregory, *The Surrogate Proletariat: Women and Revolutionary Strategies in Soviet Central Asia 1919–1929* (Princeton: Princeton University Press, 1974).

MEEHAN, Elizabeth M., *Women's Rights at Work: Campaigns and Policy in Britain and the United States* (London: Macmillan, 1985).

MELLOR, Roy E.H., *Eastern Europe: A Geography of the Comecon Countries* (London: Macmillan, 1975).

MILLET, K., *Sexual Politics* (London: Virago, 1971).

MITCHELL, J.J., *Women's Estate* (Harmondsworth: Penguin, 1971).

MITCHELL, J.J., *Psychoanalysis and Feminism* (Harmondsworth: Penguin, 1975).

MORGAN, D.H.J., *Social Theory and the Family* (London and Boston,: Mass. Routledge & Kegan Paul, 1975).

MORGAN, Robin (ed.) *Sisterhood is Global* (Harmondsworth: Penguin, 1984).

MURDOCK, George P., *Social Structure* (New York: 1949).

NORRIS, Pippa, *Politics and Sexual Equality: The Comparative Position of Women in Western Democracies* (Brighton: Wheatsheaf, 1987).

NOVE, Alec, HOHMANN, Hans-Hermann and SEIDENSTÉCHER, Gertrude *East European Economies in the 1970's* (London: Butterworth, 1982).

NOVE, Alec, *The Economics of Feasible Socialism* (London: Allen & Unwin, 1986).

NOVE, Alec, *The Soviet Economic System*, 3rd edn (London: Allen & Unwin, 1986).

OAKLEY, Ann, *Telling the Truth About Jerusalem: A Collection of Essays and Poems.* (Oxford: Basil Blackwell, 1986).

OAKLEY, Ann, *Housewife* (Harmondsworth: Penguin, 1974).

OAKLEY, Ann, *The Sociology of Housework* (Oxford: Martin Robertson, 1974).

PARKES, Alan S., *Patterns of Sexuality and Reproduction* (Oxford University Press, 1976).

PARKIN, Frank, *Class, Inequality and Political Order* (New York: Praeger, 1971).

PASCALL, Gillian, *Social Policy: A Feminist Analysis* (London: Tavistock, 1986).

PHILLIPS, Eileen (ed.), *The Left and the Erotic* (London: Lawrence & Wishart, 1983).

PRIYA, Jacqueline Vincent, *Birth Traditions and Modern Pregnancy Care* (Dorset: Element, 1992).

RADICE, G. *Community Socialism* (London: Fabian Society, 1979).

RAKOVSKI, Marc, *Towards an East European Marxism* (London: Allison & Busby, 1978).

RICH, Adrienne, *Of Woman Born: Motherhood As Experience and Institution* (London: Virago, 1972).

RICH, Adrienne, *Compulsory Heterosexuality and Lesbian Experience* (London: Only Women Press, 1981).

RIGBY, T.H. and FEHÉR, F. (eds), *Political Legitimation in Communist States* (London: Macmillan, 1982).

ROBERTS, Helen (ed.), *Doing Feminist Research* (London: Routledge & Kegan Paul, 1981).
ROWBOTHAM, Sheila, *Women, Resistance and Revolution* (Harmondsworth: Penguin, 1972).
ROWBOTHAM, Sheila, *Woman's Consciousness, Man's World* (Harmondsworth: Penguin, 1973).
ROWBOTHAM, Sheila, *Hidden From History* (London: Pluto Press, 1977).
ROWBOTHAM, S. (*et al*), *Beyond the Fragments: Feminism and the Making of Socialism* (London: Merlin, 1979).
RUESCHEMEYER, Marilyn, *Professional Work and Marriage: An East–West Comparison* (London: Macmillan/St Antony's, 1981).
SARGENT, L. (ed.), *Women and Revolution* (London: Pluto Press, 1980).
SCHAPIRO, Leonard and GODSON, Joseph (eds), *The Soviet Workers from Lenin to Andropov* (London: Macmillan, 1984).
SCOTT, Hilda, *Working Your Way to the Bottom: The Feminization of Poverty* (London: Pandora, 1984).
SCOTT, Hilda, *Sweden's Right to be Human: Sex Role Equality: The Goal and the Reality* (London: Allison & Busby, 1982).
SCOTT, Hilda, *Women and Socialism: Experiences from Eastern Europe* (London: Allison & Busby, 1974).
SHARPE, Sue, *Double Identity: The Lives of Working Mothers* (Harmondsworth: Penguin, 1984).
SHERMAN, J. and BECK, A., *The Prism of Sex* (Madison, Wisc: University of Wisconsin Press, 1979).
SNYDER, Paula, *The European Women's Almanac* (London: Scarlet Press, 1992).
SPENDER, Dale, *Invisible Women: The Schooling Scandal* (London: Writers' and Readers' Publishing Cooperative Society, 1982).
SPULBER, N., *The Economics of Communist Eastern Europe* (Boston, Mass: MIT, 1957).
STANLEY, Liz and WISE, Sue *Breaking out: Feminist Consciousness and Feminist Research* (London: Routledge & Kegan Paul, 1983).
STEVENSON, Leslie, *Seven Theories of Human Nature* (Oxford University Press, 1974).
STONE, Elizabeth (ed.), *Women and the Cuban Revolution* (New York: Pathfinder Press, 1981).
SWAIN, Nigel, *Hungary: The Rise and Fall of Feasible Socialism* (London: Verso, 1992).
SZELÉNYI, Iván, *Urban Inequalities under State Socialism* (Oxford University Press, 1983).
SZOBOSZLAI, György, *Studies in the Field of Political Science in Hungary* (Budapest: The Hungarian Political Science Association, 1982).
TÖKÉS, Rudolf F. *Opposition in Eastern Europe* (London Macmillan/St Antony's, 1979).
TOMÁ, Peter and VOLGYES, Iván, *Politics in Hungary* (San Francisco: W.H. Freedmand and Co, 1977).
TÓTH, András and GÁBOR, László, *Research Review: Beyond the Great Transformation* (Budapest: 1991).
TROTSKY, Leon, *Women and the Family* (New York: Pathfinder Press, 1970).

UNGERSON, Clare, *Women and Social Policy: A Reader* (London: Macmillan, 1985).

VOGEL, Lise, *Marxism and the Oppression of Women: Toward a Unitary Theory* (New Brunswick, NJ: Rutgers University Press, 1983).

WALBY, Sylvia, *Theorizing Patriarchy* (Oxford: Basil Blackwell, 1990).

WEEDON, Chris, *Feminist Practice and Poststructuralist Theory* (Oxford: Basil Backwell, 1987).

WELSH, William A. (ed.), *Survey Research and Public Attitudes in Eastern Europe and the Soviet Union, Pergamon Policy Studies* (New York: Pergamon Press, 1981).

WHITE, Stephen, *Handbook of Reconstruction in Eastern Europe and the Soviet Union* (London: Longman, 1991).

WHITELEGG, Elizabeth (*et al.*), *The Changing Experience of Women* (Oxford: Open University Press).

WILSON, Elizabeth, *Hidden Agendas: Theory, Politics, and Experience in the Women's Movement* (London: Tavistock, 1986).

WILSON, E., *Women and the Welfare State* (London: Tavistock, 1977).

WOLCHIK, Sharon L. and MEYER, Alfred G., (eds) *Women, State, and Party in Eastern Europe* (Durham: Duke University Press).

WOODHEAD, Neville (ed.) *Politics and Class* (Ormskirk: G. W. and A. Hesketh, 1985).

YAZYKOVA, V., *Socialist Life Style and the Family* (Moscow: Progress, 1984).

YEDLIN, Tova (ed.) *Women in Eastern Europe and the Soviet Union* (New York: Praeger, 1980).

ZARETSKY, Eli, *Capitalism, the Family, and Personal Life* (London: Pluto Press, 1976).

Index

Note: Figures in *italics* refer to captions.